Where There Is No Psychiatrist

A Mental Health Care Manual

VIKRAM PATEL MBBS MSc MRCH

Senior Lecturer
London School of Hygiene & Tropical Medicine

Founding Member,
The Sangath Society, Goa, India

Honorary Senior Lecturer, Institute of Psychiatry, London, UK

Illustrations by Mr Wilson D'Souza
Bal Bhavan, Goa, India

GASKELL

Gaskell is an imprint of the Royal College of Psychiatrists, 17 Belgrave Square, London SW1X 8PG.
Any parts of this book, including illustrations, may be copied, reproduced, or adapted by individual persons as part of their own work or training without permission from the author or publisher, provided the parts reproduced are not distributed for profit. For any reproduction by profit-making bodies or for commercial ends, permission must first be obtained from the publisher.

British Library Cataloguing-in-Publication Data
A catalogue record for this book is available from the British Library.
ISBN 1-901242-75-7

The views presented in this book do not necessarily reflect those of the Royal College of Psychiatrists, and the publishers are not responsible for any error of omission or fact.

Gaskell is a registered trademark of the Royal College of Psychiatrists.
The Royal College of Psychiatrists is a registered charity (no. 228636).

Printed by Bell & Bain Limited, Glasgow, UK.

To Daddy and my parents
for instilling the joy of learning

And to my teachers, especially

Tony Hope
Alwyn Lishman
Anthony Mann
Ashit Sheth
Mohan Isaac

for instilling the joy of teaching

Contents

Boxes and tables

Tables

Foreword

David Werner, with a background as a school teacher, went to the mountains of Mexico as an artist to draw the fauna. He found that people there were denied any form of scientific healthcare and were exploited when they took patients to health workers. In 1977, with the help of colleagues in the health sector, the first copies of *Where There is No Doctor* (WTIND) were published in Spanish, soon to be followed by an English edition. This book met such a need that it has since been translated into over 100 languages. No other book on health has been so widely used by parents, volunteer health workers, nurses, medical assistants and even doctors. Physical, mental, community and environmental health needs are interdependent. Disturbance of one affects all. Despite this, Werner realised that doctors and the health profession in general tend to be compartmentalised and were almost totally ignorant of how to assist those with physical disability, dental problems and mental health. David Werner set about meeting this need and wrote the book *Disabled Village Children* (DVC). With this book someone with no more than a secondary school education could learn how to meet the needs of children with a wide range of disabilities. David Werner also encouraged the writing of another popular book *Where There is No Dentist* (WTIND). However, the needs of those with mental health problems were more difficult and up to now have been largely unmet. This need has now been magnificently filled by Vikram Patel's *Where There Is No Psychiatrist*.

So often desperate family members have brought to us individuals, often children or adolescents but also parents or grandparents, who were depressed, aggressive, hooked on alcohol or drugs and even suicidal. If only this book had been available, how much better these individuals could have been treated. Unfortunately the need for this book now is even greater than in the past. In today's age of globalised greed and the roll-back of collective compassion, mental illness is an increasing concern. Traditional social structures are being lost in the name of economic development. More and more people are losing the sense of belonging, of meaning and of hope, the basic requirements for mental health. The evil in many societies is seeing an opportunity to gain wealth through the spread of addictive drugs. Often communities do not appreciate the dangers of these addictions. This is particularly so in the case of nicotine addiction, which is said to be as difficult to break as heroin addiction. The advent of AIDS greatly increased mental health problems of the community. AIDS can lead to denial, shame and discrimination against those affected. In the worldwide Child-to-Child programme, children were asked what they saw as the major health problems in their society. A decade ago most would say diarrhoea, pneumonia and under-nutrition but now, in many societies, they reply 'it is violence within and outside our families'. This violence is evidence of a disruption in our societies and this book goes a long way to show why this takes place and perhaps what steps can be taken to overcome it.

Teaching-aids At Low Cost (TALC) has, over many years, been trying to encourage various groups with experience in this field to fill this important gap. Those who have worked at community level will know the importance of mental health problems. Research suggests that 40% of those attending a health centre have a mental health problem as their primary problem. Dr Vikram Patel was familiar and inspired by the approach to health care that David Werner had developed in *WTIND* and the subsequent publications. In his many years of service in Zimbabwe and India he saw the need for a book which would meet the needs of health workers at many levels as they encounter a variety of mental health problems in clinical practice. He brings to this book both an Asian and African understanding of mental health problems. I have often felt the dire need for an easy-to-understand handbook on how to deal with common (and even not so common) mental disorders. For years David Werner and I have urged mental health practitioners to write such a handbook. Now, at last, we have this very comprehensive yet remarkably user-friendly book, *Where There is No Psychiatrist*. Dr Vikram Patel is to be congratulated on putting together information so widely needed worldwide and particularly in the poorer countries where mental health professionals are scarce. The publishers are to be congratulated in taking steps to see that the book will be made available at a price that can be afforded and so much lower than most books in the health field.

David Morley
TALC

Preface

Health in its broadest sense includes physical and mental health. Even though many health workers agree with this broad conception of health, in reality the focus is mainly on physical health. There are many reasons for this. Probably the most important reason is that health workers do not understand much about mental health and are therefore less comfortable dealing with mental health problems. However, in recent years there has been growing awareness about various types of mental illnesses. Many health workers have become more interested in dealing with these problems. Mental illnesses have been shown to be common, occurring in all societies and in all sections of any society. We now know that mental illnesses cause great suffering and disability. As well as in the general adult population, mental illnesses have been found to occur in children, in the elderly and in mothers. Mental health is no longer a subject for the specialists; in fact, it is a basic aspect of care for any health worker in any community. It is essential that, just as with physical illnesses, the health worker is well informed about mental illnesses. It is with this goal in mind that this manual has been written.

Why this manual?

This manual was written for two key reasons. The first is that there are no practical, clinically oriented manuals for mental health care designed for general health workers. Those that exist focus entirely on medical practitioners or are in the form of local handouts or leaflets, and so lack depth. The second reason is that in my years of working in developing countries I have realised that the single biggest obstacle to achieving our shared goal of mental health for all is the increasingly complex and technical language of psychiatry. I have sought to break down the wall that psychiatry has built around itself, with the aim of liberating mental health from its hold. In the process, I hope this manual will serve to empower health workers to feel confident to deal with mental illness.

What readership?

This manual has been written with the needs of the general health worker in mind. Who might this be? It would include anyone who works in a health care setting, or who works with people who are ill, but who is not specially trained to work with persons with mental illness. Thus, this manual can be used by the community health worker, the primary care nurse, the social worker and the general practitioner. This fairly diverse group of health workers will have different levels of training and skills. However, they all often have in common a low level of awareness about mental illnesses and their treatments. Furthermore, because the 'medical' treatment of most mental illnesses is relatively straightforward, this is one topic that can be communicated to both medical and non-medical health workers in a similar medium. Of course, some readers may find the manual too simple, while others may find it too complex. I only hope that most find it easy to follow and use in their day-to-day clinical work.

Where will this manual be most useful?

Given that all societies have similar mental illnesses, the manual should be of use anywhere in the world. But clearly, the main region for its use will be in the developing world. Even though this term includes nations and societies far more diverse and varied than nations in the developed world, there are many features that they share which make this manual applicable to them all. The majority of developing countries have relatively few mental health professionals. Indeed, in many countries, there is about one psychiatrist for every half million people or more. These few mental health specialists spend most of their time caring for those with severe mental disorders. The vast majority of common mental disorders are not seen in specialist settings. In these circumstances, it is obvious that mental health specialists cannot even remotely achieve the goal of providing mental health care for all. On the other hand, many countries have large numbers of general health workers and medical practitioners who are the actual front line of mental health care.

Another important feature shared by most developing societies is that psychiatry, as a medical speciality, is an alien subject which has been imported relatively recently, often as a result of colonial rule. The theories that underlie psychiatry are deeply rooted in European and North American medical systems. This has had a profound effect on what mental illnesses are called and how they are recognised. Take depression as an example. Even though we know it is the commonest mental illness in the world and that it occurs in all societies, we also know that it is rarely recognised, let alone treated, in many general health care settings. The reason is simple: few patients with depression openly complain of feeling depressed! Indeed, many non-European languages do not have words for the 'diseases' of depression and anxiety. This poses a challenge to those who are concerned with training health workers on how to recognise and manage these disorders. In my view, rather than take a top-down, diagnosis-based approach, the alternative bottom-up, symptom-based approach could be one way around this obstacle.

The approach taken

Thus, to make training on mental illness realistic and practical, there is a need to adopt a more clinically relevant, problem-based approach. The current ICD–10 classification devised by the World Health Organization is an example of how complicated we have succeeded in making the diagnosis of mental illness. Even the primary care version has 24 categories of psychiatric disorder; few health workers are likely to have patience with this list. The problem-oriented approach that I have taken in this manual is to begin with common or important clinical presentations that have a mental health component and then to identify how to deal with these problems. A basic understanding of mental illness forms the core of Part I, since a simple theoretical foundation is essential for managing any health care problem. Another approach taken in the manual is to describe the relevant mental health issues as they arise in specific health care contexts. Health workers may often find themselves working in a special setting, say in a reproductive health clinic. What are the mental health issues relevant to this setting? These problem- and context-oriented approaches are two key deviations from the traditional approach to writing manuals on mental health for general health workers. Part IV allows users to personalise the manual, by allowing space for relevant information on the local area to be recorded.

Writing this manual has been a formidable challenge for me. It has involved several months of attempting the task of boiling down the basic truths from a large volume of academic and clinical literature. References to this literature are not cited throughout the text in support of the assertions made. There is a large evidence base for the approaches recommended in this manual, but it is not the aim of the book to introduce readers to this research. The Bibliography at the end of the book lists some general sources.

In being immersed in the process of writing drafts, sending them for review to friends and colleagues, revising here and there and then revising yet again, preparing this manual has taught me much about communicating complex issues in everyday language. Some of the reviewers have rightly pointed out that the language of the material may not reach out to all kinds of health worker. However, in my experience, I have found that most community health workers and primary care doctors possess a sophisticated level of understanding of health. I was determined to ensure that, while trying to keep the language simple and clear, the content of the manual would not become so simplistic that it failed to demonstrate the variety and diversity of mental health problems in the community. I am fully aware that, as an academic psychiatrist, my goals may be too ambitious and my style may not satisfy every reader. I only hope that comments and criticisms are forthcoming so that, in the end, the manual may be improved and revised to ensure that it can reach out to more users around the world.

Vikram Patel
Goa, April 2001
vikpat@goatelecom.com
vikram.patel@lshtm.ac.uk

Acknowledgements

I must acknowledge the inspirational source for this manual: *Where There Is No Doctor* (by David Werner) and two companion successor books (*Disabled Village Children*, again by Werner, and *Where Women Have No Doctor*, by Burns *et al* – see Bibliography) are classic examples of how the subject of health care can be reduced from lofty volumes to practical training manuals. Unlike the earlier books, however, this manual is targeted not only at community health workers but at general practitioners as well.

I also thank the funding agencies which have supported my research and, in this way, expanded my horizons on mental health services where there is no psychiatrist. In particular, I am grateful to the Beit Medical Trust, the Wellcome Trust and the MacArthur Foundation for their generous support of my work in Zimbabwe and India.

Finally, I would like to thank Wilson D'Souza, a Goan artist, for his unique talent and patience with my constant requests concerning the drawing and redrawing of the illustrations.

I also acknowledge the valuable comments of the reviewers from around the world listed below, and a wealth of handouts, leaflets and mental health books that have been important sources of information. I must also acknowledge the support of Gaskell right from the beginning when I first submitted a sketchy book proposal. In particular, I am grateful to Dave Jago, without whose support I doubt I would have been able to complete this exercise. During the later stages of revising the manuscript, the words of encouragement and support from David Morley and David Werner provided tremendous lift to my own mental health.

Reviewers

- Dr Melanie Abas, New Zealand;

- Professor Wilson Acuda, Zimbabwe;

- Dr Ricardo Araya, Chile;

- Dr Metin Basoglu, UK;

- Professor C. R. Chandrashekar, India;

- Professor Andrew Cheng, Taiwan;

- Dr Gauri Divan, India;

- Dr Solvig Ekblad, Sweden;

- Dr K. S. Jacob, India;

- Professor C. Kumar, UK;

- Dr Mauricio Silva de Lima, Brazil;

- Dr Paul Linde, USA;

- Dr Rajiv Menon, UK;

- Dr Deb Pal, UK;

- Dr Charles Parry, South Africa;

- Dr Jack Piachaud, UK;

- Dr Sunanda Ray, Zimbabwe;

- Professor Brian Robertson, South Africa;

- Dr Shekhar Saxena, India;

- Dr K. Shaji, India;

- Dr Nandita de Sousa, India;

- Professor Shoba Srinath, India;

- Professor Leslie Swartz, South Africa;

- Dr R. Thara, India;

- Dr Charles Todd, Zimbabwe;

- Dr Matthew Varghese, India.

I am also grateful to the anonymous reviewers who commented on the original book proposal and the entire manuscript.

How to use this manual

The manual is divided into four parts. It is important that readers familiarise themselves with Part I before reading the other parts. This is because much of the rest of the manual requires an understanding of the basic concepts presented in Part I. Part IV contains a guide on medicines, a glossary of terms for mental illnesses and symptoms, and information on local resources. An appendix provides flow charts that can be used for quick reference to clinical problems. Throughout the manual, extensive use is made of cross-referencing with *Where there is no Doctor* (WTIND; Werner, 1994*a*), *Where Women have no Doctor* (WWHND; Burns *et al*, 1997) and *Disabled Village Children* (DVC; Werner, 1994*b*), in order to make the book more practical.

Part I
An overview of mental illness

Part I of this manual provides the essential foundation on which the rest of the manual is built. Its three chapters cover the three broad areas of knowledge needed to give you the confidence to provide mental health care. Chapter 1 deals with the different types of mental disorder, using a simple classification that is geared for use in community and general health care settings. It also discusses issues such as cultural influences on mental health. Chapter 2 discusses how you can assess a person with mental illness. It covers key questions such as how to recognise and diagnose a mental illness. Chapter 3 discusses the major types of treatments of mental disorder. The chapter covers both medical treatments (i.e. medicines) and psychological treatments (i.e. talking) for mental disorders.

Most readers will need to go through Part I at least once before reading the rest of the manual, because many of the later chapters assume that you are already familiar with the basic information on the types and treatments of mental disorders.

Chapter 1

An introduction to mental illness

1.1 Mental health and mental illness

There is more to good health than just a physically healthy body: a healthy person should also have a healthy mind. A person with a healthy mind should be able to think clearly, should be able to solve the various problems faced in life, should enjoy good relations with friends, colleagues at work and family, and should feel spiritually at ease and bring happiness to others in the community. It is these aspects of health that can be considered as mental health.

Even though we talk about the mind and body as if they were separate, in reality they are like two sides of the same coin. They share a great deal with each other, but present a different face to the world around us. If one of the two is affected in any way, then the other will almost certainly also be affected. Just because we think about the mind and body separately, it does not mean that they are independent of each other.

Just as the physical body can fall ill, so too can the mind. This can be called mental illness. Mental illness is "any illness experienced by a person which affects their emotions, thoughts or behaviour, which is out of keeping with their cultural beliefs and personality, and is producing a negative effect on their lives or the lives of their families".

There are two important points that form the basis of the material in this manual:

- There have been tremendous advances in our understanding of the causes and treatment of mental illnesses. Most of these treatments can be provided effectively by a general or community health worker.

- Mental illness includes a broad range of health problems. For most people, mental illness is thought of as an illness associated with severe behavioural disturbances such as violence, agitation and being sexually inappropriate. Such disturbances are usually associated with severe mental disorders. However, the vast majority of those with a mental illness behave and look no different from anyone else. These common mental health problems include depression, anxiety, sexual problems and addiction.

1.2 Why should you be concerned about mental illness?

There are many reasons why you need to be concerned about mental illnesses.

- *Because they affect us all.* It is estimated that one in five of all adults will experience a mental health problem in their lifetime. This shows how common mental health problems are. Anyone can suffer a mental health problem.

- *Because they are a major public health burden.* Studies from nearly every corner of the world show that as much as 40% of all adults attending general health care services are suffering

Mental illness is common: at least two of these people are likely to suffer from a mental illness at some time in their life.

from some kind of mental illness. Many of the people attending general or community health services seek help for vague physical health problems, which may be called 'psychosomatic' or something similar. Many of them are actually suffering from a mental health problem.

• *Because they are very disabling.* Even though the popular belief is that mental illnesses are less serious than physical illness, they do in fact produce severe disability. They can also cause death, as a result of suicide and accidents. Some people suffer from a mental illness and a physical illness; in such persons the mental illness can make the outcome of the physical illness worse. The World Health Report from the World Health Organization in 2001 found that four out of the ten most disabling conditions in the world were mental illnesses. Depression was the most disabling disorder, ahead of anaemia, malaria and all other health problems.

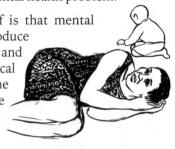
Mental illness can affect a person's ability to do things at home and at work.

• *Because mental health services are very inadequate.* There is a severe shortage of psychiatrists, psychologists and other mental health professionals in most countries. These specialists spend most of their time caring for people who suffer from severe mental disorders ('psychoses'). These are quite rare, but are also the very diseases that the community associates with mental illness. Most people with the much commoner types of mental health problems, such as depression or alcohol problems, would not consult a mental health specialist. General health workers are ideally placed to treat these illnesses.

• *Because our societies are rapidly changing.* Many societies around the world are facing dramatic economic and social changes. The social fabric of the community is changing as a result of rapid development and the growth of cities, migration, widening income inequality, and rising levels of both unemployment and violence. These factors are all linked to poor mental health.

• *Because mental illness leads to stigma.* Most people with a mental health problem would never admit to it. Those with a mental illness are often discriminated against by the community and their family. They are often not treated sympathetically by health workers.

• *Because mental illness can be treated with simple, relatively inexpensive methods.* It is true that many mental illnesses cannot be 'cured'. However, many physical illnesses, such as cancers, diabetes, high blood pressure and rheumatoid arthritis, are also not curable. Yet, much can be done to improve the quality of life of those who suffer these conditions and the same applies to mental illness.

Most mental illness can be treated.

1.3 The types of mental illness

To detect and diagnose a mental illness, you have to depend almost entirely on what people tell you. The main tool in diagnosis is an interview with the person (☞ Chapter 2). Mental illness produces symptoms that sufferers or those close to them notice. There are five major types of symptoms:

• *Physical – 'somatic' symptoms.* These affect the body and physical functions, and include aches, tiredness and sleep disturbance. It is important to remember that mental illnesses often produce physical symptoms.

A person can be worried about the future: a *thinking* complaint …

which can make her feel scared: a *feeling* complaint …

which can make it difficult for her to sleep: a *physical* complaint.

- *Feeling – emotional symptoms*. Typical examples are feeling sad or scared.

- *Thinking – 'cognitive' symptoms*. Typical examples are thinking of suicide, thinking that someone is going to harm you, difficulty in thinking clearly and forgetfulness.

- *Behaving – behavioural symptoms*. These symptoms are related to what a person is doing. Examples include behaving in an aggressive manner and attempting suicide.

- *Imagining – perceptual symptoms*. These arise from one of the sensory organs and include hearing voices or seeing things that others cannot ('hallucinations').

In reality, these different types of symptoms are closely associated with one another. See the figures, for example, of how different types of symptoms can occur in the same person.

  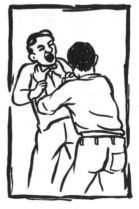

A person can hear people talking about him: a complaint of *imagination* …

which makes him think that his life is in danger: a *thinking* complaint …

which makes him attack others to protect himself: a *'doing'* complaint.

There are six broad categories of mental illness:

- common mental disorders (depression and anxiety);

- 'bad habits', such as alcohol dependence and drug misuse;

- severe mental disorders (the psychoses);

- mental retardation;

- mental health problems in the elderly;

- mental health problems in children.

1.3.1 Common mental disorders (depression and anxiety)

Case 1.1

Lucy was 23 when she had her first baby. During the first few days after the baby was born, she had been feeling tearful and mixed up. The midwife reassured her that she was only passing through a brief phase of emotional distress, as experienced by many mothers. She suggested that Lucy and her husband spend a lot of time together and care for the baby and said that her mood would improve. As expected, Lucy felt better within a couple of days. Everything seemed fine for the next month or so. Then, quite gradually, Lucy began to feel tired and weak. Her sleep became disturbed. She would wake very early in the morning, even though she felt tired. Her mind was filled with negative thoughts about herself and, to her fright, about her baby. She began to lose interest in her home responsibilities. Lucy's husband was becoming irritated with what he saw as her lazy and uncaring behaviour. It was only when the community nurse visited for a routine baby check that Lucy's depression was correctly diagnosed.

> Even though I should be so happy with my baby, I just feel tired all the time.

What's the problem? Lucy was suffering from a kind of depression that can occur in mothers after childbirth. It is called postnatal depression.

Case 1.2

Rita was a 58-year-old woman whose husband had suddenly died the previous year. Her children had all grown up and left the village for better employment opportunities in a big city. She had started experiencing poor sleep and loss of appetite soon after her husband died. The symptoms worsened once her children left the village after the funeral. She started experiencing headaches, backaches, stomachaches and other physical discomforts, which led her to consult the local clinic. There she was told she was well, but was prescribed sleeping pills and vitamins. She felt better immediately, particularly because her sleep improved. However, within two weeks her sleep got worse again and she went back to the clinic. She was given more sleeping pills and injections. This went on for months, until she could no longer sleep without the sleeping pills.

> I feel pain all over my body and I cannot sleep at night.

What's the problem? Rita had a 'physical' presentation of depression resulting from the death of her husband and loneliness because her children were no longer living with her. The clinic doctor had not asked about her emotions and gave her sleeping pills. This led to Rita becoming dependent on sleeping pills.

Sometimes my heart beats so fast, I feel as if I am going to die.

Box 1.1. The key features of depression

A person with depression will experience some of the following symptoms:

Physical
- tiredness and a feeling of fatigue and weakness
- vague aches and pains all over the body

Feeling
- feeling sad and miserable
- a loss of interest in life, social interactions, work, etc.
- guilty feelings

Thinking
- hopelessness about the future
- difficulty making decisions
- thoughts that he is not as good as others (low self-esteem)
- thoughts that it would be better if he were not alive
- suicidal ideas and plans
- difficulty in concentrating

Behaving
- disturbed sleep (usually reduced sleep, but occasionally too much sleep)
- poor appetite (sometimes increased appetite)
- reduced sex drive

Case 1.3

Ravi was 30 when he had a serious road accident. He was riding his motorcycle with a close friend on the pillion seat. The bike was hit by a bus from behind, and Ravi and his friend were thrown off the bike. To Ravi's horror, his friend fell under the wheels of the bus and died instantly. After a few days of deep sadness and shock, Ravi began to experience spells of fear. These started when he had been shopping in the market. Ravi suddenly experienced a choking sensation and felt his heart beating hard. His father had a heart complaint and Ravi became worried that he had a heart problem too. This made him scared and fearful. The doctor sent him for tests which showed that he had a healthy heart. Ravi also started getting nightmares, when he would see the whole accident played out. Sometimes, even when he was awake, he would get images of the accident in his mind and he would feel scared and tense. His sleep began to suffer and soon he began to feel suicidal.

What's the problem? Ravi was suffering from an anxiety illness that may occur after a person has been involved in a traumatic event. This is sometimes called 'post-traumatic stress disorder.'

Common mental disorders consist of two types of emotional problems: depression and anxiety. Depression means feeling low, sad, fed up or miserable. It is an emotion that almost everyone suffers from at some time in their life. To some extent it can be thought of as 'normal'. But there are times when depression starts to interfere with life and then it becomes a problem. For example, everyone gets spells of feeling sad but most people manage to carry on with life and the spell goes away. Sometimes, however, the depression lasts for long periods, even more than a month. It is associated with disabling symptoms such as tiredness and difficulty concentrating. The feeling starts to affect daily life and makes it difficult to work or to look after small children at home. If depression starts to get in the way of life and lasts for a long period of time, then we can assume that the person is suffering from an illness. The key features of depression are shown in Box 1.1.

Anxiety is the sensation of feeling fearful and nervous. Like depression, this is normal in certain situations. For example, an actor before going on stage or a student before an examination will feel anxious and tense. Some people seem to be always anxious but still seem to cope. Like depression, anxiety becomes an illness if it lasts long (generally more than two weeks), is interfering with the person's daily life or is causing severe symptoms. The key features of anxiety are shown in Box 1.2.

Most people with a common mental disorder have a mixture of symptoms of depression and anxiety. Most never complain of feeling or thinking symptoms as their main problem but instead experience physical and behavioural symptoms (as in Case 1.2). This could be for many reasons. For example, they may feel that psychological symptoms will lead to them being labelled as 'mental' cases (☛ 5.1.1).

Three varieties of common mental disorders may present with specific or unusual complaints:

- Panic is when anxiety occurs in severe attacks, usually lasting only a few minutes. Panic attacks typically start suddenly. They are associated with severe physical symptoms of anxiety and make sufferers feel terrified that something terrible is going to happen or that they are going to die. Panic attacks occur because people who are fearful breathe much faster than usual. This leads to changes in the blood chemistry which cause physical symptoms.

- Phobias are when a person feels scared (and often has a panic attack) only in specific situations. Common situations are crowded places such as markets and buses (as in the case 1.3), closed spaces like small rooms or lifts, and in social situations such as meeting people. The person with a phobia often begins to avoid the situation that causes the anxiety, so that, in severe cases, the person may even stop going out of the house altogether.

- Obsessive–compulsive disorders are conditions where a person gets repeated thoughts (obsessions) or does things repeatedly (compulsions) even though the person knows these are unnecessary or stupid. The obsessions and compulsions can become so frequent that they affect the person's concentration and lead to depression.

Advice on the various ways depression and anxiety present in health care settings and how to manage these problems is given in Chapters 5 and 7.

1.3.2 'Bad habits'

Case 1.4

Michael was a 44-year-old man who had been attending the clinic for several months with various physical complaints. His main complaints were that his sleep was not good, that he often felt like vomiting in the mornings and that he was generally not feeling well. One day, he came to the clinic with a severe burning pain in the stomach area. Antacids were not as much help as they had been before. He was seen by the doctor, who prescribed more antacids and ranitidine, a medicine to help stomach ulcers heal. When he was about to leave the clinic, the doctor noticed that Michael was sweating profusely and his hands appeared to be shaking. The doctor asked Michael if he had any other problems. Michael sat down and started crying. He admitted that his main problem was that he had been drinking increasing amounts of alcohol in the previous few months as a way of coping with stress at work. However, now the drinking itself had become a problem. He could not pass even a few hours without having to have a drink.

Box 1.2. The key features of anxiety

A person with anxiety will experience some of the following symptoms:

Physical
- feeling her heart is beating fast (palpitations)
- a feeling of suffocation
- dizziness
- trembling, shaking all over
- headaches
- pins and needles (or sensation of ants crawling) on her limbs or face

Feeling
- feeling as if something terrible is going to happen to her
- feeling scared

Thinking
- worrying too much about her problems or her health
- thoughts that she is going to die, lose control or go mad (these thoughts are often associated with severe physical symptoms and extreme fear)
- repeatedly thinking the same distressing thought again and again despite efforts to stop thinking them

Behaving
- avoiding situations that she is scared of, such as marketplaces or public transport
- poor sleep

What's the problem? Michael was dependent on alcohol. Many of his complaints were due to the direct damage caused by alcohol to his body. Some symptoms were caused by the distress he felt because of withdrawal symptoms.

Case 1.5

Li was an 18-year-old high school student. He had always been an average student, hardworking and honest. Recently, however, his mother had noticed that Li had been staying out till late at night, his school grades had been falling, and he was spending more money. The previous week, his mother noticed that some money was missing from her purse. She was worried that Li might have stolen it. She had also noticed that Li was spending less time with his old friends and family, and seemed to be hanging around with a new group of friends, whom he did not introduce to his parents. His mother had suggested to him that he should see a counsellor, but he refused. The health worker decided to visit Li at home. Li was very reluctant to discuss anything at first. However, as he became more trusting of the health worker, he admitted that he had been using heroin regularly for several months, and now he was 'hooked'. He had tried to stop on many occasions, but each time he felt so sick that he just went back to the drug. He said he wanted help but did not know where to turn.

What's the problem? Li had become dependent on heroin. Because of his dependence, his school performance had suffered and he had been seeing new friends who also use drugs. He had been stealing things to pay for the drug.

A person is said to be dependent on alcohol or drugs when their use harms the person's physical, mental or social health. Typically, it becomes difficult for people to stop using these substances because they may develop physical discomfort and an extreme desire to consume the substance ('withdrawal syndrome'). Dependence problems cause great damage to sufferers, their families and ultimately to the community. Alcohol, for example, not only harms the drinker through its physical effects, but is also associated with high suicide rates, marriage problems and domestic violence, road traffic accidents and increased poverty. For most heavy drinkers, alcohol misuse is rarely the main reason for seeking health care. Instead, you have to be alert and ask people about their drinking habits, particularly when the clinical presentation suggests that the illness may be related to drinking. The key features of alcohol dependence are shown in Box 1.3.

Different types of drugs may be abused. Other than alcohol, the commonest drugs of misuse are: cannabis, opium and related drugs such as heroin; cocaine and other stimulants, such as 'speed'; and sedative medicines. The key features are shown in Box 1.4.

There are other habits that can damage people's health. These include smoking cigarettes, dependence on sleeping pills, and gambling.

Advice on how to identify and help people with habit problems is given in Chapter 6.

1.3.3 Severe mental disorders (psychoses)

This group of mental disorders consists of three main types of illness: schizophrenia, manic–depressive disorder (also called bipolar disorder) and brief psychoses. These illnesses are rare. However, they are characterised by marked behavioural problems and strange or unusual thinking. This is why these are the disorders most typically associated with mental illness. The majority of patients in psychiatric hospitals suffer from psychoses.

Box 1.3. The key features of alcohol dependence

A person with alcohol dependence will experience some of the following symptoms:

Physical
• stomach problems, such as gastritis and ulcers
• liver disease and jaundice
• vomiting blood
• vomiting or sickness in the mornings
• tremors, especially in the mornings
• accidents and injuries
• withdrawal reactions, such as seizures (fits), sweating, confusion

Feeling
• feeling helpless and out of control
• feeling guilty about his drinking behaviour

Thinking
• a strong desire for alcohol
• continuous thoughts about the next drink
• thoughts of suicide

Behaving
• sleep difficulties
• the need to have a drink in the daytime
• the need to have a drink early in the morning, to relieve physical discomfort

Box 1.4. The key features of drug misuse

A person who misuses drugs will experience some of the following symptoms:

Physical
• breathing problems, such as asthma
• skin infections and ulcers if she injects drugs
• withdrawal reactions if the drug is not taken, such as nausea, anxiety, tremors, diarrhoea, stomach cramps, sweating

Feeling
• feeling helpless and out of control
• feeling guilty about taking drugs
• feeling sad and depressed

Thinking
• a strong desire to take the drug
• continuous thoughts about the next occasion of drug use
• thoughts of suicide

Behaving
• sleep difficulties
• irritability, such as becoming short-tempered
• stealing money to buy drugs; getting in trouble with the police

They are all talking about me ... in fact, there is a plot to kill me.

Case 1.6

Ismail was a 25-year-old college student who was brought by past year and had started locking himself in his room. Ismail used to be a good student but had failed his last exams. His mother said that he would often spend hours staring into space. Sometimes he muttered to himself as if he were talking to an imaginary person. Ismail had to be forced to come to the clinic by his parents. At first, he refused to talk to the nurse. After a while he admitted that he believed that his parents and neighbours were plotting to kill him and that the Devil was interfering with his mind. He said he could hear his neighbours talk about him and say nasty things outside his door. He said he felt as if he had been possessed, but did not see why he should come to the clinic since he was not ill.

What's the problem? Ismail was suffering from a severe mental disorder called schizophrenia. This made him hear voices and imagine things that were not true.

Box 1.5. The key features of schizophrenia

A person with schizophrenia will experience some of the following symptoms:

Physical
• strange complaints, such as the sensation that an animal or unusual objects are inside his body

Feeling
• depression
• a loss of interest and motivation in daily activities
• feeling scared of being harmed

Thinking
• difficulty thinking clearly
• strange thoughts, such as believing that others are trying to harm him or that his mind is being controlled by external forces (such thoughts are also called 'delusions')

Behaving
• withdrawal from usual activities
• restlessness, pacing about
• aggressive behaviour
• bizarre behaviour such as hoarding rubbish
• poor self-care and hygiene
• answering questions with irrelevant answers

Imagining
• hearing voices that talk about him, particularly nasty voices (hallucinations)
• seeing things that others cannot (hallucinations)

Box 1.6. The key features of mania

A person with mania will experience some of the following symptoms:

Feeling
• feeling on top of the world
• feeling happy without any reason
• irritability

Thinking
• believing that she has special powers or is a special person
• believing that others are trying to harm her
• denying that there is any illness at all

Behaving
• rapid speech
• being socially irresponsible, such as being sexually inappropriate
• being unable to relax or sit still
• sleeping less
• trying to do many things but not managing to complete anything
• refusing treatment

Imagining
• hearing voices that others cannot (often, these voices tell her that she is an important person who can do great things)

Schizophrenia is a severe mental disorder which usually begins before the age of 30. Sufferers may become aggressive or withdrawn, may talk in an irrelevant manner and may talk to themselves. They may feel suspicious of others and believe unusual things, such as that their thoughts are being interfered with. They may experience hallucinations, such as hearing voices that others cannot. Unfortunately, many people with schizophrenia do not recognise that they are suffering from an illness and refuse to seek treatment voluntarily. Schizophrenia is often a long-term illness, lasting several months or years, and may require long-term treatment. The key features of schizophrenia are shown in Box 1.5.

Case 1.7

Maria was a 31-year-old who has been brought to the clinic by her husband because she had started behaving in an unusual manner a week previously. She was sleeping much less than usual and was constantly on the move. Maria had stopped looking after the house and children as efficiently as before. She was talking much more than normal and often said things that were unreal and grand. For example, she had been saying that she could heal other people and that she came from a very wealthy family (even though her husband was a factory worker). She had also been spending more money on clothes and cosmetics than was normal for her. When Maria's husband tried to bring her to the clinic, she became very angry and tried to hit him. Finally, his neighbours had helped him to force her to come.

What's the problem? Maria was suffering from a severe mental disorder called mania. This made her believe grand things and made her irritable when her husband tried to bring her to the clinic.

Manic–depressive illness or bipolar disorder is typically associated with two poles (or extremes) of mood: 'high' mood (or mania) and 'low' mood (or depression). The illness usually begins in adulthood and mostly comes to the notice of the health worker because of the manic phase (Box 1.6 lists the key features). The depressed phase is similar to depression in common mental disorders except that it is usually more serious. A typical feature of this condition is that it is episodic. This means that there are periods during which sufferers are completely well, even if they are not taking treatment. This is in contrast to people with schizophrenia, who may, in the absence of medication, often remain ill.

Case 1.8

Ricard was a 34-year-old man who suddenly started behaving in a bizarre manner three days earlier. He became very restless, started talking nonsense and behaved in a shameless manner, taking his clothes off in public. He had no history of a mental illness. The only medical history was that he had been suffering from fever and headaches for a few days before the abnormal behaviour began. When he was brought to the clinic, he appeared confused and did not know where he was or what day it was. He was seeing things that others could not and could not answer the health worker's questions sensibly. He also had high fever. He was found to have cerebral malaria.

What's the problem? Ricard was suffering from a severe mental disorder called delirium, confusion or acute psychosis. In his case, the problem had been caused by the infection of his brain by malaria.

An acute or brief psychosis appears similar to schizophrenia (☛ Box 1.7), but is different in that it usually starts suddenly and is brief in duration. Thus, most sufferers recover completely within a month and do not need long-term treatment. Brief psychoses are typically caused by a sudden severe stressful event, such as the death of a loved person. Sometimes, a severe medical or brain illness can cause the psychosis; when this happens, the condition is also called 'delirium' (☛ Box 1.8). Delirium often needs urgent medical treatment.

Box 1.7. The key features of acute or brief psychoses

The symptoms are similar to those of schizophrenia and mania (see Boxes 1.5 and 1.6). The key is that the symptoms begin suddenly and last less than a month. The typical symptoms seen are:
• severe behavioural disturbance such as restlessness and aggression
• hearing voices or seeing things others cannot
• bizarre beliefs
• talking nonsense
• fearful emotional state or rapidly changing emotions (from tears to laughter)

Advice on how to deal with severe mental disorders can be found in Chapter 4.

1.3.4 Mental retardation

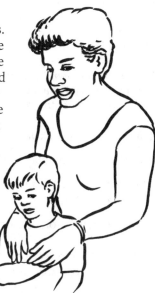

The term 'mental retardation' is being dropped by many health workers. This is because it is often used in a discriminatory way. Instead, the term 'learning disability' is preferred. In this manual, we will use 'mental retardation' because it is the most widely used and understood term to describe the condition of delayed mental development.

Mental retardation is not a mental illness in the strict sense of the term. This is because an illness usually refers to a health problem that begins and ends. Mental retardation, on the other hand, is a state, i.e. a condition that is present from very early childhood, and remains present for the rest of the person's life. Mental retardation means that the brain development (and thus mental abilities) of the child is slower or delayed compared with that in other children. People with mental retardation are often brought to health workers by concerned relatives for many reasons such as self-care, school difficulties and behavioural problems such as aggression (☞ Box 1.9).

Case 1.9
Baby Rudo was born after a very difficult labour. Her mother was in labour for more than two days and the baby was getting stuck in her birth passage. After the village midwife said that the mother needed medical help, she was put in a taxi and taken to the hospital, about three hours away. At the hospital they had to do an operation to remove the baby. The baby did not breathe for many minutes after being born

Box 1.8. The key features of delirium (acute psychosis caused by a brain or medical illness)

A person with delirium will experience some of the following symptoms:
• disorientation (he does not know where he is or what time it is)
• fever, excess sweating, raised pulse rate and other physical signs
• poor memory
• disturbed sleep pattern
• visual hallucinations (seeing things others cannot)
• symptoms that vary from hour to hour, with periods of apparent recovery alternating with periods of severe symptoms

---

Box 1.9. Key features of mental retardation

A person with mental retardation will experience some of the following symptoms:
- delays in achieving milestones such as sitting up, walking and speaking
- difficulties in school, especially coping with studies and repeated failures
- difficulties in relating to others, especially other children of the same age
- in adolescence, inappropriate sexual behaviour
- in adulthood, problems in everyday activities such as cooking, managing money, finding and staying on in a job, etc.

---

and it was only because of the doctor's treatment that she lived at all. She was a very precious baby indeed! Both parents took great care of Rudo, who seemed quite normal for the first few months. However, they later noticed that Rudo took longer to learn to sit up by herself and to walk than had their son, Thabo. For example, whereas Thabo had been able to walk by the time he was just one year old, Rudo began walking when she was nearly two. Even her speaking seemed much delayed. She could not call her mother even when she was two years old. It was then that they realised something was not right. They took Rudo to a children's doctor, who asked them many questions about Rudo's few years of life.

What's the problem? The doctor carefully explained that Rudo was suffering from mental retardation. This had probably happened because Rudo's brain had been damaged as a result of the great delay in getting her mother to a hospital during her difficult labour.

There can be various degrees of mental retardation:

- mild retardation may lead only to difficulty in schooling but no other problems;

- moderate retardation may lead to failure to stay in the school system and difficulties in self-care such as bathing;

- severe retardation often means the person needs help even for simple activities such as eating.

Whereas persons with mild retardation may spend their entire lives without being referred to health workers, those at the severe end are diagnosed in early childhood because of the obvious severity of the disability. Whereas those in the mild category may be able to live alone and work in certain types of jobs, those in the severe category will almost always need close supervision and care.

Advice on how to help children with mental retardation is given in section 8.1, and information on how to prevent mental retardation is given in section 10.2.

1.3.5 Mental health problems in the elderly

Case 1.10

Raman was a 70-year-old retired postman who was living with his son and daughter-in-law. His wife had died some 10 years previously. Over the past few years, Raman had become increasingly forgetful, something his family passed off as 'just growing old'. However, the forgetfulness kept getting worse, until one day he lost his way around his own home. He started forgetting the names of his relatives, including his favourite grandchildren. His behaviour became unpredictable; on some days, he would be irritable and easily lose his temper, while on others he would sit for hours without saying a thing. Raman's physical health began to deteriorate and one day he had a fit. Raman's son brought him to hospital, where a special scan of the brain was done; this showed changes in the structure of the brain which confirmed that Raman had dementia.

Box 1.10. Key features of dementia

A person with dementia (who will rarely be under the age of 60) will have some of the following symptoms:
• forgetting important things like names of friends or relatives
• losing her way in familiar areas such as in the village or home
• becoming irritable or losing her temper easily
• becoming withdrawn or appearing depressed
• laughing and crying for no reason
• having difficulty following conversations
• not knowing what day it is or where she is (disorientation)
• talking inappropriately or irrationally

What's the problem? Raman was suffering from a kind of brain disease typically found in older people, called dementia. This illness begins with forgetfulness. It continues to get worse as time passes and leads to behaviour problems.

I can't seem to remember things. I even forget what day it is or what I had for breakfast

The elderly suffer from two main types of mental illness. One is depression, which is often associated with loneliness, physical ill health, disability and poverty. This is similar to depression in other age groups. The other mental health problem in the elderly is dementia (Box 1.10). This is typically a disease of older people only.

The clinical problems associated with dementia are discussed in section 4.7. Integrating mental health in health care for the elderly is discussed in section 9.9.

1.3.6 Mental health problems in children

Certain types of mental health problems that typically occur in childhood:

• dyslexia, which affects learning abilities;

• hyperactivity, where children are overactive;

• conduct disorders, in which children misbehave much more than is normal;

• depression, in which children become sad and unhappy;

• bed-wetting, in which children wet the bed at an age when they should not.

Children will also come to your attention when they have been the victims of abuse.

The main thing to remember is that these child mental health problems (Box 1.11), unlike mental retardation, often improve, and some children completely recover. Thus, it is important not to assume that any child with a behaviour problem is mentally retarded.

For more information on these topics ☞ Chapter 8, and also sections 9.6, 9.7, 10.3.

Box 1.11. Key features of mental illness in children

The key signs that suggest mental illness in children are:
• a child who is doing badly in studies even though she has normal intelligence
• a child who is always restless and cannot pay attention
• a child who is constantly getting in trouble or fights with other children
• a child who is withdrawn and does not play or interact with other children
• a child who refuses to go to school

1.4 The causes of mental illness

In many cultures, both medical and traditional explanations are used to understand the causes of ill health. Traditional models are often related to spiritual or supernatural causes, such as bad spirits or witchcraft. You should be aware of the beliefs in your culture. However, you should also be aware of the medical theories and use these to explain mental illness to the people who consult you. It is useful to keep in mind the following main factors that can lead to mental illness:

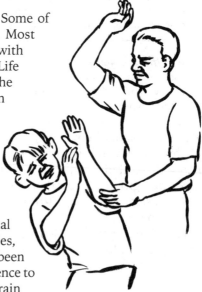

- *Stressful life events.* Life is full of experiences and events. Some of these may make a person feel worried and under stress. Most people will learn how to deal with such events and carry on with life. However, sometimes they can lead to mental illness. Life events that cause great stress include unemployment, the death of a loved one, economic problems such as being in debt, loneliness, infertility, marital conflict, violence and trauma.

- *Difficult family background.* People who have had an unhappy childhood because of violence or emotional neglect are more likely to suffer mental illnesses such as depression and anxiety later in life.

- *Brain diseases.* Mental retardation, dementias and emotional problems can result from brain infections, AIDS, head injuries, epilepsy and strokes. No definite brain pathology has yet been identified for many mental illnesses. However, there is evidence to show that many illnesses are associated with changes in brain chemicals such as neurotransmitters.

- *Heredity or genes.* Heredity is an important factor for severe mental disorders. However, if one parent has a mental illness, the risk that the children will suffer from a mental illness is very small. This is because, like diabetes and heart disease, these disorders are also influenced by environmental factors.

- *Medical problems.* Physical illnesses such as kidney and liver failure can sometimes cause a severe mental disorder. Some medicines (e.g. some of those used to treat high blood pressure) can cause a depressive illness. Many medicines when used in large doses in elderly people can cause a delirium.

1.5 Culture and mental illness

There are many ways in which culture can influence mental health issues.

- *What is a mental illness?* Concepts about what a mental illness is differ from one culture to another. The group of disorders most often associated with mental illness is the severe mental disorders, such as schizophrenia and mania. The commonest mental health problems in general or community health care are the common mental disorders (depression and anxiety) and problems associated with alcohol and drug dependence. These disorders are rarely viewed as being mental illnesses. Although you should be aware of these mental illnesses, you need not add to the sufferer's problems by using labels with a potential stigma attached to them. Instead, you can use locally appropriate words to describe stress or emotional upset as a way of communicating the diagnosis. (For more on the main mental health problems in a primary care clinic ☞ section 9.1.)

- *Words used to describe emotional distress.* The descriptions of human emotions and illness are not easy to translate into different languages. Consider the word 'depression'. This word means sadness and is used to describe both a feeling ('I feel depressed') and an illness ('the patient is suffering from depression'). In many languages, however, while there are words to describe the feeling of sadness, there are no words that describe depression as an illness. Thus, it is important to try to understand the words in the local language that best describe depression as a feeling and as an illness. Sometimes, different words may be found for these two meanings. Sometimes, a phrase or series of words will need to be used to convey the meaning of depression as an illness. The Glossary in this manual provides the words in English to describe various mental health problems and symptoms. Space is provided next to each word and its meaning for readers to write down the term in their local language.

- *Beliefs about witchcraft and evil spirits.* People in many societies feel that their illness has been caused by witchcraft or evil spirits or is the result of some supernatural cause. There is little to gain from challenging such views (which are often shared by the community). Such an approach will only make the person feel uncomfortable. Instead, it would be better to understand these beliefs and explain the medical theory in simple language.

- *Priests, prophets and psychiatrists: what do people do when in distress?* Sick people seek help from a variety of alternative, religious and traditional health care providers. Examples include: homoeopathy, Ayurveda, traditional Chinese medicine, spiritual healers, shamans, priests, pastors and prophets. This is for several reasons. First, medical health care does not have the answers for all health problems, and this is especially true for mental illness. Second, many

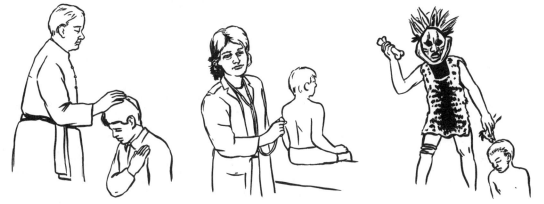

People with mental illness seek help from different sources.

Box 1.12. Things to remember about mental illness

• There are a number of different types of mental illness. Mental illness can produce severe disability and can lead to death.

• The commonest types of mental illness in the community or general health care settings are the common mental disorders, and disorders related to alcohol dependence; however, many patients and health workers may not consider these conditions as mental disorders.

• Schizophrenia, manic–depressive illness and acute psychoses are conditions that are most often recognised by the community and health workers as mental illnesses, because of the disturbed behaviour associated with them.

• Stressful events, changes in brain function and medical factors such as brain infections are the main causes of mental illness.

• Some people may believe that spirits or supernatural factors cause mental illness. You should not challenge these beliefs but try to put forward the medical explanations for these problems.

• It is not essential that you label a person with a mental illness diagnosis. What matters is that you recognise the existence of a mental health problem, attempt to identify the type of mental illness and then offer appropriate treatment.

---

persons associate their emotional upset with spiritual or social factors and thus seek help from non-medical persons. Traditional treatment may help some people get better quicker than would medical treatments.

• *Counselling people with mental health problems.* In many Western societies, counselling to help people with emotional problems is based on psychological theories which have evolved from within their cultures. These theories are foreign to the cultural beliefs in many non-Western cultures. This does not mean that counselling therapies will not be useful in these cultures. You will need to search for resources and methods that have evolved in your own culture because these are likely to prove more acceptable. Only a simple form of counselling that can be applied in most cultures is described in this manual (☛ section 3.2).

Box 1.13. Voices from the edge

"It was so frightening when it first happened. I was sitting on a bus, when all of a sudden my heart started beating so fast that I felt I was having a heart attack. I had difficulty breathing, and then I started feeling as if ants were crawling on my hands and feet. My heart started pounding even faster, my body felt hot and I was trembling all over. I just had to get off the bus, but it was moving fast and I began to choke. My biggest fear was that I might collapse or go mad. Then the bus came to a stop and I rushed to get off even though I was still far from home. Since then, I have never been able to get on a bus … just the thought of using a bus makes me feel sick. For the past two years, I have stopped going out of the house because of this fear and now I have few friends and almost no social life … I didn't know what to do and I was too scared to see a psychiatrist … after all, I am not a mental case."
A 24-year-old woman with panic attacks and phobia

"I was only 17 when I first started hearing the voices. At first, I wasn't sure whether they were in my mind or real. But later, I used to hear strangers talking about me, saying nasty things. Once I heard a voice telling me to jump into a well and for days I would stand near the well feeling that I should obey the voice. I used to feel that my thoughts were being controlled by the TV and, sometimes, I was sure that my food was being poisoned and that gangsters were out to kill me. I used to get angry and it was when I lost my temper so badly and hit my neighbour that I was taken to the hospital."
A 23-year-old man with schizophrenia

"It started quite gradually, but before I knew it I had lost all interest in life. Even my children and family didn't make me feel happy. I was tired all the time. I could not sleep … I used to wake up at 2 or 3 in the morning and then just toss and turn. I lost the taste for food which I used to love and I lost weight. I even lost interest in reading because I just could not concentrate. My head ached. I felt so lousy about myself, that I was a burden on the family and so on. The worst thing was that I felt embarrassed about the way I felt and could not tell anyone … my mother-in-law used to complain that I had become lazy. Once I felt like ending my life and it was then that I got so scared that I told my husband … that was two months after I started feeling ill."
A 43-year-old woman with depression

"I used to feel as if I had so much energy that I did not need to sleep at all. In fact, I hardly slept in those days. I would rush about with all my schemes and plans, but never really managed to finish any of them properly. I used to lose my temper if anyone tried to stop me. Once I got into a big fight with my business partners over one of my crazy schemes. But when I was high, I never realised how wrong I was. I even felt sometimes that I had special powers to heal others. The worst thing about my illness was how I would spend so much money that I almost bankrupted the family."
A 38-year-old man with mania

"I don't know what's happening. I seem to forget things so easily. The other day, my wife came to give me my morning tea and, for a moment, I did not know who she was. And then, I was walking home from the market and, even though I was in my village, I suddenly found I had no idea where I was. I always thought I was getting absent minded as I grew older, but this is too much … and then I remember my father who died after years of losing his memory and now I am scared that I may have the same problem."
A 68-year-old man with dementia

"My problems started at work when I started taking too much sick leave. I kept getting stomach upsets and, recently, I had jaundice. It was then that I started worrying about my drinking. What frightens me is that I wake up feeling terrible. It's like I must have a drink to get myself going in the day. These days I am starting to drink even before lunch. I don't know exactly how much I am drinking but it never seems to be enough."
A 44-year-old man with a drinking problem

Chapter 2

Assessing someone with a mental illness

This chapter is about how you can carry out an interview to diagnose a mental illness. It covers the main symptoms of mental illness and gives tips on how to manage difficult interviews, such as those in crowded primary care clinics or with people who refuse to talk. It describes the questions you can ask to confirm the presence of a mental illness.

2.1 Can you examine a mentally ill person?

The assessment of mental health need not be done by a specialist. It requires nothing more than compassion, good listening skills and some basic knowledge, as described in this manual.

Some health workers have mixed feelings about assessing a mentally ill person. They may experience:

- fear that the person may attack them;

- disgust with the person's lack of personal hygiene;

- frustration that the interview may take longer than a regular examination;

- amusement at the odd behaviour shown;

- anger that the person is wasting their time with 'no real illness'.

Such feelings will usually make it harder for you to provide help for mental illness. These attitudes will also make the person less comfortable and less likely to share feelings with you. A person with a mental illness should be treated with the same respect and compassion as anyone else. Working with the mentally ill is a challenge that will be both fulfilling and rewarding. The most important aspect of assessing mental illness is to give the person enough *time*.

2.2 Will you have the time to talk to someone who may have a mental illness?

The first thing to remember is that time spent finding out why someone has come to see you may actually save you time later on. We know that many mental illnesses, especially common mental disorders and alcohol problems, are rarely recognised by health workers. Health workers in a busy clinic will often simply accept

Don't be in a hurry! Time spent now can save you more time later!

someone's complaints and give medicines for them. Thus, painkillers are prescribed for aches and pains, vitamins for fatigue and sleeping pills for sleep problems. However, this may mean that the real problem, the mental illness, has not been treated. Many of these people will keep returning to the clinic and will take up more time. Thus, time spent finding the true problem may actually be a saving of time in the long run! Besides, you will get the reward of seeing the person improve rather than keep coming back for more pills. The second important thing to remember is that it does not take a long time to ask about mental illness. The key to using time sensibly is to be well informed about how to ask about mental illness, and this is described below.

2.3 Who will have a mental illness?

The commonest image of a mentally ill person is someone who is talking nonsense and behaving bizarrely. In reality, the vast majority of people with a mental illness look, behave and talk no differently from those with a physical illness. Mentally ill people are no more dangerous than physically ill people, and you should never feel that you are at risk of being harmed simply because you are talking to a person who is suffering from a mental illness.

You should consider using some kind of screening procedure to identify people who may be suffering from a mental illness. Then you can spend more time with such people to find out what the problem is and start treatment. There are two approaches to screening people in a busy clinic. First, there are some kinds of clinical presentations that are typical of mental illness. If anyone presents with these, you should suspect a mental illness (Box 2.1). Second, you can ask a set of 'golden questions' to help detect the two commonest types of mental health problems in general health care, namely the common mental disorders and alcohol dependence (Box 2.2) (☛ section 9.1). If the answer to any of these questions is positive, you should then ask more questions about these conditions.

> **Box 2.1. Clinical presentations that suggest a mental illness**
>
> • When the person or relatives complain directly of mental illness, such as depression or alcohol problems.
> • When the person or relatives suspect super-natural causes.
> • When a specific cause of mental illness, such as alcohol misuse and family violence, is obvious.
> • When you know that the person has relationship problems, such as marital and sexual problems.
> • When you know that the person has life problems, such as unemployment or the death of a close friend.
> • When there are many physical complaints (especially more than three) that do not fit into a pattern of any known physical illness.
> • When there is a personal or family history of mental illness.

Box 2.2. Golden questions to detect mental illness in general health care settings

• Do you have any problems sleeping at night?
• Have you been feeling as if you have lost interest in your usual activities?
• Have you been feeling sad or unhappy recently?
• Have you been feeling scared or frightened of anything?
• Have you been worried about drinking too much alcohol recently?
• How much money and time have you been spending on alcohol recently?

If any of the answers are 'yes', ask more detailed questions to confirm the diagnosis.

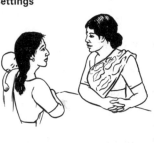

2.4 What to ask a person with a probable mental illness

A standard form of interview can be used for people who, as a result of the screening process, you suspect have a mental illness (Box 2.3). There are three types of information you will need to understand the problem. This information should also suggest ways in which the person can be helped.

- Basic information on age, address, family details and employment should be collected for anyone who consults you.

- Information about the illness itself should begin with finding out about the symptoms, for example how long they have been present and how they affect the person's life.

- Then you should ask about the person's social situation. This should include who the person is living with and who are the main sources of social support. Questions about recent life events such as a death in the family may help explain why the person is suffering from a mental illness.

2.5 Symptom checklists to diagnose mental disorders

The following symptom checklists may be used for the diagnosis of three major types of mental disorders described in Chapter 1.

2.5.1 To diagnose a common mental disorder (depression or anxiety)

The person must have had at least one of the following symptoms for at least two weeks:

- feeling sad;

- loss of interest in daily activities;

- feeling tense or nervous or worrying a lot.

Other symptoms that are frequently present and should be asked about include:

- disturbed sleep;

- tiredness;

- loss of appetite;

- poor concentration;

- suicidal thoughts;

- palpitations (heart beating fast), trembling, dizziness;

- aches and pains all over the body.

Box 2.3. Information to collect from people with a probable mental illness

General information
- Sex
- Age
- Occupation
- Marital status

History of current complaint
- When and how did it start?
- Is it getting worse?
- Are medicines (or other treatments) being taken?
- The person's beliefs about the illness – what the person feels the illness is and why it has happened. You may ask questions about beliefs regarding stress and supernatural factors causing the illness.

Other information
- Is there any history of mental illness (if so, ask for old prescriptions or old clinic notes)?
- Relevant medical history, such as recent head injury.
- Recent major life events, such as separation, death in the family, unemployment.
- Social support – specifically, who does the person live with, who cares for the person, and is there any form of support from outside the home, such as religious or spiritual support and friends?

2.5.2 To diagnose a severe mental disorder

The person must have at least two of these symptoms:

- believing things that are untrue, for example that his thoughts are being controlled by outside forces or that people are trying to poison him (delusions);

- hearing or seeing things that no one else can (hallucinations); often these are frightening;

- agitation and restlessness or withdrawal and lack of interest.

If these symptoms have been present for less than a month, the diagnosis may be of an acute psychosis. If they have been present for more than a month, schizophrenia is possible. If there is a history of episodes in which the person seems to recover completely, bipolar disorder may be the diagnosis. The 'high' or manic episode can be diagnosed on the basis of:

- increased speed of talking;

- restlessness;

- irritable mood (getting angry easily);

- grand ideas (out of keeping with reality).

2.5.3 To diagnose alcohol (or drug) dependence

The person must have at least two of the following symptoms for at least one month:

- drinking (or drug use), which has led to personal problems such as losing his job or health problems such as accidents or jaundice;

- difficulty in controlling the use of alcohol (or the drug) even though there are problems being caused by the use;

- alcohol (or the drug) is used throughout the day;

- feeling sick or unwell unless he drinks alcohol (or takes the drug);

- using gradually increasing amounts of alcohol (or the drug).

Section 6.1 gives more details on how to diagnose alcohol dependence; for the diagnosis of other types of mental illnesses such as confusion, dementias and child mental health problems, refer to specific chapters in the manual.

2.6 What to look for during the interview

During the interview, you should note any of the following:

- facial expressions of sadness or fear (with schizophrenia and depression);

- restlessness, i.e. unable to sit relaxed (with psychoses, depression, drug and alcohol dependence and as a side-effect of some psychiatric medicines);

- strange movements (associated with schizophrenia and as a side-effect of some psychiatric medicines);

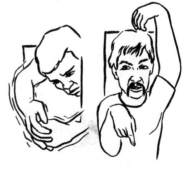

- irrelevant answers to questions (associated with all the psychoses);
- a very fast rate of talking (associated with the psychoses, especially mania);
- a very slow rate of talking (associated with depression, drug dependence and schizophrenia);
- the person's general hygiene and self-care (poor in depression, drug and alcohol dependence, and schizophrenia).

2.7 How to conduct interviews

Here are some hints on how to help people feel comfortable discussing their feelings and symptoms:

- You should introduce yourself to the person. Some people may be confused or suspicious. You should clearly state your professional role and say that you wish to talk about the person's recent health.

- To establish rapport, you can begin the interview with a general subject such as a recent news event. Many people feel more comfortable discussing personal issues when they can identify with the health worker, for example speak the same language and live in the same area.

- Empathy simply means imagining what it must feel like to be in another person's place. Understanding a person's symptoms and the social and family situation will help you be more sensitive in dealing with illness and will help the person feel more comfortable in talking to you.

- The golden questions should be asked of anyone who consults you. Any positive responses should lead to a more thorough assessment, using the checklists in section 2.5.

- It is helpful always to keep in mind the main types of mental illnesses and their symptoms (☛ section 1.3). This is especially important because many sufferers may not openly discuss emotional complaints unless specifically asked about them.

- You must not appear pressured for time, for example by constantly checking a wristwatch! Remember that just ten minutes is often all that is needed to understand a person's problem and guide treatment choices. Of course, it is better if you can spare more time.

- Give the person a chance to talk without the relatives present. Never consider people 'unreliable' simply because they suffer from a mental illness.

- Try to speak to the relatives as well. Some people with a mental illness may deny they have a problem. Some may not be fully aware of the nature of their behaviour. Relatives and friends can often give information that is valuable in making a clinical decision.

- Look at the person during the interview. Eye contact can help make people feel confident that a health worker is interested in what they are saying.

- Try to ensure privacy; this may be impossible in crowded clinics, but even here you can speak softly so that discussions of personal problems are not overheard by others in the room. Alternatively, ask the person to wait till the clinic is less crowded and then talk in private.

And how long have you been hearing voices, Mr Rao?

Try to ensure privacy – discussions of personal problems should not be overheard.

- Record key information for future reference, especially the main symptoms, current diagnosis and important information, such as the presence of any marital problems.

2.8 How to reach a diagnosis

There are only a few types of diagnosis that need to be made in a general health care setting. Part II will describe how you can diagnose various mental illnesses based on the problems people complain of to health workers. Be familiar with the types of mental disorders (☞ section 1.3) and the questions to assess mental health as discussed in this chapter. Practice the questions first with colleagues. Remember that diagnoses are important for two reasons:

- to help guide you in selecting the right treatments;
- to help explain to people the cause of their complaints.

2.9 Special situations in assessment

There are some special situations in assessing mental illness. These include:

- assessing someone who refuses to talk;
- assessing physical complaints in a person with a mental illness;
- assessing someone on the telephone;
- assessing someone with the family present;
- assessing the violent person (☞ section 4.1);
- assessing the confused person (☞ section 4.2);
- assessing the suicidal person (☞ section 4.4);
- assessing children with mental health problems (☞ Chapter 8).

The first four situations are discussed below. The remaining four situations are discussed in the other parts of this manual.

2.9.1 Assessing someone who refuses to talk

Sometimes you may be faced with people who refuse to talk. This could be for many reasons. They may be angry for having been brought to the clinic. They may be scared that talking to a health worker might mean they will be labelled a 'mental case'. They may be suspicious of your motives.

The general advice in such situations is to allow more time. Interview the person in a private room if possible. If this is not possible, at least ask any relatives to stand far away so that the conversation cannot be heard by them. This may help the person feel more confident about sharing personal problems. Do not threaten the person, for example by saying that you do not have time to waste. Instead, reassure someone who refuses to talk that you are interested in their problems. If the person refuses to talk and you have other work to attend to, say you need to go to complete the work and that you will return later when you have more time. This will allow the person some more time to think. It will also demonstrate your concern.

Do not threaten the person (left) by saying that you do not have time to waste. Instead, reassure someone who refuses to talk that you are interested in their problems (right).

2.9.2 Assessing physical complaints in a person with a mental illness

Imagine that someone whom a health worker knows has a mental illness comes to the clinic with a new complaint of a headache. Often health workers will assume that the complaint is just another symptom of the mental illness. However, this attitude may lead to a serious physical illness being missed. It is important that the physical health of a mentally ill person is given due attention. Do not dismiss new physical complaints without properly assessing them and, if required, carrying out necessary tests. Remember that mentally ill people may neglect their physical health. Some kinds of mental health problems are closely associated with physical health problems. The most important examples are:

• alcohol and drug dependence, which can seriously damage physical health (☞ Chapter 6);

• women who have been subject to violence or rape (☞ sections 7.2, 7.3);

• confusion and agitation, which can often be caused by physical health problems (☞ section 4.2);

• disturbed behaviour in elderly people (☞ section 4.7).

2.9.3. Assessing someone on the telephone

Where telephones are available, people may call you for advice. In fact, this can save time for both you and the caller by avoiding unnecessary visits to the clinic. Sometimes, a person may call you with a problem that is related to mental health. Examples of such calls could be:

• a person who wishes to die;

• a child who is in need of help;

• a person who is drunk and confused;

• a person who is angry and abusive.

Avoid giving vague advice or reassurance on the telephone. You should approach callers as follows:

Why are you so distressed? Can you come to the clinic to talk to me?

- Find out their name, age, address and which telephone number they are calling from.

- Ask them to tell you exactly what the problem is, how it started, what has happened recently. Get an idea of the situation they are facing.

- Find out about any close friends or relatives to whom they can talk. Encourage callers to share their distress with them now.

- If they are abusive or confused, explain that you would like to help but cannot if they do not change their attitude. If callers remain difficult, hang up the telephone.

- Ask them to come to the clinic if you feel they are in need of a face-to-face assessment.

- With children in distress, immediately inform a local child welfare team or the local police. Ask children to stay where they are and say that someone will come to help them.

2.9.4 Assessing someone with the family present

Families are an important factor in assessing and treating people with mental illnesses. You must balance the need to involve the family in the assessment with the need to ensure the person's privacy. As a rule, it is important that you have a chance to speak to the person alone on at least one occasion. During this interview, you will have a chance to find out about family relationships and stresses. Later on you may discuss the problem with other family members. However, care must be taken not to discuss matters that the person has said should remain confidential.

There are some situations when the family can be a key to providing information about the person. For example, some people with severe mental disorders or dependence problems cannot give a clear or accurate account. In such cases, talking to relatives can provide you with the information needed to reach a diagnosis. Relatives can play an important role in monitoring the health of the person and encouraging the taking of prescribed treatment.

Box 2.4. Things to remember when assessing someone with a mental illness

- The most important factors in assessing mental illness are to give enough time to talk to the person and to be able to listen patiently to the person.
- Most mentally ill people can give a clear and complete history of their problem. Relatives can also provide useful information.
- A systematic assessment interview can be the first (and a very important) step in the treatment of the person with a mental illness.
- Most common mental health problems can be easily diagnosed by asking questions about specific complaints.
- Mentally ill people may also suffer from a physical illness; never dismiss a physical complaint just because a person also has a mental illness.

Chapter 3

The treatment of mental illness

There was a time when many people with mental disorders were locked up in asylums and treated in a degrading manner. People blamed mentally ill people for the way they behaved and would abuse them. Even today, many mentally ill people suffer human rights abuses in their homes and in some mental hospitals. Many people think that mental illnesses are untreatable. Some people cannot understand how 'talking' to someone can be considered a 'medical' treatment.

The truth is very different. Most mental disorders can be effectively treated. The real problem is that many people with mental disorders rarely see health workers. Even when they do, they tend to receive treatments that are not effective or may even be harmful. Like medicines for physical illnesses, medicines for mental illness work only when taken in the right doses for the right period of time. 'Talking' can be as effective a treatment as a pill, depending on how the talking treatment is carried out and for what reason.

There are two important points for you to remember while reading this chapter.

• The treatment of the vast majority of mental illnesses can be done with confidence by any general health worker armed with the basic knowledge described in this manual. Thus, the diagnosis of a mental illness does not mean that the person needs specialist care. It only means that you now know what type of treatment is needed.

• There are many effective ways of treating mental illnesses. The usual approach to mental illness, of treating only the different physical symptoms – for example sleeping pills for sleep problems, tonics and vitamins for tiredness, and painkillers for aches and pains – is often the least helpful in the long run. Diagnosis of the type of disorder and providing specific treatments are just as important for mental disorders as they are for physical disorders.

Even today, mentally ill persons are treated inhumanely in many places.

3.1 Drug treatments

3.1.1 When to use medicines

These tablets will help you feel much better if you take them as I tell you.

First, you must decide whether to use a medicine. Sometimes, medicines are prescribed even when a health worker feels they are not needed. Do not use a medicine only because the person expects a medicine. If some people expect medicines, it is often because they are used to getting medicines every time they consult a health worker. They may believe that the only way to help a sickness is by drugs and injections. They may not be aware of the important roles played by knowledge, lifestyle changes and emotional support. If you do not take this chance to educate them and, instead, use unnecessary medicines, the person's problem may take much longer to improve. In the long run the person may come to see you more often and for much longer and take up more of your time.

On the other hand, some people are very reluctant to take medicines at all! They will offer many reasons and excuses. The most common reason for refusing medicines, though, is ignorance.

Some health workers may feel that medicines for mental illnesses are too dangerous. There are different types of drug treatments available for different mental illnesses. There are some general rules that you should follow (Box 3.1). If these are followed properly, then medicines for mental illness are as safe as any other medicines. Do not make the error of avoiding medicines when there is clear evidence that the person suffers from an illness that would benefit from them.

As a rule of thumb, the following mental illnesses will benefit from medicines:

- severe mental disorders, including schizophrenia, manic–depressive illness and acute psychoses (☞ Chapter 4);

- common mental disorders, particularly when these have lasted more than a month and are seriously affecting the person's day-to-day life (☞ Chapter 5);

- acute stress situations, such as excitement and restlessness following a death of a close relative (☞ Chapter 7).

Box 3.1. The steps in using medicines for mental illness

- Try to identify the *type* of mental illness. Knowing the diagnosis can help make the choice of treatment much simpler.
- Depending on the type of mental illness, decide whether a drug treatment is required.
- Use the guidelines in section 3.1.2 to choose a specific medicine.
- Explain to the patient how to take the medicine and for how long.
- To limit side-effects, some medicines may need to be started in a small dose which is increased in steps until the recommended average dose is reached.
- Always keep a close watch for side-effects (although most psychiatric medicines are quite safe).
- Never exceed the maximum dose.
- Avoid using some drugs for too short a period (e.g. antidepressants) and some for too long a period (e.g. sleeping pills).
- Resist the temptation to continue medicines 'as before' in follow-up clinics. If you see someone taking a medicine for years, review the person's health.
- Be aware of the common trade names and costs of medicines in your area. Space is provided for this information in Part IV.

3.1.2 Which medicines to use

The next step is deciding which medicine to use. There are four major groups of medicines for mental illness:

- drugs to treat depression (antidepressants);
- drugs to treat anxiety (anti-anxiety medications, including beta-blockers);
- drugs to treat severe mental disorders (antipsychotic medications);
- drugs to control manic–depressive illness.

Sometimes the medicine used will depend on the diagnosis of the type of mental illness. Thus, antidepressants may be used to treat common mental disorders. Sometimes medicines are used to treat symptoms. Thus, sleeping pills may be used to help someone sleep irrespective of the diagnosis. Similarly, antipsychotic drugs may be used to treat disturbed behaviour which may occur in severe mental disorders or mental retardation. Below are the general guidelines on which drugs to use for specific types of mental illnesses. Details of trade names, costs, doses and side-effects can be found in Part IV.

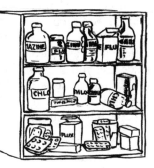

Antidepressants

These medicines are used for depression and anxiety. These disorders often present as medically unexplained physical complaints, such as tiredness and sleep problems. In addition, they are useful for panic disorder, obsessive–compulsive disorder and phobias. They can also be used when depression occurs along with other mental illnesses such as alcohol misuse or schizophrenia.

There are three main types of antidepressants that you can use:

- tricyclic antidepressants, such as imipramine, amitriptyline, norimipramine, nortriptyline, dothiepin and desipramine;
- serotonin 'boosters', such as fluoxetine, sertraline and fluvoxamine;
- new drugs, such as venlafaxine, paroxetine, bupropion and citalopram.

There are some points you should remember when prescribing antidepressants:

- Antidepressants take three to four weeks to act.
- Treatment must be continued for at least six months to avoid relapse.
- They act only if given in the right dose.
- Tricyclic antidepressants can cause drowsiness; tell patients to avoid alcohol.
- Side-effects are often short lived. Encourage patients to continue medicines if they do experience side-effects.
- Avoid tricyclics in people with prostate enlargement or glaucoma.
- 'Serotonin boosters' cause fewer side-effects but may be more expensive.

Anti-anxiety medicines

These medicines are also called 'sleeping pills'. They include diazepam, nitrazepam, lorazepam, clonazepam, alprazolam and oxazepam. They are used to treat sleep problems and anxiety.

When you prescribe these drugs, there are some points you should remember:

• the patient should avoid alcohol;

• avoid giving them to a woman in the last stage of pregnancy;

• as a general rule, do not give them for more than four weeks because they can produce a dependence problem (☛ section 6.3).

Beta-blockers

These medicines are usually used to treat high blood pressure and cardiac disorders. Of them, propranolol has also been found to be helpful to control the physical symptoms of severe anxiety (e.g. trembling hands and palpitations).

There are two points to remember when prescribing them:

• avoid giving them to people with breathing problems and heart failure;

• avoid giving them to a woman in the last stage of pregnancy.

Antipsychotic medicines

There are many types of antipsychotic medicines. A simple way of grouping them is:

• older antipsychotics, such as chlorpromazine, thioradazine, trifluoperazine and haloperidol;

• newer antipsychotics, such as olanzapine, clozapine and risperidone.

As a general rule, the older drugs produce more side-effects but are much cheaper than the newer drugs.

Antipsychotic drugs are used to treat the severe mental disorders and to help calm people who are aggressive or confused. Thus, they can also be given to people with mental retardation or dementia who have disturbed behaviour.

You should note the following points when prescribing these drugs:

• They can take several weeks to reach full effect.

• In brief psychoses, treatment may be reduced gradually after as little as two weeks. If symptoms recur, return to the original dose, continue for three months and then try to withdraw them again.

• Treat schizophrenia for at least one year (many patients will need treatment for much longer).

• Treat mania until symptoms subside and for three months thereafter. During this period, start a different medicine to *prevent* further episodes (see below).

• Side-effects are common but are mild for most people.

• Small reductions in dose can help reduce side-effects.

• Use procyclidine or benzhexol to reduce the side-effects of tremor and stiffness. Some mental health specialists advise giving these medicines to all patients to make sure that there are fewer side-effects. This may help improve compliance.

• For severe muscle spasms (e.g. neck spasms), use procyclidine or benzhexol by injection.

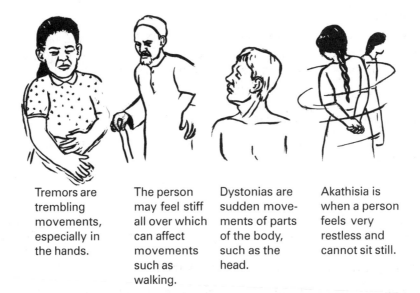

| Tremors are trembling movements, especially in the hands. | The person may feel stiff all over which can affect movements such as walking. | Dystonias are sudden movements of parts of the body, such as the head. | Akathisia is when a person feels very restless and cannot sit still. |

The side-effects of antipsychotic drugs (above) and the steps to take to stop or reduce them (below).

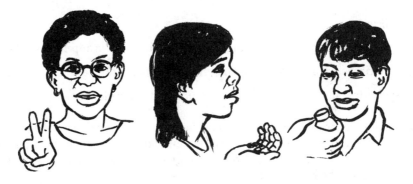

| Reduce the amount of medicine. | Or try a medicine to reduce the side-effects. | Or change to another medicine for the mental illness. |

Medicines for the prevention of manic–depressive or bipolar disorders

Manic–depressive disorder is the only mental disorder for which there are specific medicines that can be used to prevent the illness from recurring. One of three medicines may be used:

- lithium carbonate;

- sodium valproate;

- carbamazepine.

Each of these medicines needs to be taken for a long period (usually a minimum of two years) and those taking them will require monitoring of the levels of medicine in the blood. Ideally, the decision to start using them should be made by a specialist. Lithium must not be used if there are no facilities for testing blood levels of the drug. If no specialist facilities are available, carbamazepine or valproate are safer to use than lithium. None of these medicines should be given to pregnant women.

3.1.3 What if the person does not improve?

If the person's condition does not improve, consider the following possible reasons for this:

- *Poor compliance.* Make sure the person has understood the dosage and reason for the prescription. Poor compliance with medicines may occur because the person feels better and decides that there is no more need for medicines. Another reason may be that the person is worried about becoming addicted to the medicines. Side-effects can also make a person stop taking a medication (see below).

Some people refuse medicines.

- *Not enough medicine.* This is especially important with antidepressants, which are often prescribed in too small a dose.

- *Medicines not taken for long enough.* Again, this problem applies mainly to antidepressants. These medicines take at least two weeks at the recommended dose before a positive response is obtained.

- *Wrong diagnosis.* People may be withdrawn and tired because they are depressed or, in some cases, because they are psychotic. An antidepressant may not help in the latter case. Reconsider your diagnosis only if you are sure that the patient has been taking the full recommended dose for at least one month.

Medicines must be taken in the right dose.

If, despite the above considerations, your patient still fails to improve, you may need to consider a referral to the nearest specialist centre.

Medicines must be taken for the right amount of time.

Review the diagnosis if there is no improvement.

Consider referring to a mental health specialist.

3.1.4 What if there are side-effects?

First, make sure that the complaints really are side-effects. For example, someone may say that she has felt tired since starting the medicine, but sympathetic questioning may show that the symptoms were present even before the medicine was started and are therefore likely to be a result of the illness. In such cases, reassure the person by pointing this out. Remember the common side-effects of psychiatric medicines; if a complaint does not match one of these side-effects, consider other reasons for it.

Once you are sure that the person does have side-effects, you have the following options:

- Are the side-effects intolerable? Most medicines produce some side-effects, but most side-effects are minor and temporary. Ask the person how much distress the side-effect causes. Often they will say that they can tolerate the symptoms, provided the benefit of the medicines will also be evident in a short time.

- Can the dose be reduced? Sometimes, a small reduction in the dose may be tried and could lead to a reduction of side-effects without causing a worsening of the illness.

- Can the person be switched to another medicine? Many types of medicine can be used to treat the same mental illness. If intolerable side-effects occur with one type of medicine, try switching to another.

- Is the medicine necessary? In some people the need for medicine may be less evident on follow-up. You may consider stopping the medicine and seeing them again after a week to ensure they are still feeling better.

3.1.5 When are injections needed in the treatment of mental illness?

Injections have a very limited role in the treatment of mental illness (☞ Box 3.2). Besides these situations, it is advisable not to use injections in the treatment of mental illness. Avoid using unnecessary injections such as vitamins for complaints of tiredness and weakness, which are often the result of a common mental disorder rather than a vitamin deficiency.

The diagrams on the next page give some guidance on how to give injections.

Box 3.2. Injection treatments in mental illness

In violent or agitated people who refuse to take oral medicine
Any of the following:
- diazepam, 5–10 mg as an intramuscular or slow intravenous injection
- haloperidol, 5–10 mg intramuscular injection
- chlorpromazine, 25–100 mg intramuscular injection

In people with schizophrenia who are poorly compliant with oral medicines and fall ill frequently (ideally, refer any such person to a specialist)
Any of the following:
- fluphenazine decanoate, 25–75 mg every four weeks
- flupenthixol decanoate, 25–200 mg every four weeks
- haloperidol decanoate, 25–100 mg every four weeks
- zuclopenthixol decanoate, 100–400 mg every four weeks

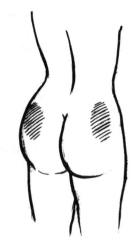

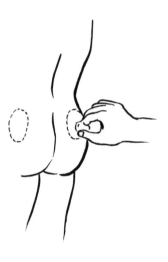

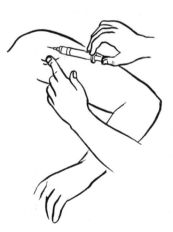

Give the injection in the upper arm or buttocks, into the muscle.

If this is the first time the patient is receiving this medicine, always give a test dose of a quarter of the full dose you want to give.

Clean the injection site.

If there is no allergic reaction after one hour, give the rest of the dose.

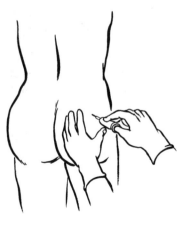

3.1.6 Cost of medicines

Many new psychiatric medicines have some advantages over older ones, namely fewer side-effects and better clinical effects. However, a major limitation (as with new medicines for other health problems) is their cost. This should always be considered when deciding which medicine to use, since the difference in side-effects may be less important to the person who needs the drug than the difference in costs between medicines. In Chapter 11 there is space for you to note down the costs of different medicines in your region so that you can choose the right medicines for the people who come to consult you.

3.1.7 How to make sure people take medicines

The most important thing you can do is to educate people about their illness and the medicine. Some important points are:

- Explain how the symptoms are caused by an illness and, just as with physical disorders, how medicines can be of help.

- Involve the family (with the patient's permission) in encouraging the patient to take the medicines.

- Take steps to minimise the risk of side-effects by starting with a small dose and gradually increasing it to the required level.

- Explain that many medicines for mental illnesses take some time to act (for example, antidepressants usually require at least two weeks to begin to take effect).

- See patients at least once a week until they show signs of recovery.

- If side-effects occur, follow the steps outlined earlier (☞ 3.1.4).

- Stick to simple dosage schedules; many psychiatric medicines can be given once a day (most antipsychotics and antidepressants, for example).

- If you know how many days have passed since the last appointment, you can check on whether the expected number of pills have been taken by counting those left over in the medication bottle/strip.

3.2 Talking treatments and counselling

Some health workers feel that 'proper' health care should involve something more than 'just talking'. Many doubt that talking can even be considered a treatment at all. This is why many health workers give medicines to just about anyone who comes to the clinic, and many people expect to be given medicines when they visit the clinic. Some may even tell you that they need an injection! It is important to clear up a few doubts and myths about talking treatments in health.

Talking treatments are more commonly called 'counselling'. The term 'counselling' is used in different ways and can mean different things to different people. Thus, a caring person with no formal training could 'counsel' friends who are distressed. In this kind of counselling, counsellors often simply follow their own instincts and knowledge. While this approach has its own strengths, it is so particular to each individual that it may not be useful as a 'treatment' for others to learn and use. Counselling as a treatment is, in fact, more than 'just' talking to a friend. This is for two main reasons:

- There is a method to counselling. All counselling methods are based on a theory that explains why a person has mental illness and seeks solutions to problems.

- Counselling is given by health workers to whom people have turned for help. When advice and reassurance are given in this situation, it has a healing potential in itself. Counselling is a skill that can be learned by any health worker who has an interest and an open mind.

There is evidence that counselling does help people with mental illness. However, counselling is not a 'competitor' to medication. If you consider educating and giving proper reassurance as key components of counselling, then you counsel everyone you work with. After all, everyone should understand something about their sickness. The process of education can make all the difference between a person feeling satisfied with your help or being unhappy and seeking help from some other health worker.

Some other types of psychological treatment, such as problem-solving (see below), are simple, useful strategies that may be applied to a wide variety of clinical situations. Thus, as a general rule, the basic elements of counselling should be used for all the people who see you, regardless of their health problem. In some, you may also choose to use medicines on top of that.

There are some mental illnesses where more specific psychological treatments may be used with great effectiveness. In particular, these illnesses are the common mental disorders and alcohol and drug dependence. The specific steps of a counselling treatment are as follows:

- give reassurance;

- provide an explanation;

- give relaxation and breathing exercises;

- give advice regarding specific symptoms;

- teach problem-solving skills.

While the discussion below deals mainly with common mental disorders, many of the principles will have more general use.

3.2.1 Give reassurance

Often, people suffering from depression and anxiety are dismissed by health workers as being 'mental' or 'neurotic'. These remarks suggest that they do not have a 'real' medical problem. It is important for you to avoid the mistake of saying "There is nothing wrong with you". Most people will be upset with this sort of remark. After all, there *is* something wrong with them. Many are worried that they are suffering from a serious physical illness. This makes them even more tense and unhappy. Thus, you should reassure them that you do understand that they are suffering from a number of distressing symptoms, but that these symptoms will *not* result in a life-threatening or dangerous illness. You should reassure them that the illness is very common and that you will explain the cause and treatment of the problem.

After childbirth, many women feel pain and discomfort now and then. In fact, it is quite common to feel tired and have sleep problems. Some women may also become sad and lose interest in their baby.

3.2.2 Provide an explanation

Explaining the nature of the problem helps to make the person aware of the reasons for the symptoms and to clear any doubts. First, explain in *general terms* that everyone experiences symptoms of bodily discomfort at some time or other. Take the example of Lucy in case 1.1, shown right:

You can then move on to focusing on the specific symptoms the person has told you about. You can also give some further meaning to the nature of the symptoms if you know how they started. For example, you could say to Rita, from case 1.2:

When you are tense, you breathe faster than normal. When you breathe faster, this produces changes in your body which make your heart beat fast and make you feel scared that something terrible may happen.

> "When a person is feeling stressed or upset or unhappy about things, she will often experience sleep problems, aches and pains and worries. You have been feeling tired and unhappy in the past month. This is because you have been under stress ever since your husband died and your children left the village. You have become depressed. This is not because you are lazy or are a mental case. This is a common problem which affects many people in our community. All the problems you described are because of this emotional illness."

Or, taking the example of Ravi in case 1.3:

> "Your symptoms of difficulty breathing, dizziness, heart beating fast and fear are because of attacks of anxiety. These are quite common problems and are not signs of a dangerous illness. In fact, they occur because you are tense or worried about something. When you are tense, you breathe faster than normal. When you breathe faster, this produces changes in your body which make your heart beat fast and make you feel scared that something terrible may happen. Actually, if you had controlled your breathing, you could have stopped the attack quickly. You are probably suffering these attacks of anxiety because of the shock of the accident in which your friend died. This can happen to anyone and is not a sign that you are going crazy."

Or, consider the case of Michael in case 1.4:

> "Your complaints of sleep problems, sickness in the mornings and burning pain in the stomach are all related to your drinking too much. Alcohol is highly addictive so that now you are feeling like drinking all the time. This is why you wake up feeling sick: it is part of the withdrawal from alcohol that makes you sick. This is why you feel better when you have a drink in the morning. You have become depressed and unhappy because you feel you have lost control of your drinking and because you are feeling sick and unwell. If you were to stop drinking, these problems would go away and you would feel much better."

It is important that you also ask the person what he feels has caused the illness and what treatment he thinks might help. Understanding his views can help you plan treatment much better. Consider the example of someone who feels that her illness was caused by bad spirits. You could suggest that she consult her priest for spiritual guidance, but that her symptoms were also caused by stress and, for this, she should take treatment as directed by you. Do not dismiss the person's views even if they appear non-scientific. By listening to and understanding the person's models of illness, you will achieve a better outcome. After your explanation, always give the person a chance to clarify doubts or concerns.

Have you understood why you are suffering these symptoms? Do you have any questions or doubts?

3.2.3 Relaxation and breathing exercises

Relaxation is a very useful way of reducing the effects of stress on the human mind. It is used in traditional types of meditation as well as in modern psychology. Most methods of relaxation use some form of breathing exercise. It is these exercises that are of most value in helping people with emotional problems.

Before you teach the exercise below, try it yourself. You will feel relaxed and calm. It is one treatment that you can take without having to feel you have a sickness!

The exercise can be done at any time of the day. The person should devote at least 10 minutes a day to the exercise. It is best done in a room that is quiet and where the person will not be disturbed. The steps are as follows:

• Begin the exercise by lying down or sitting in a comfortable position. There is no special position; any position which the person finds comfortable is the right one.

• The person should close his eyes.

• After about 10 seconds, he should start concentrating his mind on his breathing rhythm.

• Then he should concentrate on breathing slow, regular, steady breaths through the nose.

• If he asks how slow the rhythm should be, you can suggest that he should breathe in until he can count slowly to three, then breathe out to the count of three and then pause for the count of three, until he breathes in again.

• You can suggest that each time he breathes out, he could say in his mind the word 'relax' or an equivalent in the local language. People who are religious can use a word that has some importance to their faith. For example, a Hindu could say 'Om', while a Christian might say 'Praise the Lord'.

• Demonstrate to the person how to breathe steady, deep breaths.

• Explain to him that if he practises daily, he will begin to feel the benefits of relaxation within two weeks. With adequate experience, he may even be able to relax in a variety of situations, for example while sitting on a bus.

(A) (B) (C)

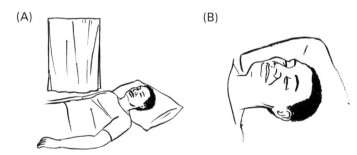

(D)

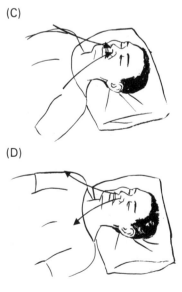

(A) Lie down in a room that is quiet and where you will not be disturbed.
(B) Close your eyes and concentrate your mind on your breathing rhythm.
(C) Now, concentrate on breathing slow, regular, steady breaths through the nose, taking a deep breath in.
(D) Then let go of the breath slowly.
Try to spend at least 10 minutes a day doing this exercise.

3.2.4 Advice for specific symptoms

Counselling will be more effective if it is sensitive to the person's symptoms. The following are examples on how to manage specific symptoms which are described in more detail later in the manual:

- *Panic attacks* (☛ section 5.2). Panic attacks result from rapid breathing. Breathing exercises are a helpful way of controlling these attacks.

- *Phobias*. A phobia is when a person experiences fear, often panic attacks, in specific situations and begins to avoid them. The best way of dealing with phobias is to face up to the fearful situation and not run away (☛ section 5.2).

- *Tiredness and fatigue*. Depressed people often feel tired and weak. This leads to withdrawal from activities and worsens the feeling of tiredness and low mood. To break this vicious cycle, a depressed person can be encouraged gradually to increase the amount of physical activity she is doing (☛ section 5.4).

- *Sleep problems*. These are very common. Simple advice on proper sleep routines can help many people recover their normal sleep patterns (☛ section 5.3).

- *Worry about physical health* (☛ section 5.1). This is also common, especially when a person has many physical symptoms, such as aches and pains.

- *Irritability*. Some people complain that they have difficulty in controlling their temper. Tips on how to manage their anger may help (☛ section 7.2, Box 7.6).

3.2.5 Problem-solving

Problem-solving is a method that teaches how problems in a person's life can make him feel anxious or depressed and how these emotions can then make it harder to solve the problems. The aim is not that you should try to solve a particular problem. Instead, you should teach the person these skills so that he can effectively overcome the problems himself.

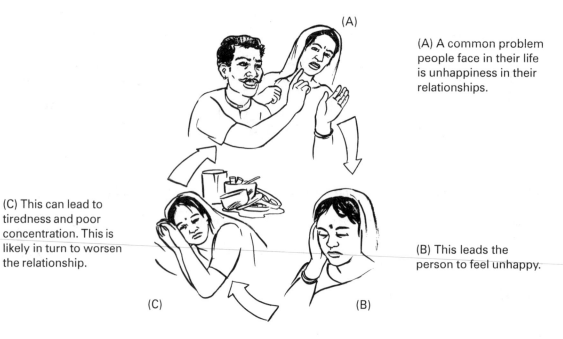

(A) A common problem people face in their life is unhappiness in their relationships.

(C) This can lead to tiredness and poor concentration. This is likely in turn to worsen the relationship.

(B) This leads the person to feel unhappy.

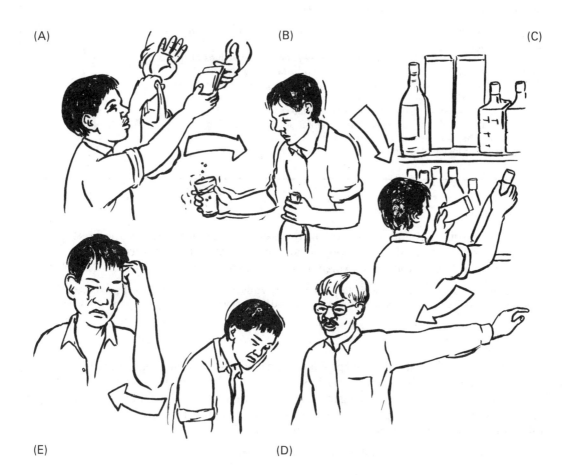

(A) A common problem is not having enough money to meet daily needs.
(B) This could make someone turn to alcohol.
(C) The person becomes even poorer because he spends precious money on alcohol.
(D) His work suffers and he loses his job.
(E) This makes him sad and desperate and worsens the drinking and financial problems.

The steps in problem-solving are as follows:

- explain the treatment;

- define the problems (what are the different problems faced by the person?);

- summarise the problems (how are these problems related to the person's symptoms?);

- select one problem and choose the goals (why should the person overcome the problem?);

- define solutions (the action to be taken to overcome the problem);

- review the outcome of the action taken (did it make the problem less, or did it help improve the person's mood?).

Box 3.3. The kinds of problems people face in life

• Relationship problems with a spouse, such as lack of communication, arguments, violence in the family and poor sex life
• Relationship problems with others, such as in-laws, children, relatives or friends
• Employment problems, such as not having a job or feeling overworked
• Financial problems, such as not having enough money, being in debt
• Housing problems, such as living in a noisy neighbourhood
• Social isolation, such as being alone in a new place or not having friends
• Physical health problems, especially when painful and long-standing
• Sexual problems, such as loss of interest in sex
• Bereavement or losing a loved one
• Legal problems

Explain the treatment

The first step in this technique is to explain the treatment by pointing out the links between problems a person faces in life and emotional symptoms, which in turn affect the ability of the person to solve problems. You could explain how the technique works like this:

> "People with complaints like yours can be helped by looking at the way in which they handle stress and deal with problems. I would like to discuss some of your problems and think of ways in which you can try to deal with them."

Define the problems

Ask the person a question about which problems she has been experiencing in her life. Ask about family life as a way of probing on problems. It is a good general principle is to start with a relatively 'safe' area (such as work) before tackling more personal areas (such as sex). Remember, though, to ask questions about personal problems – they are often the most upsetting and important. A useful method of asking personal questions is to say something like:

> "Sometimes when people feel unhappy they have less interest in sex: has this happened at all to you?"

Or

> "It is quite common for people who are worried to drink more alcohol than usual: how much are you drinking?"

This method of introducing a personal subject demonstrates that you are not going to be shocked if the person says 'yes'. Some common areas of difficulty for people presenting to health workers with mental health problems are listed in Box 3.3.

Summarise the problems

Once you have collected information on problems, summarise the key problems for the person by saying something like this:

> "You have told me that your baby's arrival has changed a lot of things in your life. You are not working now, you're up half the night and you see less of your friends. All this has also affected your relationship with your husband."

Doing this serves several functions. It confirms to the person that you have been listening. It shows that there is some structure to the problems. It is also a useful means of getting more personal information.

Select a problem and choose a goal

The next step involves selecting a specific problem worth tackling and choosing the goals the person would like to set. Here are some hints on how to select an appropriate problem:

- Ask the person to make a list of all his problems. Identify those that are of most concern to him.

- Target a problem that has a potential solution in the short term. For example, if the problem is related to a long-standing difficulty in the relationship with the spouse, it is not a good problem to tackle first. On the other hand, a recent problem in coping at work or feeling socially isolated may be a useful one to start with.

- Remember that the aim of the treatment is to teach the person problem-solving skills, not to try to solve all his problems.

- Once a problem area is selected, confirm with the person that this is indeed the problem he wishes to tackle during therapy.

Define solutions

This consists of the following steps:

- generate solutions – think up various solutions with the person;

- reduce the number of solutions – if many options are available, focus on those that are most practical given the person's social situation;

- identify consequences – consider what might happen as a result of carrying out the solutions;

- choose the best solution;

- plan how to carry out the solution;

- set specific targets that are achievable before the next meeting with you;

- consider what might happen in the worst-case scenario, for example if the solution fails completely.

Encourage the person to come up with the solutions to his problems. In this way, you will help improve his self-confidence. For example, if he has said that being lonely is a major problem, do not say "I think you should sort this out by visiting some friends" – even if this is a perfectly logical and sensible solution to the problem. Instead say "Now we've identified an area you want to tackle, how do you want to go about it?"

Often, it is difficult to identify solutions and you may need to assist the person either through more questions or with more direct advice, as follows:

- Identify key social supports so that he can be made aware of the people who care about him.

- Identify individual strengths, such as examples from his past that illustrate his coping skills.

- It is important that you are familiar with all the helping agencies in the area so that practical advice for specific problems may be given. A list of all helping agencies in your area can be entered in the resources section in Part IV.

- You may need to take a more direct role with some people, for example by writing letters to other agencies on behalf of those who are illiterate.

- You may need to be provide ideas for solutions to the person's problems, especially at the beginning of the treatment. However, efforts should be made to make him take a leading role in problem-solving at some stage.

  Solutions to some common problem areas are suggested in other parts of the manual:

- violence in the family (☛ section 7.2);

- loneliness and isolation (☛ section 4.4.8)

- bereavement (☛ section 7.4);

- relationship problems (☛ section 10.7);

- alcohol and drug misuse (☛ sections 6.1 and 6.2);

- caring for a sick relative (☛ section 9.10, also 4.7).

Review

Briefly review all that has been covered during the meeting with the person. In particular, review the target and plan for problem-solving.

Subsequent sessions

The main aims of the subsequent sessions are:

- to evaluate how well the person managed in completing tasks;

- if progress has been made, to apply new solutions to the same problem or look at solutions to a new problem;

- if progress has not been made, to identify what went wrong and set new goals.

When assessing progress, be specific. It is no use asking "How did you get on?" and accepting a shrug of the shoulder and a vague answer like "OK". You should ask for details of exactly how the person did, as follows:

- What did she do towards achieving the target?

- Was it easy or difficult?

- How did it affect her feelings and emotions?

- Do you and the person agree that the task was satisfactorily done and want to move on to another goal?

- What went wrong if it was not done?

3.2.6 Counselling in a crisis

A crisis is a situation when a person feels completely overwhelmed or defeated by the problems he is facing. What one person may see as a crisis would not necessarily be regarded as a crisis by someone else. Thus, the definition of a crisis is based on the person's view of his situation, and on how the situation has affected his ability to cope with the problems.

Crisis counselling should help such people cope better during this period of extreme distress. The key steps in crisis counselling are:

- *Get more information.* What has happened? Why did she come to the clinic? Who are the people who can support her at this time? Get information from the family or others who have come with her.

- *Establish rapport.* Allow her to tell her story at her own pace. Do not appear to be in a rush. See her in private.

- *Assess the person's mental health.* By talking to and observing her, see if she is behaving in an odd or unusual way. Is she saying things that are irrelevant? Is there any sign that she is drunk?

- *Assess what is the main problem that has caused the crisis.* Usually, there is a single major problem that causes the crisis. Most often, the problem is a relationship breakdown, bereavement or the result of violence.

- *Try to suggest solutions.* These could include sharing the problem with others, reassuring her that she is not going mad, making contact with the police or other helping agencies, and referring to a hospital for a short admission in severe situations.

- *Give medication if appropriate.* For example, if she is very agitated and has not slept well, you can prescribe a few days' supply of sleeping medication.
- *Always ask to see the person again for review in a day or two.* Many people will be much calmer on review and more in control of the situation. A more thorough mental health assessment should then be made.

3.2.7 Rehabilitation for the mentally ill

Mental illnesses can interfere with the ability of a person to function at home, at work and in social situations. Severe mental disorders can disable the person for a number of reasons:

- 'feeling' symptoms can make the person feel there is no point in working or meeting up with friends;
- 'thinking' symptoms can make it harder for a person to concentrate, make decisions properly or carry on conversations with others;
- abnormal behaviour can make the person isolated from others;
- stigma and discrimination make it harder for people with a mental illness to get jobs or marry.

Rehabilitation is the process of helping people find ways of returning to the normal life they led before the illness started. There are a number of things you can do to help a person achieve this goal:

- ensure that the illness is being correctly treated;
- plan the rehabilitation with him and his family;
- suggest activities that he would be able to do and find pleasurable (as he succeeds in these activities, suggest new and more challenging activities);
- always keep in mind his actual abilities before he fell ill when planning rehabilitation.
- counsel the family regarding treating him as a responsible adult (this means allowing him to make decisions for himself);
- encourage social contact with others, such as friends, neighbours, relatives;
- if he is religious, encourage contact with spiritual activities as long as they do not interfere with his medical treatment;
- refer him to local employers who you know are sensitive to giving jobs to people with a disability;
- refer him for vocational training, such as carpentry or some other skill;
- monitor his progress regularly, and use these meetings to counsel him regarding mental health problems and life difficulties that are bothering him.

3.2.8 The importance of follow-up in the treatment of mental illness

Proper diagnosis and treatment will cure some health problems. Examples of such curable problems are bacterial infections. However, this is not the case for most mental illnesses. Seeing a person with a mental illness on many occasions is often the key to ensuring recovery. When you see a person on many occasions you have an opportunity:

- to establish a good relationship with her;

- to make contact with family members who can help support her;

- to give her a feeling that her problem is being taken seriously and that you are concerned about her well-being;

- to monitor the progress of the illness;

- to monitor whether treatment is being taken – many treatments take time to work, and once they work they need to be continued for some time; stopping medicines early is often a problem and this can be prevented if you keep in touch.

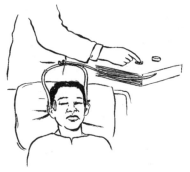

3.3 Other treatments

There are some other treatments that are used to help people with a mental illness. Even though these treatments are unlikely to be used by the general health worker, it is helpful to know a little bit about them.

- *Electroconvulsive therapy (ECT)*. This is the technical name for the much-feared 'shock' therapy. There is no doubt that ECT is often given to people who do not need it. It may also sometimes be given without anaesthesia, which is un-acceptable, unethical practice. Despite these incidents of bad practice, the fact remains that that ECT is one of the most dramatic and effective treatments in medicine, when used for the disorders for which it is indicated, namely severe depressive illness and acute manic episodes. It is also remarkably safe: if properly given under anaesthesia, side-effects are rare.

- *Psychotherapy*. Especially in developed countries and in urban, upper-class areas of developing countries, a number of specialised psychotherapy clinics are now available. Psychotherapy is a more complex type of counselling. The real drawback of this treatment is that it is not accessible to the majority of people because very few professionals practise it, and it can be expensive and time-consuming.

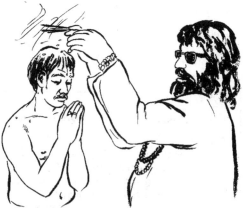

- *Spiritual 'therapy'*. In many cultures the mind and spirit are considered to be the same and the treatment of emotional problems often involves priests and healers. Even if biomedical treatments are easily available, many people often choose spiritual help for depression, anxiety, family problems and so on. You should try to build bridges with spiritual healers. You may not agree with the way they diagnose or treat health problems, but they are still your partners in health care. Some spiritual healers, however, insist that medical treatments be stopped. Warn anyone against visiting such healers.

3.4 Referring to a mental health specialist

There are various types of mental health specialist:

- Psychiatrists are medical doctors who, after completing basic medical training, have specialised in the treatment of mental disorders. In many countries, the majority of psychiatrists are almost entirely based in hospitals. These may be general hospitals with a psychiatric ward or a hospital specialising in mental health problems. Psychiatrists' main skills are in the diagnosis and treatment of severe mental disorders. They mainly use medicines and ECT and a variable amount of 'talking' treatments.

- Psychologists are trained in treating mental health problems using theories based on how human beings learn about life, feel emotions and behave towards others. Psychologists use only 'talking' treatments.

- Psychiatric nurses are nurses who have specialised in psychiatry. They may work either in hospitals or in the community. Their main roles are in providing talking treatments and the treatment and rehabilitation of people with severe mental disorders.

- Psychiatric social workers tend to work either in hospitals or in the community and deal with social problems and life difficulties faced by people with a mental illness. Both social workers and nurses can provide talking treatments.

In most developing countries, there are few mental health professionals. Thus, the majority of people with a mental illness will need to be treated by general health workers. Of course, the majority of them do not need to see a specialist mental health professional at all. Most mental illnesses can be recognised and treated by general health workers. However, there are some situations in which you may need to refer someone to a specialist. Specific situations are discussed throughout this manual. As a general rule, refer to a mental health specialist in the following circumstances:

- people with abnormal behaviour and evidence of a physical illness such as head injury or high fever;

- people who are so disturbed that they can no longer be managed at home;

- any child whom you suspect is suffering from mental retardation or other brain problems;

Box 3.4. Example of a referral letter, for Raman in case 1.10

Dear Doctor,
Please advise Raman, a 70-year-old retired man living with his son and daughter-in-law. He has been complaining of memory problems for the past few years. Recently he has started behaving oddly, for example wandering out of his house and not being able to find his way back home. At present, his memory is very poor and he does become angry without any reason. I gave him sleeping pills and vitamins but this has not made any difference. Raman is living with his family who are very concerned but also very supportive ...

Box 3.5. Things to remember about the treatment of mental illness

• Most people with a mental illness can be treated just as well by the general health worker as by the mental health specialist.
• People need at least a basic explanation of their illness; other counselling methods such as breathing exercises can be easily taught in general health settings.
• Medicines for mental illnesses are effective and safe if used properly.
• The commonest reasons to use medicines are for the treatment of psychoses and depression and anxiety disorders.

• people who are taking large amounts of alcohol or drugs, so that stopping suddenly may lead to a severe withdrawal reaction;

• people whose illness is continuing to have a serious effect on their personal life or work, despite your efforts to provide treatment.

In addition, people who have made a serious suicide attempt must be referred to an emergency medical unit to make sure their life is not in danger. Once this is done, and if they still have suicidal feelings, refer to a mental health specialist.

People with a convulsion should, ideally, be assessed by a specialist doctor (a neurologist or psychiatrist) before they start to take regular anticonvulsant medication.

Remember that when you refer someone it can be very helpful if you write a short note explaining a little bit about the background to the problem and what treatments you have already tried. An example referral letter is given in Box 3.4. You can also ask the specialist to write to you, advising on how someone should be cared for in the community.

Part II
Clinical problems

Part I of this manual discussed the general issues that apply to all mental illnesses and treatments. Part II will take you through the common types of clinical problems associated with mental illness. A problem-solving approach is taken. This means that mental health issues are discussed according to how you would approach a person presenting with a particular kind of problem. Diagnoses are not used as the starting point since this would assume that you will already know what the illness is! Instead, we begin with clinical problems that you are likely to encounter and then work our way to finding out how you can help the person with the problem. It is important that you are familiar with Part I before you use the problem-solving approach used in Part II.

The clinical problems associated with mental health have been grouped into five major groups. Flow charts that describe how you should deal with each group of problems can be found in the Appendix.

Chapter 4 covers the most disturbing and worrying clinical problems that you will encounter. The commonest causes of such severe behaviour problems are the psychoses.

Physical symptoms such as tiredness, aches and pains, and dizziness are among the most common of all health problems in general health care, and these are looked at in Chapter 5. Often, no 'medical' or physical explanation can be found for these symptoms. The commonest causes for such symptoms are depression and anxiety disorders.

Common problems affecting any community are alcohol and drug dependence. These are discussed in Chapter 6, along with sleeping pills, tobacco and gambling.

Chapter 7 examines problems arising from loss and violence. Violence can do a great deal of harm to mental health. Losing someone through death (bereavement) is also a trauma, especially when the loss is sudden and unexpected. The commonest mental illnesses associated with these experiences are depression, anxiety and post-traumatic stress disorder.

There are a number of important mental health issues in childhood, many of which can affect the child's ability to complete education and to relate to others in the family. Childhood mental health problems can also lead to problems in adjusting in later life. These issues are the subject of Chapter 8.

Chapter 4

Behaviours that cause concern

4.1 The person who is aggressive or violent

Aggression and violence are behaviours that hurt others. These terms include a variety of different behaviours. Verbal aggression is hurtful through talking, such as shouting, abusing and using foul language. Physical aggression includes pinching, hitting, slapping, kicking and punching. More serious physical aggression can involve the use of weapons such as sticks, knives or guns.

4.1.1 Why do mentally ill people become aggressive?

A common belief is that people with a mental illness are dangerous because they can suddenly become aggressive. In reality, they are no more dangerous than anyone else. It is true that, in some instances, the symptoms of a mental illness can lead to aggressive behaviour, but this is rare. Let us consider some important examples of how mental illness can lead to aggression.

- *Hearing voices and becoming angry.* Imagine that you were hearing voices that said nasty things about you and made you feel that others were plotting to kill you. You would feel scared and attack those who you believed were trying to harm you. This is what can happen, sometimes, in people who have a psychotic illness.

- *Being stopped from carrying out your plans and dreams.* Imagine that you had great plans and dreams to do things that would change your life. If someone tried to stop you, or told you that you were 'sick', you would probably be quite angry. This is what can happen, sometimes, in people with a manic illness.

- *Being unable to get a drink in time.* Imagine that you were so dependent on alcohol (or a drug) that you began to feel physically sick because of your desire for a drink. You might become aggressive if someone tried to stop you from getting a drink.

- *Suffering from confusion.* Imagine that you have difficulty remembering things. You do not know where you are, what time or day it is, or who is speaking to you. You may become frightened and feel you need to defend yourself from these strangers. Such a state of confusion can be caused by drinking too much alcohol, low blood sugar, brain infections and brain damage (☞ section 4.2).

Like anyone else, those who have a mental illness usually have a reason for becoming aggressive. If you can find out why a person is angry, then you are more likely to find ways to help.

4.1.2 *How to deal with this problem*

Questions to ask the family or friends

- What happened? One person's description of violence may be quite different from another's. Find out exactly what happened.

- How did it start? Has the person been irritable for several days, or was this a sudden outburst? Sudden aggression is often caused by a specific trigger, such as an argument about drinking. Aggressive behaviour without any warning is rare, but may happen in people with a severe mental disorder.

- Has this ever happened before? If so, then the chances are that further violence may occur.

- Has the person suffered from a mental illness in the past? Is he on any medication? This is of obvious importance since it may provide important clues for treatment.

- Whom does he trust? This person could be an important ally in helping him calm down.

- Does he have a drug or alcohol problem?

Questions to ask the aggressive person

- What happened? You may get a different point of view from the aggressive person than from friends and family. In particular, ask whether there were any reasons for her becoming violent.

- Do you still feel angry? If yes, ask her if she would prefer to spend some time alone before you ask any more questions.

- Have you been feeling under stress? Have you been feeling as if people around you were behaving strangely? That they were talking about you? Or doing things that could hurt you? These questions help assess whether she has a psychosis.

- Have you heard people talking about you? Can you hear voices even when there is no one around? Hallucinations are an important sign of psychoses.

- Have you been drinking alcohol (or, if appropriate, taking drugs) recently? How much? When was your last drink?

Interview suggestions

- Be aware of the signs of impending violence. These include:
  - talking louder or becoming abusive or threatening;
  - fists opening and closing;
  - breathing rapidly;
  - fidgeting;
  - tapping or punching or slapping tables, walls or the floor.

- Listen for signs that the person's speech is not making any sense or is too fast – this is a sign of intoxication or psychosis.

- Be aware of the smell of alcohol or of skin marks of injections (a sign of drug misuse);

Make sure that the door to the clinic room is accessible to you and the person you are interviewing.

- Look for signs that the person is losing balance or has slurred speech, which would suggest intoxication with drugs or alcohol.

- Be sensitive to your own feelings; if you feel scared, then you should stop the interview.

- Make sure that both the interviewee and you have access to the door of the clinic room.

- Speak in a clear, calm tone; do not shout in an attempt to calm the person.

- Never threaten the person. This can only worsen the situation.

- Ensure that another health worker is available during the interview. If this is not possible, get a trusted relative or friend to sit with you.

- If the person has a weapon, reassure him that you are a health worker and that there is no need for a weapon in the clinic. If he refuses to hand over the weapon, leave the room and call the appropriate security staff to disarm him.

- If the person becomes violent, first try to tell him to calm down by firm reassurance. If this is not possible, you will need to restrain him.

What is the mental illness?

When violence is associated with a mental illness, there are three major causes to remember:

- People can become violent either when they are intoxicated by a drug or when they are in a withdrawal state (☛ Chapter 6).

- People with a psychosis, whether they are suffering from schizophrenia or a manic illness, can become very agitated and, occasionally, aggressive (☛ section 4.3).

- People in an acute confusional state, such as that which follows an epileptic seizure, may become aggressive (☛ section 4.2).

What to do immediately

First try to calm the person by talking, reassuring and listening to her. Do not be in a hurry to get the situation under control. The aim is to encourage the person to take a sedative and calm down. If she agrees, then try giving an anti-anxiety drug (e.g. lorazepam, 1–2 mg, or diazepam, 5–10 mg, orally) or an antipsychotic drug (e.g. haloperidol, 5 mg, or chlorpromazine, 50–100 mg, orally).

If she refuses to take medicines orally and is becoming more disturbed, you will need to restrain her (☛ picture on following page) and give an injection. Always prepare the injection before you restrain someone. The drugs of choice are: diazepam, 5–10 mg, intramuscular or slow intravenous injection; haloperidol, 5–10 mg, intramuscular injection; chlorpromazine, 25–100 mg, intramuscular injection.

When to refer

If you suspect that the violence is associated with confusion and may be the result of brain injury or other brain disease, the person should be referred to a general hospital, preferably accompanied by a health worker.

How to restrain a patient: make sure you have enough people and hold the person down firmly using hands. Always prepare the injection before you restrain someone.

What to do later

- Once the person is sedated, explain to the family or friends what happened.

- As he may become agitated when he awakes, ask someone who is familiar to him to stay with him.

- When he awakes, talk to him about what happened and explain the need to take oral medication (the choice will depend on what kind of illness he has).

- Offer him something to eat and drink.

- Refer to a mental health professional for further advice and treatment, particularly if he has a psychosis.

Box 4.1. Things to remember in dealing with an aggressive person

- Mentally ill people are not 'naturally' violent; a number of different reasons can lead a person with a mental illness to become violent.
- Psychoses, alcohol and drug misuse are the important mental health problems that may be associated with violence.
- Violence almost always affects friends and relatives. Remember to counsel those affected and explain what you are doing and why.
- While you should be concerned about the safety of others, your primary goal must be to protect, understand and help the person.
- Use of medicines and restraining techniques may be required to calm someone with a mental illness who becomes aggressive.

4.2 The person who is confused or agitated

People who are confused or agitated are not fully aware of their surroundings. They do not make sense and cannot make sense of what you are saying. Confusion is also called delirium. The main features of a person who is confused are:

I don't know what day it is ... I get frightening visions at night.

- she is not as aware of her surroundings as you would expect her to be;

- she is not able to remember things that happened recently;

- she does not know what day it is, or where she is;

- she does not sleep properly at night and may be drowsy in the day;

- she may be uncooperative or fearful;

- she may suffer hallucinations and be suspicious;

- she may be restless and aggressive.

Being confused is not the same as being muddled in thinking or talking about irrelevant matters. When people are muddled or irrelevant, they are still aware of what is going on around them. Examples of muddled thinking are discussed later (☛ sections 4.3, 4.7). However, sometimes it is difficult to make this distinction. Careful questioning and observation are the key to recognising a state of confusion.

4.2.1 What are the causes of confusion and agitation?

Confusion and agitation are common conditions, especially in emergency or casualty settings and in medical and surgical wards in hospitals. The commonest causes are:

- side-effects of some medicines, especially in older people;

- withdrawal from alcohol in a dependent person;

- a brain illness, particularly strokes, head injury, epilepsy or infections;

- another medical illness, particularly high fevers, severe infections, dehydration, AIDS, breathing problems, kidney or liver disease;

- being drunk or high on drugs;

- severe anxiety or stress, such as after a sudden shock.

Confusion is especially common in people who are physically sick.

4.2.2 How to deal with this problem

Questions to ask the family or friends

- How did it start? Typically, confusion starts suddenly and the person is brought to the clinic quickly because the family is worried.

- Has it happened before? If there is a history of similar episodes, he may be suffering from repeated strokes, or from alcohol misuse.

- Has he been taking any new medicines recently? Which medicines?

- Has he been suffering from any physical illness recently? Has he had a stroke or heart problem? Has he had a head injury or a seizure recently?

- Does he have a drink or drug problem? If so, when was the last time he had a drink?

- Has he been sleeping well recently? Confusion is almost always associated with disturbances of sleep.

Questions to ask someone who is confused or agitated

- Begin by introducing yourself and clearly stating where you are (for example, "My name is Marina. I am a nurse. This is the clinic in your village of …").

- Have you had any problems recently? The answer may give you a clue to whether the person is aware of what has been happening recently.

- Could you tell me what day it is? Could you tell me my name? Could you tell me where we are right now? These questions test whether the person is disoriented.

- Have you been drinking alcohol recently? When was your last drink?

- Do you have pain anywhere in your body? Where? Pain may be a sign of a medical illness.

- Do you feel worried for your safety? Are you hearing or seeing things that others cannot? Suspicious thoughts and hallucinations are typical features of confusion.

Things to look for during the interview

- The person's attention keeps wandering, for example she does not seem to pay attention to your questions and may not answer them sensibly.

- Her orientation is poor; she may make mistakes about what time it is, where you are or what your name is.

- Her talking may be difficult to follow and may not make sense.

- She may have unusual or suspicious beliefs (delusions).

- She may talk to herself or appear to be talking to an imaginary person.

- She may make movements that suggest she is seeing imaginary things.

- She may be restless and fidgety.

- Her emotions may suddenly change from laughter to crying for no reason.

Always perform a basic physical examination. This must include:

- pulse;

- temperature;

- blood pressure;

- check the person's breath for the smell of alcohol;

- look for signs of physical illnesses, particularly paralysis (due to strokes), injuries, especially on the head, swelling of the feet, jaundice.

What to do immediately

- Rule out an emergency that needs immediate medical attention. This would include serious infections, strokes or head injuries or alcohol withdrawal syndrome with complications such as fits. These conditions may need urgent transfer to a hospital.
- Place the person in a private room, if possible, with a health worker or relative to monitor him. The room should not be too dark or too brightly lit.
- Keep the family well informed about what is happening.
- Make sure the person is taking enough fluids; if there is any concern about dehydration, insert an intravenous line for fluids. This line can also be used for medication.
- Remind the person where he is, and what day and time it is. Reassure him that he is safe with you in the clinic.
- Some confused people can become aggressive or hurt themselves, for example, by pulling out their intravenous tubes. You may need to restrain them on a clinic bed. Drugs can also be used to calm them – diazepam, 5–10 mg, by intramuscular injection three or four times a day, and then orally once the person improves, or haloperidol, 2.5–5 mg, by intramuscular injection three or four times a day, and then orally once the person improves.

When to refer

Confusion is often a sign of a medical emergency, particularly in elderly people or children. It is best, if you have reasonably quick access to a hospital, to refer anyone with these symptoms to the hospital. If this is not possible, follow the steps described above, and once the person is stable, refer.

What to do later

- If the person was on multiple medicines, reduce these to a reasonable number to reduce the chances of future drug-induced confusion.
- If the person has a drink problem, follow the guidance in section 6.1.
- If the person is elderly and you find that, even after the confusion has passed, there seem to be memory problems, follow the guidance in section 4.7.

Box 4.2. Things to remember when dealing with a confused or agitated person

- Confusion is not being aware of one's surroundings.
- The most common causes of confusion are strokes, medical illnesses, brain infections and injuries, side-effects of medicines and alcohol dependence.
- Confusion can be a medical emergency and often needs hospital admission.
- The elderly are at a greater risk of becoming confused.
- The key to treatment is to identify and treat the cause of the confusion, give medicines to calm the person and start intensive nursing care. If nurses are not available, ask a relative to stay.

4.3 The person who is suspicious, has odd beliefs or is hearing voices

Sometimes, people think that others are talking about them, trying to hurt them, or plotting to harm them. Occasionally the thought lasts for a short time, especially when people are under stress. At other times, this thought lasts for a long time and becomes a firm belief. No matter how much you try to reassure them that there is nothing to worry about, the suspicious thoughts do not go away. Such thoughts are called delusions. People may try to protect themselves from the imagined people who are trying to harm them. Some people can also believe other sorts of odd things that make no sense either to you or to their family. Examples include a person thinking that his thoughts are being interfered with by aliens or that the radio or television is making comments about him or that he possesses superhuman or special powers.

She is a bad person. She will be taught a lesson for her sins.

4.3.1 What is 'hearing voices'?

'Hearing voices' is when someone hears people talking even when there is no one around. This experience is called a hallucination. Often, these voices take on an unpleasant character. For example, the voices may say nasty things about the person. Occasionally the voices may talk directly to the person and tell her to do things, such as to hurt herself or others.

4.3.2 Why do some people have these experiences?

These experiences are not common. They are typically associated with severe mental disorders:

- *Schizophrenia.* There will often be a long history of illness, usually more than six months.

- *Manic–depressive illness.* Typically, there is a history of sudden onset and of similar episodes in the past.

- *Drug psychoses.* These occur after intoxication with certain drugs, such as stimulant tablets and cocaine.

- *Confusional states and brief psychoses.* Confused and agitated people may also hear voices and become suspicious (☞ section 4.2).

4.3.3 Can 'normal' people have these experiences?

Yes. In some communities there are individuals who claim to have an ability to communicate with supernatural forces and spirits. These people may experience hearing of voices, particularly of spirits or God. They may also have beliefs which seem unusual, for example that the spirits are angry with someone. These beliefs may be appropriate for that community. Examples of such people include the traditional healers in some societies and the charismatic priests in some evangelical churches. However, these people do not go to

A priest who is speaking in tongues – it is important not to confuse such experiences with an illness.

health workers for help, since they are using their experiences in a manner that is beneficial to their own health and may help others in distress. It is important not to confuse these experiences with an illness. An illness should be defined by its adverse effect on the person's life or that of the family.

4.3.4 How to deal with this problem

Questions to ask the family or friends

- When did it start? This will tell you whether the illness is sudden, which would be a sign of mania or brief psychoses, or long-standing, which would suggest schizophrenia.

- Have you noticed any odd behaviours? For example, the person appearing as if he is talking to himself?

- Has the person been saying odd things? For example, accusing you of trying to harm him?

- Has he been using drugs or alcohol recently?

- Has he been violent? If so, ☛ section 4.1.

- Does anyone else in the family suffer from these sorts of problems? Schizophrenia and manic–depressive disorder can run in families.

Questions to ask the person who is suspicious or has odd beliefs

- Have you been feeling under stress recently? Start with a general question instead of asking a direct question about delusions or hallucinations.

- Have you felt as if something odd was going on around you? Have you felt as if others were talking about you? That some people were trying to hurt you? These questions will help identify delusions.

- Have you heard people talk about you behind your back? Have you heard people talk about you even when there is no one around? These questions will help identify hallucinations.

- Do you get thoughts of wanting to kill yourself? Remember that the risk of suicide is higher in a person with a psychotic illness.

- Have you been drinking or taking drugs recently? If so, ☛ sections 6.1, 6.2.

Things to look for during the interview

- The person's general appearance may indicate poor self-care.

- She may make strange movements with her arms or body.

- She may do things that suggest she is hearing voices, for example suddenly looking in a different direction as if someone is speaking to her from there.

- Her talk may not make sense to you; answers to your questions may not be relevant.

- She may talk far too much or may not talk at all.

- She may laugh or cry or talk to herself without reason.

Special interview suggestions

- A person who is already suspicious needs to be approached in a gentle manner; the aim must be to win his trust by asking general questions first.

- Never confront him by challenging the beliefs. For example, do not say "Don't be ridiculous. No one is talking about you." The experiences that may appear ridiculous to you are very real to him.

- Never agree with the content of the beliefs; thus, even though you should not challenge them, you should not agree with them either.

- Never mock or laugh at the beliefs; the person will lose faith in you.

What to do

- If the person acts violently, treat as described in section 4.1.

- Explain to the family that the symptoms are the result of an illness in the brain.

- Encourage the person to take the appropriate medication. Because he will often be convinced that his beliefs are real, it is not helpful to say that he needs medicines because he has a mental problem. Instead, you can reassure him that, because of his beliefs, he must be under stress and the medicines will help to calm him down.

- Antipsychotic medication is very helpful. Try any of these:
  - haloperidol, 5–10 mg, twice a day, orally;
  - trifluoperazine, 5–10 mg, twice a day, orally;
  - chlorpromazine, 100–200 mg, three times a day, orally.

- Start on a low dose, say haloperidol, 5 mg once daily.

- Educate the person's family about side-effects and give them a supply of procyclidine or similar medicines to counter the muscle side-effects, such as sudden spasms of the neck or tremors (☛ Part IV).

When to refer

- If you suspect the person is in a confusional state.

- If the person is suicidal; people who are suspicious and also have suicidal thoughts are at a high risk of harming themselves.

- If the person is violent; refer after taking steps to control the behaviour (☛ section 4.1).

- If the person develops a high fever or severe side-effects.

What to do later

- Call the person back to the clinic in a week to assess progress. You can increase the dose of the medicine if symptoms are not under control.

- If possible, refer to a specialist mental health team. Many people with a psychosis will need long-term care.

- If there is no mental health team, make a long-term plan to help the family and sufferer cope with the illness.

Schizophrenia and other psychotic disorders may last several years and may be often associated with considerable disability. These are some principles of care:

- If possible, allocate a particular health worker to the person's care. Since these are rare illnesses, it is likely that only a few cases of psychosis will need long-term supervision.

- Visit the person (or ask the person to visit the clinic) at least once every two months.

- Educate the family about the illness and the need to ensure compliance with medication.

- Medication is an essential part of long-term care. At each visit, check on compliance and side-effects.

- Rehabilitation, in the form of assisting the person to get a job, is often a key element in helping the person stay well. The kind of job suitable for the person may depend on education, previous work experience and the severity of the illness (☛ section 3.2).

- If work outside the home is not possible, encourage the person to keep occupied in other ways, for example by helping in the house or garden, or being involved in church activities.

- Refer to organisations that work with mental disorders or disabilities (refer to resources in your area – ☛ Part IV). In some places, organisations run sheltered workshops or facilities where a person can learn new skills and meet others.

> **Box 4.3. Things to remember when dealing with someone who is suspicious or has odd beliefs**
>
> - Suspiciousness and hearing voices are symptoms of a severe mental disorder.
> - The commonest types of severe mental disorder are schizophrenia and manic–depressive disorder. Acute psychoses can also cause these symptoms.
> - Such people often suffer discrimination and stigma by others in the community.
> - Antipsychotic medicines are the best treatment for these illnesses.
> - If the family want to take the person to a traditional healer, encourage them to combine the traditional treatment with the medicines you will give.
> - If possible, refer people with these symptoms to a specialist mental health team.

4.4 The person who is thinking of suicide or has attempted suicide

Suicide is ending one's own life. Only a small proportion of those people who try to end their life succeed. This section is about helping people who have been thinking about or have tried to end their life. The role of a health worker is to understand why the person wanted to end her life and to support her in the difficult period soon after a suicide attempt.

4.4.1 Why do some people want to end their life?

Many of us feel, at some time in our life, that we have had 'enough' of living. If you think of all the difficult situations in which you might not want to continue your life, you will find that these are the same reasons for the people who come to consult you with this complaint. There is one big difference, of course. For most of us, thoughts of suicide pass quickly, and are often a reaction to a recent unhappy event. Most of us will talk it over with friends or relatives, or work out solutions to our problems and the thoughts will go away. For some, however, suicidal thoughts or plans become more persistent and are associated with mental illnesses and severe life difficulties.

The following mental illnesses are associated with suicide:

- *Depression*. This is the most important cause of suicide. Depression can make a person feel miserable, lose interest in life and lose hope for the future.

A woman in an unhappy relationship may feel her situation is hopeless and believe she would be be better off dead.

- *Alcohol and drug misuse*. Although many people drink alcohol and take drugs to feel better, in fact these substances act as depressants on the brain. The despair of not being able to stop the addiction, physical illness and financial problems make the person feel suicidal.

- *Long-term health problems*. Illnesses that cause pain or which are terminal are more likely to make the sufferer feel suicidal.

- *Severe mental disorders*. People with a psychosis are also at a risk of ending their life through suicide.

Social and personal factors play an important role in the cause of the mental illness. Important social factors that can make a person unhappy and suicidal include:

- unhappy relationships, particularly an unhappy marriage;

- poverty and economic difficulties, particularly when these happen suddenly, such as when a person loses a job;

- losing a loved one, for example through bereavement (☛ section 7.4);

- not having friends with whom to share problems and feelings.

Teenagers may become suicidal when they fail in school or have fights at home with their parents (☛ section 8.7).

4.4.2 Gender and suicide

Women are more likely to suffer from depression and the social stresses that can make a person unhappy. Thus women are more likely to attempt suicide. However, the risk of death by suicide is usually higher in men. This is particularly the case for older men with a drinking problem who are living alone or in unhappy marriages. One reason for this difference is that men may choose more dangerous methods of suicide and are, therefore, more likely to succeed in their attempt. However, women are also more likely to be discriminated against because of the suicide attempt. Take all suicide attempts seriously, whether by men or women.

4.4.3 How to deal with this problem

Questions to ask the family or friends

- What happened? Was it a dangerous attempt? If someone tried to hang himself or take insect poison, it would be considered as a fairly serious attempt; on the other hand, if he scratched his wrist with a pen, it would be less serious.

- Has it happened before? People with a history of suicide attempts are more likely to attempt it again, and repeated attempts may be a sign of a long-standing difficulty or mental illness.

- Is there a history of a mental illness or a serious physical illness?

- Has he had a recent loss, for example separation from his spouse?

Questions to ask the person who attempted suicide

- What happened? Did you want to end your life? Why?

- Did you have a plan? How long were you planning it? Did you tell anyone else about your plan? Attempts that have been carefully planned and kept secret from others are more serious.

- How do you feel now? Many people are relieved that their attempt did not lead to death. Those who are not relieved are more likely to try again.

- Have you been feeling depressed recently? Have you lost interest in life? Ask these questions to detect depression, as outlined in Chapter 2.

- Do you feel you drink too much alcohol (or take drugs)? Ask questions about problem drinking (☛ Chapter 2, 6.1).

- What reasons are there for you to continue living? This is an important way of trying to get the person to think of the good things in life. Some people are so depressed that they cannot see anything positive. This is a sign of how serious the illness is; it does not mean there is nothing for them to look forward to!

Judging the likelihood of further suicide attempts

It is difficult to predict whether a person will attempt suicide again. Factors that should make you concerned about the risk of repeated attempts are:

- a serious, planned attempt, where there was an effort to hide the attempt from others and a dangerous method such as hanging was used;

- continued suicidal thoughts;

- hopelessness about the future;

- evidence of severe depression;

- evidence of severe life difficulties and losses;

- lack of social support;

- alcohol misuse or severe physical illness;

- previous suicide attempts;

- older age of the person attempting suicide.

Inappropriate (left) and recommended (right) interview questions (and below).

Special interview suggestions

- Suicide is a sensitive and personal matter. Talk to the person in private. Give her enough time to feel comfortable and to share her reasons frankly.

- Do not make judgements about her character.

- Do not make reassuring statements without fully understanding her situation because this may make her feel even more hopeless.

- Talk to family or friends for their version of her recent life situation and health. You may need to form a trusting relationship with one person who can help support her at home.

What to do immediately

- Ensure that the person is out of immediate danger. If he has taken an overdose of tablets or poison or suffered a serious injury, emergency medical treatments must be given first (see below).

- The person must be constantly in the company of someone, such as a relative, during the hours after a suicide attempt.

- If you feel he is at risk of harming himself again, ask relatives to spend time with him and ensure that he is not left alone.

- Ensure that all dangerous items, such as poisons or knives, are kept away from him.

- Give him time to regain his calm before sending him home.

- Always ask him to come back to the clinic to see you or make an arrangement for a home visit, within a couple of days.

What to do later

- Involve the person who has attempted suicide in regular counselling until she feels better and more in control of her problems.

- Try to identify social issues that may be causing her to feel depressed. Talk to important relatives, such as a spouse.

- If she has depression or misuses alcohol, treat accordingly (☛ section 5.1 for depression, 6.1 for alcohol misuse).

- The drug treatment of depression takes three to four weeks to show effects; in the meantime, counselling and family support are essential.

- Many suicidal people face difficulties in their life which need to be tackled. Problem-solving can be very helpful (☛ section 3.2.5).

- Depressed people tend to view their life in a negative way. You can suggest positive ways of looking at the same situation (☛ Box 5.1).

When to refer

The person who has attempted suicide should, where possible, be referred to specialist mental health services if:

- the suicide attempt was serious and life-threatening;

- there are persisting suicidal ideas despite counselling;

- there is serious mental illness, such as a psychosis;

- there is a repeated suicide attempt.

4.4.4 The medical treatment of suicide attempts

The general rule is that if you have a hospital nearby, rush a person who has attempted suicide there so that time is not wasted in case medical help is needed later.

Hanging, stabbing, gunshot wounds, deep cuts or burns

These are serious medical emergencies. While you are waiting for the person to be moved to hospital, monitor his breathing, blood pressure and pulse. Insert an intravenous line if the person's blood pressure is low and administer normal saline. Oxygen should be given. If there is an open wound, clean it and apply a pressure bandage to stop the bleeding.

Overdose of insecticide or other substances

This is a common method of self-harm. If the person is awake, make an effort to make her vomit. Vomiting can be induced by:

• drinking very salty water;

• one tablespoon of syrup of ipecacuanha.

Give powdered charcoal, which will help absorb the poison.
If there are signs of severe poisoning, such as paralysis, unconsciousness, convulsions or difficulty breathing, rush the person to hospital immediately.

4.4.5 When suicide becomes a crime

In some societies, attempting suicide is an offence and suicide becomes a legal or police case. Your first concern must be the person who made the attempt. If he has a supportive family and the suicide attempt was because of a minor stressful event, you may decide not to inform the police. However, it is sometimes the case that the suicide attempt is the symptom of serious harassment or problems at home. Typically, women who are being beaten by their spouse or abused by their in-laws may try and end their life. Informing the police, after discussing this first with the woman, may help. In more serious cases, an apparent suicide attempt by burning may ultimately turn out to be an attempt to kill the woman. These are difficult situations and you should discuss them with your colleagues. If you have a good link with the local police, you may be able to get their advice without registering a formal case.

4.4.6 What to do when the family is not interested

You will need to rely on the family for supporting the person, particularly during the period just after a suicide attempt. If, however, there is conflict or violence in the family or the family is not interested, you may need to think of alternatives. Remember that you should discuss these alternatives first with the person who made the attempt and then follow one or more of the following actions:

• Refer to a women's group or shelter. Contact the local women's groups or shelters. Ask them if they can arrange for temporary relief accommodation (☛ Chapter 12 for your local resources.)

• Contact other family members. For example, if a woman is being harassed by her in-laws, you could contact her parents or other relatives.

• Contact friends, such as neighbours, or members of a religious group.

• Encourage the person to seek support through religious leaders.

4.4.7 The person who threatens or attempts suicide again and again … and again

This is the type of person who is brought to an emergency unit repeatedly. It is often easy to dislike such people because the suicide attempts are not dangerous and they are seen as 'acting' and wasting your time. However, these people are not acting; their lives are unhappy and they need help. This help may take the form of counselling with the aim getting the person to react to unhappy events by means other than attempting suicide. Identifying areas of strength, such as a supportive relationship or an occupational skill, may help the person to look on the 'brighter side' of life. Remember that such people are at higher risk of killing themselves. The best way of helping them is keeping in touch regularly and building up a trusting relationship so that, when upset or unhappy, they can talk to you rather than try to kill themselves.

4.4.8 Loneliness and isolation

Loneliness is often a cause of depression and suicide. This is particularly common among older people. Some solutions for the person are:

- to make contact with old friends, neighbours or relatives with whom the person has not been in touch;

- to contact relatives or friends and invite them for a meal or social occasion;

- to use community resources, such as clubs;

- to engage in activities that involve social contact, for example shopping in the market;

- to get involved in hobbies;

- to use time when alone in stimulating or enjoyable activities such as gardening or walking.

Box 4.4. Things to remember when dealing with a person who has attempted suicide

- Suicide is often due to mental illnesses such as depression or alcohol misuse.
- Many people who attempt suicide have a severe life problem such as marital or financial difficulties.
- Suicide is also associated with long-standing or serious physical illnesses.
- Never take a suicide threat lightly.
- Asking someone about suicidal thoughts does not make it more likely that they will end their life. On the contrary, most will feel relieved.
- Emergency treatment of the suicide attempt is a priority. Once the person is medically stable, treat any mental illness and identify relatives or friends who can provide support.

4.5 Someone with seizures or fits

Seizures or fits are when a person suddenly shows a change in behaviour or consciousness lasting for a few minutes. In some seizures, there are shaking movements of the body (called convulsions), with loss of consciousness. There are also seizures in which the person may be fully or partly awake. The only changes may be short periods of losing touch with reality or repeated movements, such as smacking the lips. Epilepsy is an illness where seizures occur repeatedly. If a person has at least two seizures in a month, one can diagnose epilepsy.

4.5.1 What types of seizures are there?

Seizures in adults are different from those in children. Childhood seizures are well described elsewhere (☛ DVC). In adults, three types of seizures are recognised:

- *Generalized seizures.* These are seizures (also called grand mal or major epilepsy) in which the person loses consciousness for a few minutes. His body becomes stiff and shakes in jerky manner. This seizure may be associated with biting of the tongue, passing urine and injury because of the sudden fall or the movements. Observers may describe him crying or screaming just before falling, the eyeballs rolling upwards, frothing at the mouth, and the person becoming blue (cyanosis) or pale. During the seizure, he is completely unconscious and will not respond to any verbal command. The seizure usually ends with him being drowsy or falling asleep. Some people may develop a temporary weakness of their limbs.

- *Partial seizures.* These may occur in an awake person or in a person who is confused or has lost touch with her surroundings. The seizures are very varied in their nature. Some can be entirely localised to one area of the body, for example jerky movements of the arm. Other seizures may involve complex behaviours such as smacking the lips and buttoning and unbuttoning a shirt. Many people experience a warning or 'aura' that the seizure is about to start. Examples of auras are an unusual feeling in the stomach area and hearing, seeing or smelling things that are unusual. Some people may have a partial seizure that then becomes generalised.

- *'Hysterical' or 'conversion' seizures.* These are more common in young women and are associated with psychological stress. Their characteristic is that they do not follow any typical pattern described above (☛ section 5.6 for more on these sorts of problems).

4.5.2 Is epilepsy a mental illness?

Epilepsy is not a mental illness. It is caused by electrical changes in the brain. However, epilepsy is often considered a mental health problem for many reasons. Many cultures consider epilepsy as being caused by supernatural forces, such as witchcraft, similar to some types of mental illness. In partial seizures, odd behaviours may be observed. Epilepsy can cause great stress on a person. Many people with epilepsy develop emotional problems. Psychoses, depression and suicidal behaviour are all commoner in people with epilepsy. Finally, one type of seizure in adults (the conversion seizure) is entirely psychological in origin. Thus, it is important not to ignore the mental health needs of people with epilepsy.

4.5.3 The important medical causes of seizures

In some persons a specific medical problem can be the causer of their epilepsy. These are:

- head injuries leading to bleeding in the brain;

- alcohol withdrawal;

- infections in the brain, such as meningitis, tapeworm, malaria, tuberculosis and sleeping sickness;

- AIDS, through direct infection by the virus, or secondary infections such as fungal infections, or tumours;

- brain tumours;

- low blood sugar levels;

- severe liver or kidney disease.

4.5.4 How to deal with this problem

Getting a clear account of what exactly happened is essential because many conditions can look like seizures. The main information you need to make a correct diagnosis is what an observer tells you about what the seizure looks like, and what the sufferer tells you about the experience of the seizure.

Box 4.5. Telling a seizure from a faint

- A seizure starts suddenly whereas a faint is gradual.
- The duration of unconsciousness is usually only seconds in a faint, but at least a few minutes in a seizure.
- Convulsions (i.e. jerky movements) are very rare in a faint but common in seizures.
- Biting one's tongue, frothing at the mouth, passing urine and cyanosis (going blue) are seen only in seizures.
- People recover quickly after a faint, whereas they may be drowsy or complain of a headache and confusion after a seizure.

Box 4.6. Telling an epileptic seizure from a hysterical seizure

- The epileptic seizure follows one of the patterns described earlier; the hysterical seizure is usually bizarre or variable in its pattern.
- Cyanosis, tongue bite, frothing, self-injury and passing urine are typical features of epileptic seizures, but not of hysterical seizures.
- People with hysterical seizures never lose consciousness. Even when they may appear to be unconscious, they resist attempts to comfort them, showing that they are still awake.
- Sometimes, the same person may have *both* types of seizure; in such situations, extra care is needed before determining which type of seizure the person has had.

Proceed as follows in dealing with the problem of a seizure:

- The first thing to be sure of is that the episode was not a faint (☛ Box 4.5).

- Next, make sure that the episode was not a conversion seizure (☛ Box 4.6 and section 5.6).

- If it is a seizure, determine whether it was the first one. A single seizure is not a rare event. For example, during severe infections, a person may have a seizure, but never have another seizure again.

- Determine the type of the seizure by interviewing both the sufferer and a person who observed the seizure, in order to identify the type of epilepsy (☛ section 4.5.1).

- Determine the age of the person. Most people with epilepsy have their first seizure before the age of 30. In such people, it is often impossible to find a cause for the epilepsy. If seizures start for the first time after the age of 30 (and especially after the age of 40), the chances that the person has another medical problem (☛ section 4.5.3) causing the seizures are high. Most of these diseases will also cause other symptoms, such as fever and headache, but sometimes the seizures may be the only sign of the disease.

What to do immediately

The vast majority of seizures are self-limited. Thus, even if you did nothing at all, the person will almost always completely recover after the seizure. During the seizure, your main objective is to ensure that the person does not injure herself. Do the following:

Keep the person on her side after a seizure.

- If possible, try to turn her on to her side.

- Do *not* try to force any object into her mouth.

- Do *not* try to hold or restrain her.

- Do *not* try to force her to take medicines or drink water.

- If the fit lasts more than five minutes, inject diazepam or phenobarbitone (see below).

- After the seizure is over, she may be sleepy. Comfort her after she wakes.

- Once she is fully conscious and calm, the most important thing to do is to assess her carefully, as described earlier.

When to refer

Ideally, all people with seizures should be assessed at least once by a medically qualified physician, if possible by a specialist in neurology or psychiatry. This is especially important for people whose first seizure occurs after the age of 30. The main reason for this is to make sure the person does not suffer from a disease that is causing the epilepsy. Since the diagnosis of epilepsy often means that the person has to take medicines for a long time, and may be restricted from doing some activities, you need to be confident that the diagnosis is correct. Specialist doctors may have access to tests such as EEGs (whichexame the electrical activity of the brain) or CT or MRI scans (special X-rays of the brain).

What to do later

The key areas in the treatment of epilepsy are education and lifestyle changes (☛ section 4.5.6) and using medicines (☛ section 4.5.7).

4.5.5 When fits don't stop: status epilepticus

This is a serious medical emergency which needs trained medical intervention. In this condition, the person has nearly continuous seizures without a break and without regaining consciousness. If left untreated, some sufferers may die or suffer serious brain damage. If emergency medical care is not available, then you should try to avert death or serious complications in this way:

- Remove false teeth and ensure an open breathing passage by inserting a plastic airway.

- Inject 100 mg of thiamine followed by a solution of 50% glucose (dextrose) rapidly, intravenously.

- Inject diazepam, 10 mg slowly, intravenously (over about two minutes).

- Wait for about five minutes.

- If seizures continue, set up an intravenous saline drip.

- Give diazepam intravenously at the rate of 5 mg per minute up to a maximum of 20 mg or until the seizures stop, whichever is first.

- Keep a close watch on respiratory rate; at any sign of distressed breathing, stop giving diazepam.

- If seizures continue, give phenytoin intravenously at the rate of 50 mg per minute up to a maximum of 1000 mg.

- Once seizures stop, immediately seek specialist medical help.

4.5.6 Advice to the person with epilepsy and family

- Epilepsy is a long-term illness which may need medication for many years.

- Epilepsy is not caused by witchcraft or spirits.

- The key to treating epilepsy is regularly taking the prescribed medicines.

- People with epilepsy can lead normal lives with some adjustments. They can marry, have children and work in most types of job.

- People with epilepsy should not drive (at least until they have had one year without a seizure and are continuing their medication), swim alone or work with or near heavy machinery.

- People with epilepsy should try to modify their lifestyle in the following ways:
  - regular sleep;
  - regular meals;
  - strict limits on alcohol intake;
  - avoiding extreme physical exercise;
  - avoiding situations that can lead to tension or sudden excitement or stress.

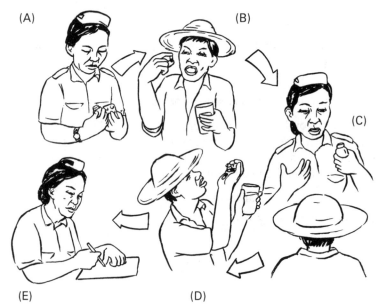

How to use drugs for epilepsy:
(A) Choose the right drug depending on cost and type of epilepsy.
(B) Start with a small dose; monitor response by counting how many seizures and side-effects.
(C) Change dose accordingly.
(D) If there is no response, increase dose to maximum of range.
(E) If there is still no response, add another drug or refer.

4.5.7 Prescribing drugs for a person with epilepsy

- Select the drug of choice for the particular type of epilepsy. In general, carbamazepine is an effective and safe drug for both main types of epilepsy in adults. Sodium valproate is another effective drug. Phenytoin and phenobarbitone are useful mainly for generalised epilepsy.

- Cost and side-effects are both important issues in selecting drugs since the medicines have to be continued for a long period. If cost is not a limitation, use carbamazepine or sodium valproate as the drug of choice. If cost is a factor, phenobarbitone may be considered (☞ Chapter 11 for drugs and their costs in your region).

- Use only *one* drug at a time. Start with a small dose and gradually increase until you reach the average recommended daily dose.

- If seizures continue without any benefit, try increasing the dose to the maximum recommended dose; if side-effects appear, do not go any higher.

- If available, use blood drug levels to help monitor the treatment.

- Educate regarding lifestyle changes before increasing drug doses (☞ section 4.5.6).

Box 4.7. Things to remember when dealing with a person who has had a seizure

- Seizures are a sudden, and brief, change in the behaviour or conscious state of the person.
- Epilepsy most often starts before the age of 30; someone with a first-ever seizure after the age of 30 may suffer from a serious brain or medical disorder and should be referred.
- Never try to restrain someone who is having a seizure; in most cases, the seizure will be over within minutes.
- Educate the person regarding the need to take the medicines regularly, to avoid driving or working with heavy machinery and to avoid alcohol.
- People with epilepsy may develop other problems, such as depression and even psychoses.
- Refer the person to a specialist before starting anticonvulsant drug treatment. If this is not possible, use the guidelines in this manual on how to diagnose epilepsy and use drug treatments.

- If seizures continue at an unacceptable frequency, add a second drug in a small dose and increase as required.

- Generally, do not consider stopping the medicine unless the person has been free of seizures for at least two years. Never stop the medicine suddenly; withdraw it slowly in small steps, for example a quarter of the total daily dose every month.

- Treat mental illnesses such as depression and psychoses as with anyone else.

4.6 The mother who becomes disturbed after childbirth

Childbirth is, for the majority of women, a positive experience. The arrival of a newborn baby is greeted with pleasure and joy. However, some mothers become mentally disturbed. There are three main kinds of postnatal mental problems.

- *The 'blues'.* This is a common emotional state which occurs within the first week after the baby is born. Typically, the mother feels tearful and sad. This is a harmless condition that lasts a few days.

- *Depression.* This is similar to depression in any other situation. It becomes obvious about a month after the baby is born. The mother may feel tired, have sleep problems and feel tearful. She may lose interest in herself and her baby. This illness can last up to 12 months if not treated.

- *Psychosis.* This is the most severe postnatal mental illness. It is similar to a confusional state. Thankfully, it is also the rarest. Symptoms become obvious within two weeks of the birth. They worsen very quickly, so that the mother may lose touch with reality, have bizarre ideas and may hallucinate. Without treatment, she may remain ill for several months.

Most mothers will be happy and satisfied when the new baby arrives.

4.6.1 Why do some mothers become disturbed after childbirth?

There are many reasons why some mothers become disturbed after childbirth:

- the extra work of being a mother, such as looking after the baby;

- childbirth is an event of great emotional significance and such events can trigger depression;

- the loss of independence for the mother;

- the change in the relationship between the mother and father;

- cultural factors, such as having a girl in some societies being a source of disappointment;

- during childbirth, a woman's body undergoes many physical and hormonal changes, which can lead to mental disturbances;

However, some mothers can become unhappy and disturbed.

Box 4.8. When mentally ill women become pregnant

When women with a mental illness become pregnant some families are concerned that the illness could affect the unborn child. Families must be reassured that mental illnesses are not 'infectious' and the baby will not be affected. Some families may ask about the genetic risk of the illness being passed onto the baby. You should say that, apart from severe mental disorders, there is no risk. For mothers with severe mental disorders, you can say that the baby is far more likely to be completely healthy than not. Mothers who suffer from mental retardation may need more time for you to explain what is happening to their bodies.

Another important issue is the dangers of medication to the baby. As a general rule, avoid any psychiatric medicine in the first three months of pregnancy. In particular, drugs such as lithium, antipsychotic medicines and anti-anxiety medicines should be avoided. Antidepressants are safer. During the period when a mother is breastfeeding her baby, avoid unnecessary medicines. In reality, there is only a tiny risk of medicines being passed into the breast milk. If the mother is disturbed or very depressed, remember that medicines may help improve her mood. This, in turn, will help her bond with her baby, which is very important for the mother and her baby.

- women who have unhappy marriages or who had difficult deliveries are more likely to develop mental health problems.

As well as childbirth itself being a cause of mental disturbance, it is of course also possible for a mentally ill woman to become pregnant, and this situation is described in Box 4.8.

4.6.2 Why is the mother's mental health important?

Mothers generally have less emotional support once their babies are born. All attention, particularly of families, is focused on the baby's needs and health. The mother may be too embarrassed to admit she is feeling unhappy because of fear of what others might think of her. Thus, you need to be especially sensitive to the mother's emotions and mood. Postnatal mental illnesses can last up to a year and affect both the mother and the baby. Babies may show problems in growth and development.

4.6.3 How to deal with this problem

Questions to ask the husband or relatives

- When did you notice the problem? The different types of postnatal mental health problems begin at different times after the baby is born.

- Is she looking after the baby as you would expect her to? In severe cases, the mother may lose interest in her baby.

- Has she been crying a lot? This is a typical feature of postnatal depression.

- Does she seem to be out of touch with reality? Does she talk to herself or to imaginary voices? If so, then a psychosis is likely.

- Has this ever happened before? Severe postnatal depression is more likely in women who have had the illness at other times in their life.

- Does she talk about killing herself? Does she talk about hurting the baby? These are signs that the illness is possibly quite serious.

Questions to ask the mother

The period after childbirth is often associated with having to be up at different times of the night to nurse or change the baby and this can interfere with sleep and make the woman tired. Many of the physical symptoms of depression, such as tiredness and sleep problems, are common in mothers who are not depressed. Therefore, it is the 'feeling' and 'thinking' symptoms that are often more important to identify the depression (☛ Chapter 2). To detect depression, you should ask questions such as:

- Have you felt sad or unhappy?
- Do you feel hope for the future?
- Have you been feeling like harming yourself?
- Are you able to enjoy the baby?

  If you suspect a psychosis, ask the following questions:

- Have you had difficulty controlling your thoughts?
- Have you been feeling as if people were talking about you or trying to harm you?
- Have you had unusual thoughts, such as feeling as if you have unusual powers?

Fathers should help look after the baby.

- Have you had thoughts of harming your baby?
- Have you been hearing voices even when there is no one around?

What to do for the 'blues'

- Reassure the mother and family that the emotional distress is very common and temporary.
- Should someone help the mother take care of the baby during those few days.
- The mother should get adequate rest.
- Talk to the mother and let her share her concerns and worries.
- If the mother does not feel better in a week, keep a closer watch because this may be a sign that her blues are becoming a more severe illness.

What to do for postnatal depression

- Reassure the mother and the family that the symptoms are the result of a common emotional illness. The illness is treatable and will do no long-term harm to the mother or the baby.
- Reassure the mother that she is not 'going mad'.
- Ask the father or relatives to help the mother in caring for the baby.
- Talk to the mother regularly about her symptoms and worries.
- Teach her breathing exercises, which she should practise twice daily (☛ section 3.2.3).
- Ensure that she gets adequate rest and food.

- Encourage her to hold and play with her baby and to breastfeed.

- If sleep problems are severe, then give the mother a sleeping medicine, such as lorazepam or nitrazepam.

- If the depression does not improve within a week, or if there are suicidal feelings, you can also use antidepressants. A safe choice during the postnatal period would be fluoxetine, 20 mg daily, for at least six months.

What to do for postnatal psychosis

- The mother may need to be hospitalised for a few days. Refer her to the nearest mental health or other appropriate hospital.

- Use antipsychotic medicines to bring the illness under control. You can use haloperidol, 5–10 mg a day, or other antipsychotic medicines (☞ Chapter 11). Sleeping medicines at night will help the woman get adequate rest.

- Advise the family that the mother should not nurse the infant if she is receiving antipsychotic medicines. The baby needs to be cared for by a relative until the mother is calmer.

- Allow the mother as much time and contact with her baby as she wishes. As she improves, encourage her gradually to take over her role of mother.

- Continue the medicines for at least six weeks.

When to refer

You should refer a mother to a mental health specialist if:

- she shows symptoms of psychosis;

- she has no family support and may be at risk of suicide or harming the baby;

- she has tried to harm the baby.

What to do later

- See the mother regularly until she is better. If she is on medication, see her at least once every two weeks until the medicines are stopped.

- Keep a close watch on the woman's mental health when she has another baby; postnatal mental health problems may recur with subsequent births.

☞ section 9.2.2 for advice on how to integrate mental health care with maternal health care.

Box 4.9. Things to remember when dealing with postnatal mental health problems

- Mothers can develop depression or psychosis after childbirth.
- Postnatal depression is a common condition. It is commoner in mothers whose marriages are unhappy or who have had a difficult delivery.
- Because mothers are expected to be happy and involved in baby care, they are less likely to share negative feelings and emotions with others.
- The majority of mothers can be helped by counselling and antidepressant medicines.
- Postnatal psychosis is best treated in a specialist unit; if this is not available, treat the mother with antipsychotic medicines and ensure that she is assisted in the baby's care by relatives.

4.7 The elderly person with disturbed behaviour

Sometimes aggression or confusion occurs in elderly people. Less often, relatives many complain that the elderly person has become sexually inappropriate, or is constantly demanding to go out of the house even though he is confused. Another type of disturbed behaviour is when a person simply withdraws from her everyday life and appears to lose interest in things. This is less likely to be considered 'disturbing' but is as important as a sign of a mental illness.

4.7.1 What can make an elderly person behave like this?

There are four main reasons why elderly people may behave unusually.

- *Depression*. The common features of depression in elderly people are withdrawal from everyday life, loss of appetite, poor sleep and physical complaints. Some can become agitated and suicidal.

- *Delirium or confusion*. The typical feature of delirium is that it is acute; the disturbed behaviour will have begun in the past few days. The person may be hallucinating and may be agitated.

- *Psychosis*. Severe mental disorders can give rise to suspicious thoughts and hallucinations. Psychosis can also occur in elderly people who suffer from dementia.

- *Dementia*. This is an illness that mainly affects older people, especially those who are more than 65 years of age. The earliest sign of the illness is memory problems. The illness usually comes to the notice of a health worker because of the disturbed behaviour. Dementia is a disease where the brain gradually degenerates. At present, there is no cure and most sufferers will gradually get worse and die within a few years. The commonest causes of dementia are Alzheimer's disease and strokes.

4.7.2 Deciding what's wrong

There are two important diagnostic decisions you must make.

First, you need to tell the difference between the four conditions that can cause disturbed behaviour. Sometimes, two of these conditions can occur together. This is especially true for dementia and delirium (or confusion) and dementia and psychosis. The first priority is to ensure that the person is not confused, because delirium can be life-threatening and is often treatable. Once this is excluded, and if you are in doubt, treat the person as if depressed. If the person was depressed, they would recover; if not, you would not have harmed them. Only if the person is neither depressed nor confused should you consider the possibility of a dementia. Sometimes it is necessary for the elderly person to be seen by a mental health specialist to make the correct diagnosis. Brain scans may also help in detecting dementia.

Second, if it is a dementia, make sure that there is no treatable medical condition that is causing it. The main ones to think of are:

- thyroid disease;

- head injuries that cause slow bleeding inside the head;

- AIDS (in younger people);
- vitamin B12 deficiency;
- chronic kidney or liver disease;
- brain cancers.

4.7.3 Memory problems in old age: when is this abnormal?

We associate growing old with becoming absent-minded, and our mental abilities do in fact fade as we grow old. However, this does not mean that we forget who our relatives are, or where we live, or other important facts. The memory loss of dementia is much more severe than in normal ageing. Thus, the person with dementia will not remember what he did the previous day, or the names of close relatives, or the address of his own home. As the disease gets worse, he may forget the day or time, what he has just said (so that he says the same thing again and again) or even who his wife or son is.

Dementia is a progressive illness, and Box 4.10 lists its stages. Box 4.11 discusses the importance of dementia in developing countries, despite their relatively small proportion of elderly people.

Box 4.10. The stages of dementia

Early stage. The person may appear confused and forgetful about things that have just happened. Concentration and making decisions become difficult. She may lose interest in her usual activities. Most families (and health workers) consider this phase as a part of 'normal' ageing.

Middle stage. Confusion, forgetfulness and mood changes become more severe. Behavioural problems such as aggression and sexual problems may occur. The elderly person may wander out of the house, his sleep becomes very disturbed and his ability to look after himself becomes affected. Even simple things like dressing may become impossible. He may have difficulty with talking and understanding everyday conversations.

Late stage. The person no longer recognises relatives or friends. Loss of weight, seizures and incontinence of urine and stool may occur. It is almost impossible to have any sensible conversation with her. She may appear confused all the time. Death usually follows soon, often through pneumonia or other infections.

Box 4.11. Dementia in developing countries: why is it important?

Alzheimer's disease is the commonest cause of dementia. It is a label that is well recognised in the developed countries of Europe, North America and in Japan. Why? Because these nations have a significant proportion of older people. Developing countries, on the other hand, have had a relatively small proportion of older people and a much higher proportion of children. This balance is changing as birth rates fall and the life span a person can expect increases. This means that dementia will become more common in the future as more and more people live to older age. Most developed countries have well-organised health and social care systems to support elderly people and their families through the long and difficult course of dementia. This is not the case in most developing countries. Thus, societies will face growing numbers of people with dementia but without much awareness or services for them. This is why dementia is an important problem for health workers in developing countries.

4.7.4 When should you suspect dementia?

Suspect dementia when an elderly person:

- is brought with complaints of disturbed behaviour;
- is forgetting things more than usual;
- has been confused or agitated or aggressive for more than a month.

4.7.5 How does dementia affect the family?

The elderly are treated with respect and love in most families. When an elderly person starts behaving in an unusual manner, it causes the family a great deal of distress. The person may forget who his closest relatives are. Aggressive behaviour, agitation and confusion, and sexually inappropriate behaviour cause great difficulty to carers. As the disease gets worse, the sufferer gradually loses the ability to care for himself. Soon, all daily activities such as feeding, bathing, dressing and toileting have to be done with help from the carers. In the final stages of the illness, the elderly person is completely bedridden and needs constant care. You can well imagine how profound the impact of the illness can be, given that dementia can last five to ten years.

4.7.6 Why is diagnosis of dementia important?

As with any other illness, knowing why a loved relative is behaving in a strange manner can make the burden less stressful. The carers can be taught what to expect in the years ahead and plan for the future. It is also important to note that in a few elderly people the dementia is caused by a treatable disease such as low thyroid function. Another important reason for accurate diagnosis is to make sure that the person is not suffering from depression, the other mental health problem seen in old age, which can be treated quite effectively.

4.7.7 How to deal with this problem

Dementia is a progressive and terminal disease. It is essential that you should diagnose this disease only if there is clear evidence (as described below).

Questions to ask the family or friends

- When did you first notice a problem? Often, a relative will recall symptoms starting several months or years before help was first sought.
- How did the illness start? Does the elderly person have a problems remembering things, such as names, or which day it is? Memory problems are the classic symptoms of dementia, but can also occur in depression.
- Does she have difficulty with everyday activities such as eating and bathing? If so, this would suggest dementia.
- Does she behave in an odd manner? For example, does she become aggressive or agitated? Again, these symptoms are more typical of dementia.
- Has she seemed sad or lost interest in daily life? These are typical symptoms of depression, but can also occur in dementia.

- Has she suffered from a mental health problem in the past? If she was depressed in the past, then there is a higher chance that she may be depressed again.

- Who is the main carer for the elderly person? How is he coping? The carer often needs counselling and asking him about his experiences is a useful way of understanding his needs.

Questions to ask the elderly person

- My name is … I would like you to repeat this. Now, please try to remember my name. These questions will check for the ability of the elderly person to remember new information.

- Can you tell me what day of the week this is? What year? This will help check for orientation to time.

- Can you tell me what this place is? For example, that this is a clinic. Where is this place? These will check for orientation to place.

- Can you tell me what you had to eat at your last meal? This tests for the ability to remember recent events.

- Now, can you tell me what my name is? This tests for whether the person was able to remember your name which you had told him earlier.

- If the person appears to understand the questions reasonably well, you should now ask questions about feelings and emotions (☞ Chapter 2 for screening questions for depression).

Special interview suggestions

Even if the elderly person has poor memory and looks confused, introducing yourself is very important. It will serve to give the elderly person some idea of where she is and to whom she is talking. Interview her with a relative who can help clarify questions that she cannot answer.

What to do immediately

- If the elderly person is depressed, psychotic or confused, treat them as you would a younger adult (☞ sections 4.2, 4.3 and 4.4). Remember though that elderly people need much smaller amounts of medicines.

- Educate the carer about dementia, and what to expect. Explain that although there is no cure, a lot can be done to make the elderly person more comfortable and life less stressful for the carer.

- Provide advice on practical issues of caring and hints on how to deal with the disturbed behaviour (☞ Box 4.12, which can apply to carers as well as health professionals).

- In cases where the behaviour is very disturbed, medicines can be very helpful to calm the elderly person. A useful medication is haloperidol. Start with a dose of 0.25 mg twice daily and increase, if needed, up to 2 mg twice daily.

- It is helpful if the elderly person sleeps well at night. If sleep is disturbed, you can use lorazepam, 0.5–1 mg, at night.

- In many countries, 'brain tonics' are sold to improve memory and brain function. However, there is no evidence that they are of any benefit. Do not use any such tonics.

Box 4.12. Practical tips for dealing with disturbed behaviour in dementia

General tips
- Establish a daily routine. This will make life a lot simpler because you will know what is to be done, how often, when and so on.
- As far as possible, let the elderly person be independent. For example, many can feed themselves, even if they are slow and unsteady.
- Never forget that the elderly person has dignity. Do not talk negatively about her in her presence.
- Preserve an elderly person's privacy during intimate activities such as bathing.
- Avoid confrontation and arguments.
- Keep tasks simple.
- Laugh with the elderly person (never at her).
- Help make the best of a person's abilities; simple tasks can be found which the person could do and which could also provide some exercise.

- Make sure that the person's eyeglasses are correct.
- Speak slowly and clearly. If the elderly person has not understood, try to say things using simpler words and shorter sentences.
- Show love and affection whenever possible. A hug is worth a hundred pills.
- Use memory aids such as labelling doors to the bathroom or a writing board in the room on which today's day and date is written every day.
- Avoid unnecessary medicines.

Bathing and personal hygiene
- Independence: let the elderly person do as much as possible unaided.
- Dignity: bathe the elderly person with underpants on.
- Safety: a chair to sit on while being bathed; a mat that does not slip on a wet floor.

Toileting
- A regular toilet routine.
- Use clothing that can be easily removed (and put back on).
- Limit drinks at bedtime.
- Keep a vessel for urine during the nights.
- Special pads for incontinence in older people can be obtained.

Feeding and eating
- Use finger foods.
- Cut up food into small, bite-size pieces.
- Do not serve food too hot.
- Remind the person how to eat (with hands or how to use cutlery).
- If the elderly person has difficult swallowing, refer to a specialist.
- Mix the food and serve it in a ready-to-eat state (for example, mixing curry and rice).

Suspiciousness and anger
- Do not argue back; keep your calm.
- Try to comfort; hold hands firmly and talk gently.
- Distract the person by drawing attention to something in the room.
- Try to find out what made the elderly person angry – and try to avoid this in future.
- Consider medication such as haloperidol.

Wandering away from home
- Use an identification bracelet or necklace.
- Keep the doors of the house locked.
- When the elderly person is found, don't show anger.

- Caring for an elderly person with dementia can be a very stressful experience. Section 9.10 provides advice that you can give carers on how to deal with this stress.
- Refer the carer to a support group for families affected by Alzheimer's disease. Such support groups are increasingly available in many countries (☞ section 10.1, Chapter 12).

When to refer

- If in doubt about the cause of the problem, refer immediately.
- When the carer is unable to manage on his own.
- When physical health problems become serious.

What to do later

Arrange to visit the family at home. You will often understand their needs far better this way. If you have given medication, check on side-effects and how much improvement has occurred. Increase the dose as needed, but always remember that the elderly are more sensitive to side-effects. As the dementia gets worse, you will need to provide more intensive nursing support and guidance.

Box 4.13. Things to remember when dealing with elderly people with disturbed behaviour

- Disturbed behaviour in the elderly can be caused by dementia, psychosis, confusion or depression. It is important to try to identify depression, psychosis or confusion since these should be treated first.
- Alzheimer's disease is the commonest cause of dementia. There is no cure for it at present.
- Practical advice, emotional support and medication for behavioural problems are the best ways of reducing the burden of care.
- The dose of most medicines for the elderly is about one-third to one-half of what you would use for younger adults.

Chapter 5

Symptoms that are medically unexplained

This chapter describes clinical problems that are often associated with depression and anxiety. Depression and anxiety are common mental illnesses that can be important in other clinical problems as well, such as someone with suicidal ideas (☞ section 4.4), when people are faced with violence or loss (☞ Chapter 7) or when someone has a drinking problem (☞ section 6.1). Chapter 2 explains how you can detect depression and anxiety, and Chapter 3 gives specific details on their psychological and drug treatment. The list below is a brief summary of the treatment options:

- *Education and reassurance.* Explain to the person that he is suffering from a common mental illness that is treatable. It is because of this illness that the person has the complaints he has. The illness does not mean he is going 'crazy'.

- *Advice about common symptoms.* Give advice about common complaints that persons with depression and anxiety suffer from, for example tiredness, sleep problems and sexual problems. You will find details of how to deal with specific complaints in this chapter.

- *Relaxation training* (☞ Chapter 3).

- *Problem-solving.* This is a simple form of counselling that helps a person identify the various problems she is facing and then tries to solve those that are most important to her.

- *Positive thinking* (☞ Box 5.1).

- *Medical treatment.* Antidepressant medicines are the best medicine for depression and anxiety. See Chapter 11 for more information and to enter information on specific medicines in your country.

5.1 The person with multiple physical complaints

Physical complaints are the commonest reasons for seeking help from a health worker or doctor. Many symptoms, such as fever or cough, can be explained as medical problems. However, there are some complaints for which it is often difficult to find any medical explanation. Examples of such complaints are:

- headaches;

- aches and pains all over the body;

- chest pain;

- heart beating fast (palpitations);

- dizziness;

- low back pain;

Box 5.1. Positive thinking: a different way of looking at life

One of the main reasons why some people become depressed when faced with difficult situations is that they see life in a negative way. It is very helpful to identify such negative thinking and encourage the person who has attempted suicide to see how the same situation could be viewed in a positive way. Here are some examples of such negative thinking and positive thinking (shown below the negative thinking, in italic):

If someone does not like me, it means there is something wrong with me.

Most of the people I know do like me. Just because this one person did not like me, it does not mean something is wrong with me.

I will always feel miserable. Nothing will change in my life.

These feelings are temporary. I feel this way because I am not well. Talking to the health worker, taking my medicines and trying to solve my problems will make me feel better.

It's my fault that I failed the exams. I do not deserve to live.

Anyone can fail an exam. I need to study harder and I will surely pass the next time.

You should try the following steps in helping the person to think more positively:
• Teach the person to be aware of these negative patterns of thinking and how they make her feel unhappy.
• She should ask herself "Is what I believe real?" To answer this, she could talk to friends or relatives whom she trusts. She could ask herself whether other people in the same situation would also think in the same way.
• Next, encourage her to come up with alternative ways of thinking. This is best done by practising with recent negative thoughts and situations as examples.

Let us take an example. A person was not selected for a job and had these thoughts:

I am useless
I will never get a job

I will always be
unemployed and poor
No one will marry me if
I am jobless

I may as well end
my life

The resulting emotions are obviously those of unhappiness and depression.

Now, look at alternative ways of looking at this situation:

There is a recession on
and many people are
finding it hard to get a job

I can see that my application
was not well written
and I should get some
help before applying again

Well, I didn't get the job
but there will be many
more opportunities
I have held jobs in
the past and done well

The resulting emotions may be more hopeful.

- abdominal pain;
- difficulty in breathing.

5.1.1 Why are physical complaints relevant to mental health?

There is a strong relationship between mental illness and physical complaints. People with mental health problems come with physical complaints for many reasons:

- Worry and tension can make a person tense his muscles for long periods. This makes the muscles tender and painful. A good example of this is the 'tension' headache as a result of tensing up neck muscles when worried.

- When a person is anxious or depressed, chemical changes occur in the body. One common change is the release of adrenalin, a chemical that is normally released in the body during exercise or when a person is scared. This causes complaints such as palpitations and chest pain.

- When people are tense, they tend to breathe faster. This produces changes in the levels of oxygen and carbon dioxide in the blood. These changes can lead to symptoms such as dizziness, palpitations, tingling or numbness of the fingers and toes, and a choking or breathless sensation. This is what happens during a panic attack (☞ section 5.2).

- Alcohol can produce physical complaints because, in large amounts, it poisons the liver and other organs (☞ section 6.1).

- People feel that if they tell a health worker that their main problem is emotional, they may not get help. Thus, they focus on the physical complaint as a way of getting medical attention.

- Many languages describe emotional pain in a physical way. For example, in English, one can say 'my heart is heavy' to describe a sad mood. Thus, the physical symptom is simply another way of expressing mental pain (space is provided in the Glossary for you to enter idioms for mental distress in your local language).

- Painful illnesses, such as inflammation of the joints, can make a person feel unhappy and worried. Here, the pain is caused by a physical illness, but it affects the person's mental health. Feeling depressed can make the pain less bearable.

5.1.2 When to suspect that physical complaints are related to mental illness

You should think of a mental illness particularly in a person who:

- has more than three complaints;
- has complaints that do not fit into any pattern which you associate with a physical disease;
- has had the complaints for more than three months;
- has consulted health workers many times for the same complaints;
- has been examined and has had tests that were normal.

5.1.3 How to deal with this problem

Questions to ask the person with multiple physical complaints

- When did this start? The longer duration of the symptoms, the more likely they are to be related to mental illness.

- How have you been feeling emotionally? Have you been worried about anything? Have you been feeling down? Have you lost interest in your daily life? Ask questions to identify depression and anxiety (☛ Chapter 2).

- Do you drink alcohol? If so, follow further questions on problem drinking(☛ section 6.1).

- What do you feel has caused your symptoms? The person's views on the illness can be a valuable way of determining whether it is an emotional problem.

Things to look for during the interview

- A worried or tense look on the face.

- Any signs of physical illness and weight loss.

What to do immediately

- Make sure that the person is not suffering from a physical illness before you assume that the complaints are due to a mental illness.

- Reassure the person that there is no life-threatening or serious physical illness. This does not mean that she is not suffering some other illness.

- Explain the link between emotions and physical experiences.

- Explain that there is no need, at present, for further tests or investigations.

When a person sees a snake, he feels scared. What often happens is that he will feel his heart beat fast and body tremble. Why? Because these are the physical experiences associated with feeling scared.

- Try to avoid using labels such as 'mental' illness, since the person may resent this. After all, many people (including health workers) do not associate complaints such as headache with mental illness. Instead, you could say "Your symptoms are being made worse by your worries and tension. You have been worried about your husband's drinking problem. This could be giving you a headache and make your heart beat fast."

- Teach the person relaxation (breathing) exercises and problem-solving (☛ section 3.2.5).

- Encourage some physical activity or exercise such as walking, shopping and household activities if these have been stopped.

- Do not prescribe vitamins or painkillers unless there is clear evidence of malnutrition or a painful physical illness.

- Antidepressant medication (☛ Chapter 11) can be used in the following instances:
  - if there are clear symptoms of depression, particularly if there are also suicidal ideas or weight loss or sleep disturbance;
  - if there are panic attacks and severe symptoms of anxiety;
  - if you have no time to provide counselling and prefer to rely on medication.

When to refer

- If you are not sure about the possibility of a physical illness, you should refer for further opinion. Some physical illnesses can produce chronic, multiple physical symptoms along with emotional effects. Examples of such illnesses are arthritis and diabetes.
- If the person is severely depressed and suicidal, refer to a mental health specialist.
- Many people with depression have social and personal problems that may be difficult to resolve in a clinic. Refer such people to other agencies (☛ Chapter 12).

What to do later

Review the person in a week and see him regularly (about once a fortnight). This will help reduce the worry that his illness may not be adequately looked after. It will also help establish trust and, once he feels comfortable with you, he will be able to share emotions that he could not at the beginning.

Box 5.2. Things to remember when dealing with a person with multiple physical complaints

- Multiple physical complaints with no clear physical cause are common in general health clinics. These include tiredness, dizziness, aches and pains, and palpitations.
- Depression, anxiety and alcohol misuse are important causes of such medically unexplained physical complaints.
- Before you say there is nothing wrong with the person, think about the possibility of a mental or social problem.
- If you have any concern that the symptoms may be caused by a physical illness, refer to a specialist for another opinion. On the other hand, if the person has already had many tests and examinations, it will probably be pointless to do more.
- Avoid unnecessary painkillers, vitamins or sleeping medicines. Treat the mental illness and this will lead to an improvement in the symptoms.

5.2 The person who worries, gets scared or panics

Worrying is thinking too much about unpleasant things that may happen in the future. Typical worries are related to money problems, relationship difficulties, children's future and health. We all worry about something, some of the time. However, when worrying becomes continuous, out of proportion to what is actually happening in a person's life, and begins to interfere with daily activities, then it is unhealthy. Excess worrying can become an illness and actually prevent the person from thinking clearly and solving problems. Depression and anxiety are important causes of such excess worrying.

We all have worries in our lives, but if a person does not find a solution for her worries, then she may become sick with worrying.

But if she thinks about the possible solutions, then she can do something about her worries and feel better.

5.2.1 Fear and panic

When we worry, we become scared that something unpleasant might happen. This is fear. Fear is an important part of learning in life. For example, when students fear failing their examinations, they may study harder for them. But if a person gets scared that he might die or that something terrible might happen to his family when there is no basis for such thoughts, fear cannot be helpful in any way.

Panic attacks are attacks of extreme anxiety and fear. Typically, the attack comes out of the blue without any warning. It is associated with such severe physical symptoms, such as the heart beating fast or difficulty breathing, that the person is terrified that she may die or go mad. Many people will have one or two panic attacks at some time during their lives. However, sometimes, panic attacks become more frequent. When they occur regularly, for example once or twice a week, then this is no longer normal.

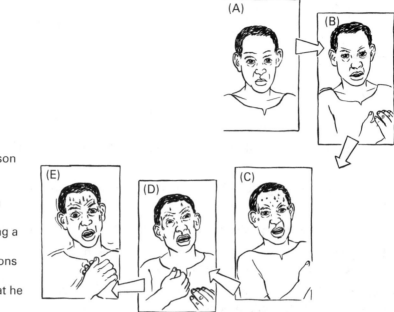

A panic attack

(A) Sometimes when a person is worried he may get palpitations of the heart.
(B) This can make him even more worried.
(C) He may think he is having a heart attack.
(D) This makes the palpitations even worse.
(E) He becomes terrified that he will die.

5.2.2 Being scared of specific situations

Some people get scared of a specific situation even though it is not dangerous. Typically, the person with these fears will avoid the situation in order to prevent getting scared. These fears are called phobias. Most people have one phobia or another, for example of spiders or snakes. However, some people have phobias of everyday situations, such as:

• crowded places, for example public buses or markets;

• open places (anywhere out of the house);

• social situations, for example meeting people on social occasions.

If a person has a fear of these situations and starts avoiding them, it will severely affect his life. This is why some phobias become health problems.

5.2.3 Why do people worry or have panic attacks or phobias?

Some of us worry when we are under stress. Examples of life difficulties that can lead to fear and anxiety are:

• relationship problems, such as marital conflict, conflict with parents;

• loss of someone close, for example due to death;

• loss of a job;

• physical illness in self;

• work difficulties;

• money problems, such as being in debt;

• sickness in the family.

The experience of trauma and violence (☞ section 7.1) can also give rise to anxiety and panic, as can alcohol misuse and other drug problems (including medicines such as sleeping pills) (☞ Chapter 6). Some people worry excessively for no obvious reason, and some may have a lifelong history of being tense or shy.

5.2.4 How to deal with this problem

Questions to ask the person who is unduly worried

- How long have you felt like this? The longer the duration, the more severe the problem is likely to be.

- How did these feelings begin? Find out whether any life events occurred that may have triggered the illness.

- Are you using sleeping pills or alcohol? If so, ask about alcohol misuse (☞ section 6.1).

- Have you been avoiding any situations because of your fear? If so, what situation? How has this affected your life? These questions relate to phobias.

- Does your fear ever get so bad that you feel you might collapse or die? If so, how often? These questions relate to panic attacks.

- Has anyone hurt you recently? If so, further advice is given in section 7.1.

- Have there been any problems in your life recently? For example, problems in your marriage or at work? Finding out about such problems is an important step in making the link between life difficulties and worry.

- Have you lost interest in daily life? Ask questions about depression (☞ Chapter 2).

Things to look for during the interview

A worried or tense look is typical of fearful people. A sad or emotionless face may suggest depression. Some anxious people are very restless and fidgety, for example constantly wringing their hands or shifting in their seat.

What to do immediately

- Reassure the person, specifically about the following:
  - The symptoms are not a sign of serious physical illness. However, it is important that this reassurance is given only if you have completed a thorough physical examination and appropriate laboratory tests.
  - The symptoms are not a sign that the person is going mad.
  - If relevant, the symptoms are not a sign of witchcraft or spirit possession.

- Explain that worrying is the cause of the symptoms and that the symptoms can make the person even more worried. The way to break this cycle is for the person to reassure herself when the symptoms start that they are only the result of worrying.

- Teach the person breathing and relaxation exercises (☞ section 3.2.3).

- Changing attitudes and ways of thinking are a very important part of treatment. It is necessary for the person to view her situation in a more positive manner (☛ Box 5.1). These are some examples of such 'positive thinking' (☛ pictures below).

- Give specific advice on panic attacks (☛ Box 5.3) or phobias (☛ Box 5.4).

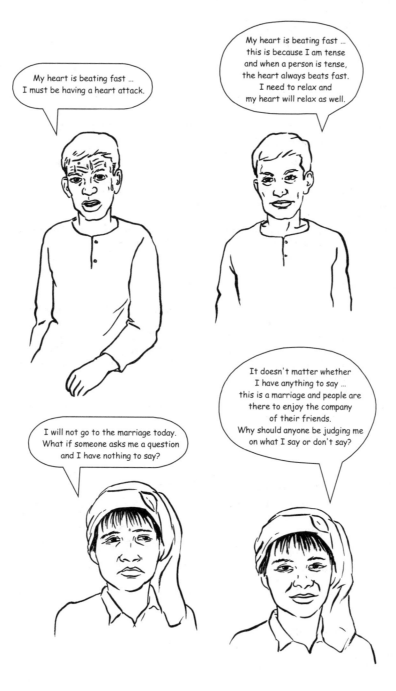

Box 5.3. Advising a person with panic attacks

Panic attacks are attacks of severe anxiety that result from rapid breathing. Sufferers should be taught the following:
- An attack begins when they start to feel the fearful thoughts or the physical symptoms.
- They should immediately remind themselves that they are breathing too fast and take control of their breathing.
- They should breathe in a *slow, steady, controlled* manner (in a way similar to the breathing rhythm described in section 3.2.3). The breathing should be continued in this manner until the symptoms of the attack subside.
- They should reassure themselves that the symptoms are due to breathing too fast and that nothing dangerous will happen.

Box 5.4. Advising a person with a phobia

A phobia is when a person experiences fear, often panic attacks, in specific situations and begins to avoid them.
- Teach people with phobias that the way of overcoming their fear is to expose themselves to the situation until the fear subsides. In this way they can become confident that there is nothing to fear about the situation.
- Explain that avoiding the situation only makes the fear worse. Exposure to the fearful situation must be done consistently to build up confidence and overcome the phobia. They can be taught to deal with the fear during exposure by breathing exercises (* section 3.2) and by reassuring themselves that the fear is temporary.
- Identify the situations that lead to fear and then grade these situations in a list from the least fearful to the most fearful.
- Expose the person in steps starting from the less fearful situations; once she has mastered this situation and can face it with no fear, encourage her to move to the next situation. For example, a housebound person could be encouraged to take a short walk to a neighbour's home as the first step. This step is practised daily until no more fear is experienced. She must not leave the situation under any circumstances. After overcoming this fear, she should move on to the next step, which could be walking further, say to the post office. Finally, she will need to walk to the marketplace.
See the figures on the next page.

When to use medication

Two types of medication can be used: anti-anxiety drugs or antidepressant drugs.

Anti-anxiety medication can be used but not for more than six weeks. It should be used only in special situations such as:

- The anxiety is so great that the person is not able to listen or understand your advice.

- The person is very tense following a severe life event such as the death of a spouse.

- The person is so tense that he has not slept well for many days and is now tired. A good night's sleep may aid recovery.

The medicines you could use are:

- diazepam, 5 mg twice daily;

- alprazolam, 0.25–0.5 mg twice daily;

- amitriptyline or imipramine, 25 mg at night.

*Steps in overcoming phobias.
1: Getting used to speaking in front of strangers*
(A) First try going with a friend to a shop and ask for an item.
(B) Once you can do this without feeling anxious, when with a friend, try asking a stranger for directions.
(C) When you feel comfortable doing that, try going to a shop and asking for an item by yourself.
(D) Once you can do that, try going to a restaurant and have a tea all by yourself.

*Steps in overcoming phobias.
2: Getting used to travelling in a crowded bus*
(A) Walk to the bus stop and wait for the bus but don't get on.
(B) Take a bus at a time when it is not crowded.
(C) When you can do this without fear, take a bus journey with a friend when it is crowded.
(D) When this no longer causes anxiety, take a bus journey alone when it is crowded.

Antidepressant medication can be very useful if:

• there are repeated panic attacks;

• the person is depressed;

• the worrying lasts more than four weeks despite your explanation and breathing exercises.

See Chapter 11 for information on how to use antidepressants.

When to refer

You should refer if:

• you are concerned that the symptoms may be the result of a physical illness;

• there are serious life difficulties that could be helped by some other agency, for example the police or women's groups (☞ Chapter 12).

Box 5.5. Things to remember when dealing with a person who is worried or scared

• When worrying and being afraid start affecting a person's daily life, then they become a health problem.
• Panic attacks are attacks of severe anxiety. They are often mistaken for a medical problem, especially a heart attack, because of the severe physical symptoms.
• Some people avoid situations that make them scared (phobias). Common situations that cause this fear are crowded places and social situations.
• Treatment consists of advice about the cause of symptoms, breathing exercises and specific advice on how to overcome the fear.
• Worrying is often associated with depression; antidepressant medication may help such people.

5.3 The person with sleep problems (insomnia)

On average, a person sleeps seven to eight hours a day. Sleep gives the body and mind time for rest and makes the person feel fresh in the morning. Insomnia is the word for the commonest type of sleep difficulty, in which sleep is no longer refreshing. Some people may have difficulty in falling asleep. Some may wake up too early in the morning and cannot get back to sleep. Some may wake up repeatedly through the night. Insomnia is one of the commonest health complaints. As a result of the excessive use of sleeping pills, many people with insomnia become addicted to them (☞ section 6.3).

5.3.1 How does insomnia affect the person?

Imagine what would happen if you had poor sleep. Insomnia leads to:

• feeling drowsy during the day;

• tiredness;

• poor concentration;

• feeling irritable and short-tempered;

• problems in thinking clearly.

5.3.2 What causes insomnia?

The commonest causes of insomnia are:

• alcohol misuse – people who drink alcohol suffer insomnia because they sleep poorly when drunk, and tend to wake up early because of withdrawal symptoms;

- depression and anxiety;

- misuse of sleeping pills (☞ section 6.3);

- medical problems, particularly those that cause pain, breathing difficulties (such as heart failure) or urinary infections that lead to increased passing of urine.

5.3.3 How to deal with this problem

Questions to ask the person with sleep problems

- What is your sleep pattern? Ask about the amount of sleep, daytime sleep and type of insomnia (for example, difficulty falling asleep, waking up in the middle of the night).

- Do you take any medicines or alcohol to help you sleep? This will give you a clue to the possibility of a sleeping pill or drink problem.

- Do you suffer from any pain or other medical problem?

- Have you been feeling like you have lost interest in things recently? Have you been feeling tense, worried or scared recently? These questions relate to depression and anxiety (☞ Chapter 2).

What to do immediately

- Explain that insomnia is a common complaint, and that everyone with insomnia will sleep normally once the cause is resolved.

- Educate the person about how to sleep better (☞ Box 5.6).

- If you identify an underlying illness that may be causing sleep problems, treat the person as indicated in other sections of this manual (the likeliest underlying mental illnesses are alcohol misuse and depression or anxiety).

Box 5.6. Advice on how to sleep better

- Keep to a regular sleep routine. Go to bed at a fixed time.
- Wake at the same time no matter how much sleep you have had during the night. Use an alarm clock if you have difficulty waking at a fixed time in the mornings.
- Do not use alcohol or sleeping medicines to get to sleep.
- Do not smoke before sleeping; coughing can keep you awake.
- Empty your bladder just before sleeping.
- Avoid tea and coffee in the evening; these are stimulants and can keep you awake.
- Try relaxation exercises before sleeping (☞ section 3.2.3).
- Avoid exercise in the evenings but do exercise in the daytime.
- Avoid daytime naps.
- Worrying about not being able to sleep worsens the sleep problem.
- Make your sleeping environment 'sleep-friendly': keep the room dark using curtains, or use eye patches; close your windows if it is noisy outside or use earplugs.
- If you cannot fall asleep, do not lie in bed; wake up, read a book or relax for 15 to 30 minutes and then go back to sleep.

When to use sleeping pills

Sleeping pills are medicines containing diazepam, lorazepam, nitrazepam and so on (☛ Chapter 11). They are among the commonest medicines used in the world. This fact alone shows us how frequent complaints of insomnia are. However, sleeping medicines produce an artificial sleep. They are all addictive, so that once a person becomes used to taking them, she will not be able to sleep without them (☛ section 6.3). The best way to avoid such problems is to follow these rules:

- Do not prescribe sleeping medicines for people with long-standing difficulties with sleep or those with a history of addictions (such as to alcohol).

- If you must use them, monitor the person closely.

- Give a week's supply of a sleeping medicine, for example diazepam 5–10 mg at night or lorazepam 1–2 mg at night. Ask the person to return in a week.

- If the person is feeling better, stop the medicine. Do not prescribe sleeping pills for more than four weeks. The prescription should be for one week at a time so that you can review the person each week.

- Give advice on how to sleep better (Box 5.6).

   For guidance on how to help a person who has been using sleeping medicines for a long time, ☛ section 6.3.

When to refer

Refer if the person is suffering a physical illness that is causing pain or other discomfort.

Box 5.7. Things to remember when dealing with a person with a sleep problem

- Sleeping problems are very common. Insomnia is a health problem if it has been present for at least two weeks and is causing difficulties.
- Depression, alcohol misuse, excessive use of sleeping medicines and painful physical illnesses can cause insomnia.
- Simple changes in lifestyle are the best way of restoring healthy sleep. If you do prescribe sleeping pills, never do so for more than four weeks at a time.
- If insomnia is part of another illness, for example depression, treat that illness.

5.4 The person who is tired all the time

Tiredness is one of the commonest reasons for feeling unwell. Tiredness can present in many ways. One way is feeling fatigued all the time. When this is severe, even minor activities such as getting dressed can seem difficult. Another common way of expressing tiredness is "feeling weak" or "having no energy" to do things. Tiredness is often accompanied by a strong desire to sleep (though often the person cannot sleep) or to just lie down.

5.4.1 Why do some people feel tired?

Many people feel tired because of viral or other common infections. In such cases, the tiredness will have started only a few days earlier. Whenever tiredness has been present for less than two weeks, you should treat it as if it is probably caused by an infection. If tiredness lasts more than two weeks, it becomes 'chronic' tiredness or 'chronic fatigue'. Box 5.8 shows the commonest reasons for chronic tiredness.

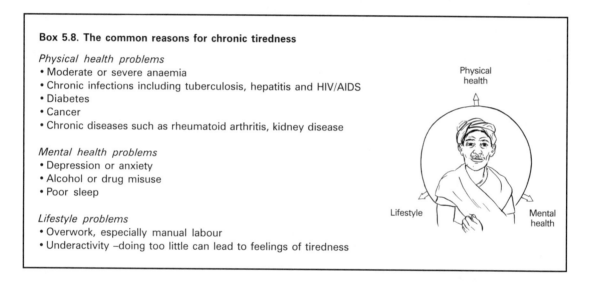

Box 5.8. The common reasons for chronic tiredness

Physical health problems
• Moderate or severe anaemia
• Chronic infections including tuberculosis, hepatitis and HIV/AIDS
• Diabetes
• Cancer
• Chronic diseases such as rheumatoid arthritis, kidney disease

Mental health problems
• Depression or anxiety
• Alcohol or drug misuse
• Poor sleep

Lifestyle problems
• Overwork, especially manual labour
• Underactivity –doing too little can lead to feelings of tiredness

Physical health

Lifestyle

Mental health

5.4.2 When to suspect that tiredness is the result of a mental illness

Never suspect a mental health problem until you have confidently ruled out the common physical illnesses (Box 5.8). Suspect a mental health cause for the tiredness:

• when there is no evidence to suggest a physical disease, such as lack of any signs of a physical disease or the absence of abnormal findings on tests;

• if there is evidence of a mental illness such as suicidal feelings;

• if the tiredness is out of proportion to the physical illness – for example, a person may be anaemic, but the tiredness is so extreme that the anaemia alone cannot explain it.

5.4.3 Is tiredness the same as laziness?

People who feel tired do not feel like doing any work. For women, this can be a great problem and can cause conflict with her partner or in-laws. When a health worker tells the family that "there is nothing wrong with her" because he cannot find any physical illness, the family assumes that the woman is pretending to be tired. Even health workers may think that the woman is lazy. Remember that tiredness is often a sign of a mental illness. Just because there is no obvious physical illness, it does not mean that the person is pretending to be sick. *Tiredness is not at all like laziness.*

5.4.4 How to deal with this problem

Questions to ask the person who is tired all the time

- Since when have you been feeling tired? If more than two weeks, the tiredness is chronic.

- Have you been feeling physically sick in any other way? For example, have you been coughing? Losing weight? Do you pass blood in your stools? These are examples of questions regarding chronic physical health problems.

- Have you been feeling under stress recently? Have you been worried about anything? Ask about symptoms of depression and anxiety (☞ Chapter 2).

- Do you drink alcohol? Do you use sleeping pills or other drugs? If so, refer to sections 6.1, 6.3.

- Tell me about the activities you have done on an average day in the past week.

Things to look for during the interview

Do a proper physical examination, and in particular check for:

- a sickly appearance;
- fever;
- abnormal pulse rate and blood pressure;
- abnormal respiratory rate;
- signs of anaemia, such as a 'washed out' or pale tongue or eyes or fingernails;
- signs of weight loss, such as thinning of the muscles of the arms or legs.

Special tests and investigations

Because tiredness can be a sign of serious physical illness, it is helpful to do tests for common illnesses:

- haemoglobin levels for anaemia;
- white blood cell counts for infections;
- urine sugar for diabetes.

What to do immediately

- Make sure the person is not suffering from a physical illness.

- Explain to the person and the family that the tiredness is real and is being caused by an illness. There is no need to specify that this is a mental illness, since this may have a negative effect on the family's support. Instead, you can say that "When we are under any type of stress we can feel tired".

- Explain that there are no specific medicines for tiredness. However, if the tiredness is caused by excess stress, medicines for stress may be given.

- If the person is not sleeping well, give advice on how to sleep better (☛ Box 5.6).

- If the person has an alcohol or drug problem, give appropriate advice (☛ sections 6.1, 6.2).

- If the person is depressed or anxious, suggest ways of dealing with this (☛ section 3).

- Gradual increase in activity levels is often a helpful way of overcoming tiredness. It is helpful to start with low levels of activity first, and to focus on activities which are fun. For example, spending 15 minutes in the morning and evening tending to the vegetable garden or going for a walk may be the first activity to be attempted. Once the person has been able to do this for a week, then move on to a higher level of activity.

- Tell the person to keep in regular touch with friends and relatives. If religious, be regular with visits to places of worship.

- Breathing exercises and problem-solving counselling can help (☛ section 3.2.3).

- In cases where nothing else seems to be working, you can try an antidepressant medicine

(A) A person who is so tired that he does feel like getting out of bed should first try a simple, enjoyable activity such as (B) watering the garden. (C) When he can manage this, he can then try something more demanding like walking to the market and shopping. (D) When he can manage this, he may be ready to return to work.

(A)

(B)

(C)

(D)

When should tonics or vitamins be used?

Tonics and vitamins are very commonly used by people who feel tired. This is because they feel that tiredness is the result of not eating enough or not having enough vitamins. However, most people with a tiredness problem will not be helped by taking tonics or vitamins. It is not helpful to give tonics or vitamins to people who are not anaemic or who do not have obvious features of malnutrition. Dietary advice, such as eating more green leafy vegetables, fish or lentils (which contain natural vitamins and minerals), is far better in the long term than tonics. Do not be fooled by the drug company marketing materials which recommend tonics for anyone who complains of feeling tired.

When to refer

If you suspect that the tiredness is due to a serious physical illness, such as tuberculosis or cancer, refer to a hospital.

Box 5.9. Things to remember when dealing with someone who feels tired all the time

- Tiredness is not always the result of an illness. If a person has been working too much, her body will get tired.
- Tiredness has both mental and physical causes. Always exclude physical causes before considering mental health problems.
- Depression, anxiety and alcohol misuse are mental illnesses that can cause tiredness lasting for more than two weeks.
- There are no specific medicines for tiredness; vitamins and tonics will not help the tired person unless there is clear evidence of anaemia or vitamin deficiency.
- Gradually increasing activities, antidepressants and problem-solving may help the person with a problem of tiredness.

5.5 The person who complains of sexual problems

Sexual health is that aspect of health that is related to the sex organs and to sexual behaviour. Sexual health includes the prevention of sexually transmitted diseases and unwanted pregnancies, the enjoyment of sex as part of intimate relationships and greater control over one's sexual decisions. In this manual, only common sexual behaviour problems are described. For a discussion of infectious diseases that affect the sexual organs see WWHND and WTND, listed in the bibliography.

Sex is an important aspect of intimate, loving relationships between people. Sex is such a personal and private aspect of our lives that it is rarely discussed with others. For many people, there is a lot of ignorance about what is 'normal' sexual behaviour and what are the types and causes of sexual problems. Sexual problems are basically problems men and women have that interfere with their ability to enjoy sex.

5.5.1 Sexual problems in men

There are two common types of sexual problems in men:

- *Impotence*. This is when the penis does not become or stay hard and erect so that the man cannot have sexual intercourse.

Box 5.10. The *dhat* syndrome – "I am feeling weak because I pass semen in my sleep"

Men in some parts of Asia believe that semen (the white liquid that comes out of the penis when the man is sexually excited) is a source of physical strength. Young men may become concerned when they notice that they are 'losing' semen by passing it in their underwear during the night, or when passing urine or stools. They may become very anxious about their desire to masturbate. If they do masturbate, they suffer guilt and tension. Many men will complain of tiredness, aches and pains, impotence and suicidal feelings. Typically, they will blame these complaints on the passing of semen (called *dhat* in South Asia) in their urine. You must spend time explaining male sexuality. An example that helps is that of a glass of milk to which more milk is being continuously added. Once the glass is full, milk will begin to dribble out of the glass. This happens with semen in the body. Education about masturbation being a normal sexual act is important. If the person has become stressed or depressed, treat with antidepressants (Chapter 11).

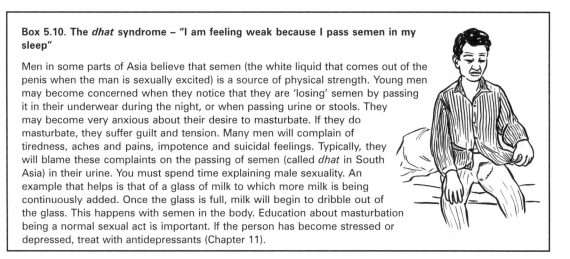

- *Premature ejaculation.* This is when the man ejaculates (passes semen) so quickly that neither partner is able to enjoy the sexual act.

The commonest causes of these sexual problems are:

- tension about sex, typically when a man is having sex for the first time with a particular person;

- misconceptions about the size of the penis, having had sexual intercourse with a woman during her menstrual period, masturbation, and so on;

- ignorance about normal sexual function is one of the main reasons for the *dhat* syndrome seen in men in Asia (☛ Box 5.10);

- depression and tiredness (it is difficult to enjoy sex when unhappy or tired);

- alcohol misuse (drinking heavily can make a man impotent);

- loss of interest in sex, which can happen if the man does not find the partner attractive;

- cigarette smoking, which can affect the blood supply to the sexual organs;

- diabetes, which can affect the nerves and blood supply to the sexual organs;

- some medicines such as antidepressants and medicines for high blood pressure.

5.5.2 Sexual problems in women

Common sexual problems in women are:

- pain during sexual intercourse – this may occur if the woman's sexual passage (the vagina) is dry, or when a man tries to have sex before she is ready or when he forces sex on her;

- loss of interest in sex.

Women's sexual problems are commonly caused by:

- lack of control over sexual decision-making – this means the woman cannot choose when she wants (or does not want) to have sex (☛ Box 5.11);

Box 5.11. Gender and sexual problems

In many places, a woman typically does not have the same control over her body and sexual life as her male partner. She may not be able to choose if and when she has sex. She may have to have sex whenever her partner desires, and yet may not feel free to ask for sex when she desires it. While there may be little you can do from a clinic to change this social problem, there are things you can do to reduce sexual problems. For example, explaining to a woman that her desire to have sex, or her desire to stimulate herself, is normal may help counter the belief that this is shameful. You may be able to explain to a woman that she has the right to protect herself from an unwanted pregnancy and teach her how to do this. You could teach a woman who wishes to enjoy sex but finds that her vagina is too dry to use butter or some other oily substance to make her vagina wet. As a health worker, there is much you can do to change negative attitudes about gender. For more on this subject, see Chapter 10.9 and WWHND.

- infections in the sexual organs;

- tension or fear about having sex;

- sexual abuse in childhood (☛ section 8.4) or other unhappy or painful sexual experiences, making enjoyment of sex difficult.

5.5.3 Abnormal sexual behaviour

Abnormal sexual behaviour is when a person shows sexual behaviour at the wrong times, for example in a public place, or in a manner that is threatening. Examples of abnormal sexual behaviour include:

- taking off one's clothes in a public place;

- showing one's sexual organs in a public place;

- an elderly person trying to have sex with his partner even though they may not have had sexual relations for several years.

When this happens, it causes great concern to the family. Sometimes, the person is abused or beaten for behaving in this manner. Many people who show abnormal sexual behaviour are either suffering from a severe mental disorder or from a brain disease. Referral to a mental health specialist may be needed.

5.5.4 How to deal with this problem

Questions to ask the person with a sexual problem

- What is the problem? When did the problem start? What have you done about it so far? Frank questions about the problem will help the person feel more comfortable in discussing this sensitive subject with you. It is also important to get a clear history of the problem.

- Tell me about your relationship. How long have you and your partner known each other? How much do you love each other? Have you enjoyed sex with each other before? What sorts of things do you enjoy doing? It is difficult to enjoy sex when the relationship is unhappy (☛ Box 5.12).

- Do you masturbate? Are you having sex with anyone other than your spouse? If the person has a sexual problem only with a specific partner, then the problem may be because of a difficulty in their relationship.

Box 5.12. Sex and relationships

Sex can be a way of expressing affection and love. Sex is the way through which a couple can have children and start a family. Sex can be a way of experiencing physical and mental pleasure. If one person has a sexual problem, the relationship with the partner is also affected. Because sex is such a sensitive issue and is rarely discussed as a 'health' issue, the problems tend to remain hidden. The couple may suffer much unhappiness and guilt. They may start blaming each other or themselves in an effort to understand why they no longer enjoy sex with each other. Sometimes, one partner may accuse the other of being unfaithful. Sexual problems can cause increasing tension in everyday life between partners and lead to depression and alcohol misuse. Finally, sexual problems can end up making relationships deeply unhappy or even lead to a break-up. On the other hand, sexual problems can be the result rather than the cause of an unhappy relationship. Thus, if there is much fighting or conflict between two partners, it is unlikely that they will have a satisfying sexual relationship.

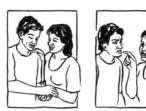

- Have you been feeling tense or worried recently? Do you feel as if you have lost interest in daily life? Ask about symptoms of anxiety and depression (☛ Chapter 2).

- Have you had any infections of the sexual organs?

  Ask a man the following:

- Do you suffer from diabetes, high blood pressure or any other medical disease?

- Are you taking any medicines?

- Do your drink alcohol?

- Do you smoke cigarettes?

- Do you get erections in the mornings? Usually, if a man does not get any erections at all, then you should suspect a medical cause for the impotence.

  Ask a woman the following:

- How much control do you have over having sex? For example, do you feel sometimes that your husband forces you to have sex?

5.5.5 Special interview suggestions

- Interview the person in private first. If he agrees, invite the partner to join the interview later.

- Allow some time to build rapport and trust. Talking about sex is not easy. Don't be in a hurry.

What to do immediately

Do some simple tests such as urine sugar and culture to exclude diabetes or infections.
  For impotence:

- explain that this is a common problem and that it is usually short-lived;

- advise against cigarette smoking and drinking alcohol before having sex;

- discuss possible reasons why the man may be tense or worried and explain the links between these emotions and impotence;

There are many ways of enjoying your lover's company besides having sex.

- advise the man to avoid sexual intercourse for two weeks, but during this time to practise pleasurable physical contact and social activities that do not involve intercourse;
- counsel the partner and encourage her to be part of this therapy.

For premature ejaculation, explain that this is a common problem and is most often caused by tension. Ejaculation can be delayed by the squeeze technique or the stop–start technique. The person is asked to recognise the sensation that he is soon going to ejaculate. The moment he feels this way, he should stop sexual movements immediately. Then, he must wait until that sensation has gone before starting sexual movements again. In the squeeze technique, just as the man begins to feel he is going to ejaculate, he squeezes his penis with his fingers (☞ picture opposite). This reduces the urge to ejaculate and helps prevent it. These techniques help the man feel more confident that he can control his ejaculation.

For women who have pain during intercourse:

- explain that this is common and most often due to tension or because she is not sexually excited;
- if she agrees, counsel the man to explain the need to stimulate the woman so that she feels sexually excited and her vagina is wet, and explain to him the need to have sex when both of them want to have sex;
- recommend the use of vaginal lubricants such as butter or oil.

A lack of sexual desire is usually a problem when one partner has less desire than the other. Counsel both separately and together, if possible. Reassure both that this problem is often a result of marital problems rather than a physical problem with the sexual organs. Explore marital problems between the partners. Encourage them to discuss their feelings and concerns. Identify

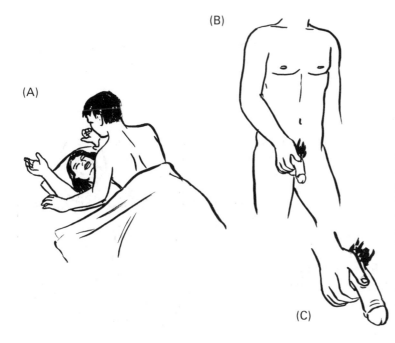

(B)

(A)

(C)

(A) When a man has a problem with premature ejaculation, it is preferable he has sex on top of the woman.
(B) When he feels that he is about to ejaculate, he should withdraw from the woman; and
(C) use his fingers to compress the penis at its base. When the desire to ejaculate goes away, he can once again continue to have to sex.

activities that both used to enjoy doing together (for example meeting friends). Suggest that they should do such activities more often (section 10.7 gives guidance on helping with marital problems). Suggest masturbation as a way of sexual release for the partner whose sexual desire is greater (Box 5.13).

When to refer

You should refer:

• anyone showing abnormal sexual behaviour, such as taking off clothes in public;

• anyone whose sexual problems continue despite education and counselling;

• if you suspect that the sexual problem is related to a serious physical illness such as diabetes or a sexually transmitted disease.

Box 5.13. Masturbation: a healthy way of giving oneself sexual pleasure

Everyone has a sexual life of their own. For example, people may have sexual fantasies or may stimulate their own sexual organs (masturbation). Some people believe that this is wrong. Some people who masturbate feel scared of being 'caught' or feel guilty that they are doing something wrong. This can cause tension and unhappiness. Impotence can be a problem when men who are masturbating cannot get their penis to go hard. In some situations, women feel very guilty when they masturbate. Some people think it is a sign of moral weakness. *Masturbation is a normal sexual activity for both men and women.* Masturbation is a safe sexual activity and does not cause any health problems.

What to do later

Review the person or couple after a week and then every two weeks to monitor how they are following your advice. Often, the explanation and the sharing of the problem makes people more relaxed and this improves sexual health.

5.5.6 Same-sex relationships and mental health

Homosexuality means sex between men and men, or women and women (lesbian relationship). There are strong views about this sort of sexual behaviour. In some places this is seen as a mental problem or even a criminal act. It is very important that, as a health worker, you treat same-sex relationships as another example of the diversity of human relationships. Homosexuality is not a mental health problem. Just as sexual problems can arise in male–female relationships, so can they in same-sex relationships. In reality, few people in same-sex relationships will discuss this with health workers because they fear being criticised or mocked. Because people who are attracted to their own gender are often persecuted, some may suffer loneliness, guilt, fear and unhappiness. If you are sensitive to this situation and can offer a space for homosexual men and lesbian women to discuss their feelings in an atmosphere of trust, you may help them cope better with their isolation and loneliness.

5.5.7 Sex and the mentally handicapped

We often assume that mentally handicapped people are 'sexless'. Just because some people are mentally handicapped, it does not mean that they do not have sexual feelings and desires. Unfortunately, because of the mental handicap, they are less likely to meet a person who wants to have sex with them. They may not be able to communicate their sexual feelings as well as others. For these reasons, they may become unhappy and angry and may show abnormal sexual behaviour. Such people (and their families) need counselling to explain sexual behaviour. In particular, you can suggest masturbation as a way of achieving sexual pleasure. Sometimes, however, the sexual behaviour can become abnormal and even dangerous to others. Refer such people to a specialist mental health service.

Box 5.14. Things to remember when dealing with sexual problems

- Sexual problems are often the result of an unhappy relationship; they can cause further problems in the relationship. As far as possible, work with the couple.
- Some sexual problems are related to serious physical disease, such as diabetes. Abnormal sexual behaviour is often caused by severe mental disease.
- Depression, anxiety, and alcohol misuse can cause sexual problems.
- Confidentiality is very important; if a person shares sexual problems that he does not want the partner to hear about, you must respect these wishes.
- People will rarely complain of sexual problems; often their main complaint may be a physical one (such as tiredness). It is good practice to ask all people a simple question such as "How has your relationship been with your partner recently?"
- Many sexual problems are the result of ignorance about sexual performance. Education is often the single most effective treatment for sexual problems.

5.6 Sudden loss of a body function

This section is about losing a physical function of the body, such as the ability to speak, or move a part of the body, or losing a mental function, such as memory or consciousness. The first cause to consider is a brain disease, particularly an injury to the brain or a stroke. This would need immediate medical attention. However, such sudden loss of function can also be due to mental problems. When this happens, the condition is called a 'conversion' disorder.

5.6.1 How can something so 'physical' happen because of mental problems?

Imagine someone, often a young woman, who is under a lot of stress. The stress could be related to failing in an examination, or to a broken love affair, or to being forced to marry someone she does not want to. It may be difficult for her to talk frankly about the cause of the stress with her family, for obvious reasons. If she were to become seriously physically ill, whatever other problems she faced would be pushed into the background.

This is precisely what happens in conversion disorder. The person's mental stress is literally 'converted' into a physical symptom. The condition usually appears suddenly and is dramatic in nature. It has also been called 'hysteria'. The commonest types of conversion symptoms are:

- loss of voice;

- loss of sight;

- loss of ability to walk or to use the arms;

- convulsions or fits (☞ also section 4.5).

Mental functions can also be suddenly affected in a conversion disorder, such as:

- the ability to remember things (the person may forget entire periods of her life);

- the level of consciousness (the person may appear confused or in a trance).

5.6.2 Can this happen like an epidemic?

Even though mental illnesses are not infectious, conversion disorder can sometimes occur in many people who are living close together. The typical example is in schoolchildren, often girls. If one girl develops a conversion symptom, some of the other girls may also develop the same symptom, and this gives the appearance of an epidemic. One reason for this is that young people may be more likely to feel that the problem is a serious disease. Because of fear and ignorance, the children feel very stressed and because they already know the nature of the symptom (by seeing it in a fellow student) this stress is 'converted' to the same symptom.

5.6.3 When to suspect a psychological cause

There are many clues to the possibility of a psychological cause for the symptom:

- if the person is less than 40 years of age, brain disease is unlikely;

- if there are no other signs of serious physical illness (for example, people with a stroke may have paralysis on one side of the face);

- if the symptoms change from time to time;

- if there is evidence of recent stress, such as an examination;

- if there is evidence that the person might be escaping from a stressful situation by becoming sick, for example avoiding getting married.

5.6.4 How to deal with this problem

Questions to ask the family or friends

- How did it start? A symptom that happened suddenly and without any previous signs of ill health is more likely to be a conversion symptom.

- Has there been any stress recently? Enquire specifically about examinations, job problems and marriage arrangements.

Questions to ask the person with a possible conversion symptom

- How did this problem start? Check on any injuries or other physical illnesses.

- Have you been worried about something recently? Ask about problems in the family and with intimate relationships. If the person is a student, ask about school difficulties and examination performance.

- Ask about symptoms of depression and anxiety (☞ Chapter 2).

Things to look for during the interview

- Look for obvious signs of brain disease, for example signs of paralysis of the limbs (such as holding them in a limp manner or signs of thinning muscles).

- Some people with conversion symptoms seem to be unconcerned about their symptoms even though they appear very serious. This apparent lack of concern may give a clue to the psychological origin of the symptoms.

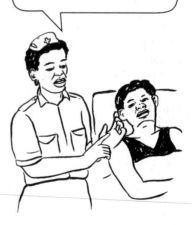

Look, I understand that you may have been worried about something recently. If you are able to talk to me about this, I can help you find some way of solving this problem. I will go away and do my other work and come back in an hour or so. I hope we can talk then.

Special interview suggestions

- The person may have personal issues that are a worry for her. She will not be comfortable to share these with you if the family or other people are nearby.

- Some people become completely mute. They do not speak at all and may even appear not to be listening to you. Never get angry because of this. They are mute because they are under stress; they are not deliberately trying to make your work harder.

What to do immediately

- Make sure that the symptoms are not caused by a medical illness.

- Explain to the family that there is no life-threatening illness. However, do not make them think that the person is pretending to be sick.

- Symptoms often resolve quickly, within hours or a few days. Use this time to establish rapport. Do not appear too concerned about the symptoms themselves. Focus, instead, on the stresses the person is facing.

- The key to quick improvement is the person talking openly about her worries or stresses and accepting that the symptoms may be related to these life difficulties.

- Encourage the person to think of ways of solving her problems (☞ section 3.2.5 for problem-solving).

- Advise against hospitalisation or prolonged rest. These may only convince the person that the illness is a serious physical illness and may prolong the symptoms.

- Avoid any medication.

- Treat people who are depressed as suggested elsewhere (☞ section 3).

When to refer

You should refer:

- if symptoms have lasted more than a week;

- if the person has a high fever, is known to have diabetes or has high blood pressure;

- if the person is injured during an attack of the symptoms or if he has not been taking food or fluids for 24 hours.

What to do later

Ask the person to visit after a week and then, depending on how she feels, review her again every month for three months. This will help you to build a relationship with her and assess how well she is coping with her difficulties.

Box 5.15. Things to remember when dealing with possible conversion symptoms

- Always think of physical diseases as the cause for sudden physical or mental symptoms. Only if these can be ruled out should you consider conversion disorder.
- Conversion disorder is the new name for hysteria. Common conversion symptoms are losing one's voice, paralysis, convulsions, loss of memory or behaving in a confused manner.
- Stress is the cause of conversion disorder.
- Most people with conversion disorder will recover on their own. Helping them to talk about stress will help them recover more quickly.
- Because of the sudden and dramatic nature of the symptoms, family members are often alarmed and worried. Explain to them what is happening.

5.7 The person who repeats the same behaviour again and again

Some people have an illness where they repeat the same thing again and again. Typically, this is washing hands or having a bath (several times a day). Other examples are the person checking whether he has done something, such as whether the door is locked. These symptoms are called 'compulsions'. Some people also have thoughts that repeat again and again. These thoughts are distressing, such as sexual thoughts or thoughts of murdering a loved relative. These are called 'obsessions'. There is often a link between the compulsion and obsession. For example, a person may have a repeated thought that she is dirty, especially when she touches a particular object. This leads to the repeated washing of hands. A person may have the repeated thought that he has not closed the door. This leads to the repeated checking of whether the door is closed. If this happens once or twice, then it is probably normal. Only if it happens many times a day, and makes the person feel distressed, is it a sign of an illness.

Obsessions and compulsions are symptoms of a mental illness called obsessive–compulsive disorder (OCD). In reality, few people will ever complain of these symptoms to a health worker. Instead, many will become very unhappy because of their symptoms and often complain of tiredness or worry or depression.

5.7.1 How to deal with this problem

Questions to ask the person may have obsessions or compulsions

- Do you have thoughts that come into your mind again and again? What kind of thoughts? Do they make you feel tense? These are questions regarding obsessions.

- Do you do things again and again? What kind of things? These are questions regarding compulsions.

- Do you feel unhappy or depressed? Have you felt as if you are losing interest in daily life? Ask about depression (☞ Chapter 2).

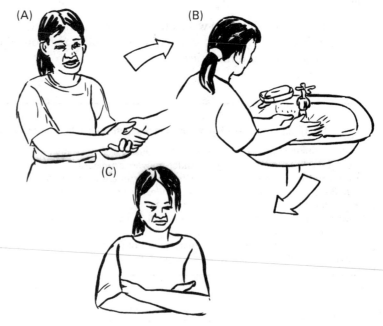

A common type of obsessive–compulsive behaviour.

(A) Some people feel that they become dirty whenever they touch something, such as when shaking someone's hand.
(B) These thoughts make them want to wash their hands each time they touch someone.
(C) This makes them feel unhappy and distressed because they know this is irrational.

What to do immediately

- Ask the person about her illness and what it does to her. This will give her an opportunity to discuss her symptoms with confidence.

- Teach her relaxation and breathing exercises (☛ section 3.2.3).

- Teach her how to resist the obsessions and compulsions (☛ Box 5.16).

- Try using medication:
  - Fluoxetine, 20 mg daily for six weeks; if there is no improvement, increase to 40 mg a day. Continue for at least six months.
  - Clomipramine, which is a tricyclic antidepressant that is found to be quite useful in OCD. It is started in a small dose, of 25 mg at night, and increased by 25 mg every three of four days to a full dose of 150 mg at night.

When to refer

If the steps above do not help, refer.

Box 5.16. Helping someone to overcome obsessions and compulsions

Exposure and response prevention

This type of treatment is based on the principle of exposing the person to the obsessional thought or situation that triggers these thoughts but preventing him from carrying out the compulsive behaviour. The person will experience the anxiety associated with the thoughts, but by resisting the response he will overcome the anxiety and learn how to cope with the thoughts appropriately. Let us take a common compulsion, that of hand washing, to illustrate how this treatment works in practice.

- Ask the person about the situations that lead to hand washing. For example, he may say that whenever he sees any dirt in the house, he must wash his hands.
- Explain the treatment to him, especially that he will feel tense during the procedure. This is to be expected and is part of the process of getting better.
- Ask him to find some dirt in the clinic. When he does, ask him to resist the urge to wash his hands. He will feel tense, but this tension will always lessen.
- After he has done this, explain that this is how he should prevent his behaviour when at home.
- See him again in a week to check on how he is responding; if he has not been able to do it, find out why and try to get him to try again.

Treating obsessional thoughts alone

Some people experience only the distressing thoughts without any compulsive behaviour. Such people often use mental rituals to distract themselves or avoid thinking the distressing thoughts. The principle of treatment remains the same: by repeated exposure to the feared thoughts and by resisting any mental rituals, the condition will gradually improve. The key, as before, is regular practice, particularly at home. The steps are:

- deliberately thinking the thoughts for a preset time period, say a minute, and then gradually increasing this time period;
- writing down the thoughts repeatedly;
- preventing any mental rituals or distraction from interfering with thoughts;
- thought-stopping.

The last, thought-stopping, is a technique where the person practises thinking the obsessional thought, and then firmly says *stop* in her mind. Instead, she thinks in detail of an alternative thought or scene that is interesting or relaxing. Before starting this treatment, she should make a list of as many obsessional thoughts and alternative thoughts as she can come up with. As with the other treatments, this should be practised first with you and then for fixed periods of time at home until she is able to stop the obsessional thoughts at any time.

Box 5.17. Things to remember when dealing with obsessions and compulsions

• Compulsions are things that a person does repeatedly; obsessions are things that a person thinks repeatedly. These occur in obsessive–compulsive disorder (OCD).
• Repeated hand washing and checking are the commonest types of compulsion.
• Although OCD is not very common, the disorder causes a lot of distress and disability.
• Simple counselling techniques and antidepressant medicines can help most people suffering from OCD.

Chapter 6

Habits that cause problems

6.1 The person who drinks too much alcohol

Alcoholic drinks are used in many cultures around the world. Some types are international, such as beer and whisky. Other alcoholic drinks are unique to the local culture, such as *chibuku* in Zimbabwe and *feni* in Goa (India). In some places, people brew alcohol at home. Illegally brewed alcohol can contain dangerous, even lethal chemicals. Most people who drink do so once in a while, in the company of friends. Some people drink more regularly but never drink more than a moderate amount every day. There are some people who drink too much. This is when you need to become concerned.

6.1.1 How much drinking is 'too much'?

When drinking starts causing health or social difficulties for the person, then the person is drinking too much. Some people may drink too much (☛ Box 6.1) yet manage to live normally. You must be concerned about such people as well, since sooner or later, the drinking problem will affect their health. Some drinkers say that they can 'hold their drink' well, as if this means that they do not have a problem. In fact, when the body becomes used to the effects of alcohol, this is called tolerance. Tolerance is itself a sign that the person is drinking too much. By the time a drinker's health is affected, the problems are very serious. Thus, the early detection of a drinking problem is an important part of health promotion and illness prevention.

People who drink too much alcohol often do so every day. There is also another type of drinking pattern which is very dangerous. This is drinking very heavily for a few days at a time. For example, some people drink only at weekends, but then consume a large amount of alcohol. This is called

Box 6.1. Drinking too much: how much is too much?

Using the chart, you can calculate the amount of alcohol the person is drinking.
• A man drinks too much if he has more than three standard drinks a day (or 21 drinks a week).
• A woman drinks too much if she has more than two standard drinks a day (or 14 drinks a week).
• People are drinking too much if they must have a drink in the morning when they wake up.
• People are drinking too much if they have one or more health or social problems related to the drinking.

A single standard drink.

A shot of spirits

A glass of beer

A 330 ml can of beer

A glass of wine

Box 6.2. Where and when alcohol should not be consumed, or only with caution

Situations when alcohol is completely prohibited
• While driving.
• While working with machines or tools.
• If the person has repeated fits (i.e. not controlled by medicines).
• Before exercise.

Situations in which alcohol can be used, but with caution
• Children should not consume alcohol except under special circumstances, as permitted by the local culture, and only with parental supervision.
• A pregnant or breastfeeding mother.
• While taking psychiatric medicines, or drugs for diabetes or epilepsy.
• If there is liver, heart or kidney disease or diabetes.

How alcohol dependence develops

(A) Most people who drink do so socially, with their friends.
(B) But sometimes the need to drink gets stronger and the person may drink more, and drink alone.
(C) Eventually he needs a drink even when he wakes up in the morning.

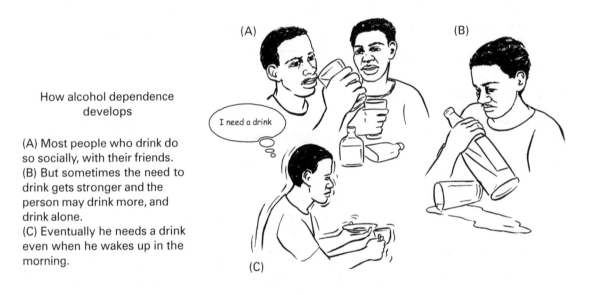

'binge' drinking. Box 6.2 describes situations where drinking alcohol should not be permitted or where it should be done with great care.

6.1.2 Why do some people drink too much?

Many people start drinking by trying out alcohol when they are teenagers (☛ section 9.6). Easy availability of alcohol and peer pressure are important reasons why they start drinking. While many teenagers only experiment with alcohol, some start drinking more regularly. Most people drink sensibly and do not damage their health or family life. Drinking can also start later in life, for example in middle age, particularly at a time of stress. Drinking problems may arise when alcohol is used to help a person cope with difficulties. Some people, especially those who drink regularly, develop a physical and psychological need to have a drink. This is called dependence or addiction. If someone with an alcohol addiction does not get a drink, he will start feeling physically sick; this is called a withdrawal syndrome. The withdrawal sickness is temporarily relieved by drinking more alcohol, but this only serves to keep the dependence going.

6.1.3 What does drinking too much do to a person and the family?

First, it seriously damages health. These are some of the symptoms that can result from problem drinking:

- blackouts – when a person has no memory of what happened after a drinking bout;
- withdrawal reactions, such as becoming tense and shaky and, in severe cases, becoming confused and having fits (☛ sections 4.2 and 4.5);
- accidents, especially while driving;
- bleeding in the stomach;
- jaundice and liver disease;
- sexual impotence (☛ section 5.5);
- depression and suicide (☛ section 4.4);
- sleep problems (☛ section 5.3);
- delusions and hallucinations (☛ section 4.3);
- brain damage;
- repeated sexually transmitted diseases and HIV/AIDS because of the greater risk of unsafe sexual behaviour;
- damage to an unborn baby (in cases where mothers drink too much).

In addition to the above physical effects of drinking, there are the social effects of problem drinking:

- increased poverty due to reduced ability to work and spending money on alcohol;
- violence in the home and community (☛ section 7.2);
- loss of job;
- neglecting the family, leading to family break-up;
- legal problems.

6.1.4 When should you suspect that a person has a drinking problem?

Many people with a drinking problem do not seek help until their health is very bad. Even when they do, the drinking problem is often undetected and untreated. It is important to be aware that many health problems are related to drinking. You should briefly ask about drinking behaviour when anyone comes to see you, but give special attention to this with people who come with any of the following:

- unexplained accidents or injuries;
- burning in the stomach area or vomiting blood;
- relationship problems in the family or with friends;
- repeated sicknesses and absence from work;
- mental health problems such as depression and anxiety;
- sleep difficulties;
- sexual difficulties, such as impotence.

6.1.5 Gender and drinking

Problem drinking is typically seen as a 'man's' problem. It is true that the majority of problem drinkers are men. However, women are also vulnerable. In many societies, problem drinking is becoming commoner in women. Drinking can affect women differently from men:

- Women are more vulnerable to the poisonous effects of alcohol; this is why the 'safe' levels of drinking are lower for women (☞ Box 6.1).

- During pregnancy drinking can lead to serious problems in the unborn child, such as mental retardation and birth defects.

- Because of the shame associated with drinking, women tend to drink at home. They are unlikely to discuss this with a health worker and so are less likely to receive help for their problem.

- Because of the gender-related stresses women face, they are vulnerable to start drinking as a way of coping.

- Women who have male partners who drink heavily may suffer physical and emotional violence from them.

6.1.6 How to deal with this problem

Questions to ask the family or friends

- Has the person been drinking alcohol recently?
- Are you worried about his drinking? Why?
- Has he been drinking in the mornings?

A 'yes' to any of these questions suggests the person may have a drinking problem.

Questions to ask the person who may be drinking too much

- Tell me about your pattern of drinking.
- Have you been drinking alcohol more than usual recently?

If so, ask these three questions:

- How often in the past year have you found that you were not able to stop drinking once you had started?
- How often during the past year have you needed a drink in the morning to get yourself going?
- How often in the past year have you failed to do what was normally expected of you because of drinking?

If any of these questions is answered 'at least once a month', then you should suspect a drinking problem and ask more detailed questions about drinking behaviour, such as:

- What type of alcohol do you drink (for example, whisky, beer)?

- How much do you drink every day? If the person drinks only on a few days a week, ask on how many days a week, and how much on those days.

- How is drinking affecting your health? This will help make the person realise how the drinking is damaging his health.

- Have you tried to stop your drinking? What happened?

- Would you like help with stopping your drinking? The last two questions will give you an idea about the person's desire to stop.

Things to look for during the interview

- Does the person look tense, nervous or fidgety? These can be signs of alcohol withdrawal.

- Check for the smell of alcohol.

- Look for bruises, scars or other signs of injuries.

- Check for signs of liver disease, such as jaundice.

- Watch for signs of brain disease, such as being clumsy or having poor balance.

Special interview suggestions

- Speak to the person in private. Spend a little time building rapport, and explain that the information the person shares is confidential. People with drinking problems are often relieved to discuss their drinking, if they feel they can trust you.

- Do not take a moral view on drinking. Even if you feel that drinking is bad, your aim is to help the person.

What to do for the person with a drinking problem

Most often, health workers treat only the physical illnesses associated with problem drinking. Unless you treat the drinking problem itself, the person will never fully recover. There are three stages to overcoming a drink problem:

- admitting there is a problem;

- stopping or reducing drinking;

- remaining sober.

To admit that there is a drink problem is an essential first step. Often the drinker comes to the clinic only because of family pressure. He may deny he has a problem. It is important not to get angry with him. Instead, talk about other issues (such as work and health) and try to get him to make the links between his drinking and its effects on his life. A person who is forced into treatment without accepting that he has a problem is less likely to give up his habit. One way of improving motivation is to help him face his problem by asking him to list all the reasons for changing his behaviour, such as "feeling healthier", "having more money to spend on other things" and "improving relations with my wife".

Once the person has admitted that there is a problem, the question to decide is whether she should stop drinking completely (abstinence) or simply reduce her drinking to the 'healthy' limit (controlled drinking – ☛ Box 6.3). There is no simple answer to this. You will need to consider the health and social situation and the history of drinking before you and the person agree on a goal. Abstinence is the preferred goal if:

- the drinking has caused serious health problems, such as repeated attacks of jaundice;

- the drinking has caused serious problems at work or at home, such as violence;

- the person has tried controlled drinking before but has not been successful.

Abstinence is an ideal goal since it is easier to monitor and less likely to lead to a relapse (becoming addicted to alcohol again). Whatever the chosen goal, it must be agreed to by the person, so that the goal is his choice. It will need regular monitoring in the months ahead.

If the person is a heavy drinker (for a man, if he has more than six drinks a day; for a woman, more than four drinks a day), suddenly stopping drinking may lead to withdrawal symptoms. Advise on how to deal with these symptoms (☛ Box 6.4). If a person has more than 10 drinks a day, it is better to refer the person to a hospital where the withdrawal reaction can be monitored more closely.

> **Box 6.3. Controlled drinking**
>
> If a person chooses controlled drinking, then there are some tips you can suggest to control the amount of drink used every day:
> - Keep a track of how much you drink (if possible by recording it in a diary).
> - Have at least two or three days in a week when you do not have any drink.
> - Alternate alcoholic drinks with non-alcoholic drinks.
> - Do not drink 'straight' alcohol – mix it with water or soda so one drink lasts longer.
> - Put less alcohol into each drink (for example, drink only single pegs).
> - Never drink in the daytime.
> - Make each drink last longer (for example, an hour).
> - Eat before you have your first drink.
> - Do not drink alcohol to quench your thirst; have water or other non-alcoholic drinks.
> - Reduce the time you spend in bars or with friends who drink heavily.

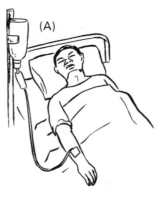

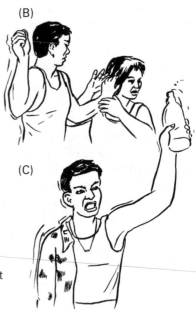

Abstinence is the goal:
(A) when the drinking has caused serious health problems, e.g. repeated attacks of jaundice;
(B) when the drinking has caused serious problems at work or at home, e.g. violence;
(C) when the person has tried controlled drinking before but has not been successful.

Box 6.4. Alcohol withdrawal and its treatment

Alcohol withdrawal occurs when a person who is dependent on alcohol suddenly stops drinking. It usually begins within 24 hours of stopping drinking and lasts between four and ten days. The worst period is usually the first two to three days. The more the person was drinking, the worse are the symptoms.

The common warning symptoms that a withdrawal reaction has started are:

• tremor;
• shakiness;
• poor sleep;
• nausea;
• anxiety;
• irritability;
• fever;
• restlessness.

As the symptoms worsen, the person becomes confused, hallucinates and may have fits (see sections 4.2, 4.5).

Treatment in the general health care setting should include:
• education about the relationship between the symptoms and the withdrawal from alcohol;
• full physical examination (if the person has a fever, has fits, cannot drink fluids, is dehydrated or has a physical disorder, or is hallucinating or confused, refer her to hospital);
• thiamine (a type of vitamin) – give 100 mg by intramuscular injection and prescribe a week's supply of thiamine tablets (50 mg daily), multivitamins and folic acid (1 mg daily);
• a four- to six-day supply of chlordiazepoxide, to be taken as follows:
  • day 1, 25 mg four times a day;
  • day 2, 25 mg three times a day;
  • day 3, 25 mg twice a day;
  • days 4 and 5, 25 mg at night;
  • days 6 and 7, 12.5 mg at night.
• alternatively, you can use diazepam, in the same way, starting from a dose of 5 mg four times a day.

Box 6.5. Dealing with difficult times while remaining sober

These are moments when it is especially difficult to stay sober. Suggest the following strategies to help the person to deal with such times.

If you drink mainly at night
Try to keep yourself busy, and go to places you cannot drink, such as a temple.

If you are in the habit of drinking with fellow workers after the day is over
Try to organise a different social activity, such as going to see a film or do a sporting activity.

If you drink heavily only with certain friends
Avoid these friends.

If you drink when alone
Reduce the time you spend alone; for example, join a support group (AA) or increase the time you spend with your family.

If you drink when you are under stress
Learn ways of coping with stress and solving problems rather than blanking them out with alcohol.

Staying sober is often the most difficult phase of treatment, because it lasts a lifetime. There are many suggestions you can make to help the person stay sober:

• Alcoholics Anonymous (AA) is an worldwide group of people who have become sober and who help each other stay sober. Anyone who has a desire to stop drinking can join. AA works through the sharing of personal experiences and giving support at regular meetings. As a health worker, you must keep relevant information on the local AA or other alcohol support groups (☛ Chapter 12).

• People with a drinking problem often use alcohol as a way of coping with difficult life situations. Teach problem-solving strategies (☛ section 3.2.5) as a healthier way of coping. Widening the social circle, for example through religious groups or friends at work or neighbours, can be a source of support in difficult times. Relationship problems are often linked to drinking behaviour; give advice on improving relationships (☛ section 10.7)

• Advise the person to find alternative activities for leisure and relaxation. Advise her on how to deal with difficult moments when she feels like having a drink (☞ Box 6.5).

When to use medicines

There are two situations in which medicines can be used to treat a drinking problem. The first is to control mild withdrawal symptoms by using chlordiazepoxide or diazepam (☞ Box 6.4). The second is to help the person stay sober: medicines like disulfiram cause a strong reaction if a person drinks and the fear of this reaction helps in keeping the person sober. This medicine should be used only by a mental health specialist.

When to refer

You should refer the person:

• for serious medical problems, such as vomiting blood, jaundice and serious accidents;

• for severe withdrawal reactions;

• when there is also a severe mental disorder, such as psychosis.

6.1.7 Living with a person who has a drinking problem

Problem drinking affects all members of the family. Some relatives blame themselves; reassure them that they are not responsible for the drink problem. Financial difficulties and sexual problems, such as impotence and rape, can cause stress in the relationship. Violence is often related to relationship difficulties caused by drinking. Relatives of drinkers often suffer mental health problems themselves, particularly depression and anxiety. Support groups for relatives are available in some places. Alternatively, the family could be encouraged to unite around this cause and encourage the drinker to seek help. The real solution lies in the drinker seeking help for a drinking problem.

Box 6.6. Things to remember when dealing with someone with a drink problem

• Problem drinking is when a person drinks alcohol at levels that are causing physical, mental or social problems.
• Problem drinking is associated with injuries, bleeding from the stomach, jaundice, repeated infections with sexually transmitted diseases, domestic violence and mental illnesses.
• Most problem drinkers come to health workers with physical problems (such as stomach ulcers) rather than the drinking itself.
• Ask everyone who comes to see you, but especially those with health problems associated with drinking alcohol, about their drinking habits.
• Counselling about stopping or controlling the drinking habit, treatment for withdrawal symptoms, referral to Alcoholics Anonymous and support to the family are the main treatments.

6.2 The person who is abusing drugs

Drug abuse is when a person uses a drug repeatedly without any medical reason and this use affects her health in a negative way. As with alcohol, repeated use of drugs that are addictive can cause dependence, which makes the person feel a strong desire to continue taking the drug, even though it may be causing her harm. When an addicted person tries to stop the drug, she feels sick (withdrawal syndrome). There are many types of drug that are abused. Of these, alcohol, tobacco and sleeping pills are described elsewhere in this chapter. These three substances are unique because, in many societies, their use is socially accepted and legal. This section deals with those drugs that are illegal.

6.2.1 Does anyone who takes a drug have a problem?

No. There are different ways in which a person could use drugs.

- Trying once or twice is very common. It is typically seen in young people.

- Casual use is the next most common type of drug use. This is especially true of drugs like cannabis (which is discussed in Box 6.7). Most people who use this drug do so only occasionally and their daily lives and health are not affected.

- Traditional use is the use of specific drugs, as accepted by the local culture, on specific occasions (Box 6.8).

- Dependence is the least common type of drug use but is, obviously, the type you should be most concerned about.

Box 6.7. Cannabis: a drug of abuse or a drug for recreation?

Cannabis or marijuana is smoked or eaten by communities around the world. It has many names, depending on where you are. For example, it is called *mbanje* in Zimbabwe, grass in the USA and *charas* in India. It is one of the commonest drugs used today but is illegal in most countries. The majority of cannabis users cannot be considered to be abusing a drug because the use is casual and controlled. However, some people may use it to such an extent that it affects their health. This can happen in two ways:
• because cannabis is usually smoked, it can damage the breathing passages and lungs;
• people with severe mental disorders (psychoses) can become more sick when they take cannabis.
Always make an effort to dissuade people from smoking (as you should for anyone smoking cigarettes), especially if they suffer from a severe mental disorder. However, be sure to explain to a concerned friend or relative the difference between cannabis and other, more serious, drugs.

Box 6.8. Traditional drugs

In many communities the use of drugs is allowed on certain occasions. Examples include cannabis in some festivals in India and Africa, and mescaline and peyote in Latin America. Some drugs, such as the *khat* leaf chewed by people in East Africa, are used as part of social interaction in everyday life. A common feature of these drugs is that they are all derived from plants. Most are used strictly for a traditional ceremony or ritual. While most people who use the drugs in this manner will have no ill effects, some people may abuse the drugs as well.

6.2.2 What drugs are abused?

• *Drugs that depress the brain.* These include opium and heroin. In small doses these drugs make a person feel relaxed. In larger amounts they make the person drowsy and unconscious. The withdrawal reaction is severe; the person may have a strong urge to take the drug, fever, restlessness, confusion, nausea, diarrhoea, anxiety and convulsions.

• *Drugs that stimulate the brain.* These include cocaine, *khat* and pills such as ecstasy and 'speed' (amphetamines). In small doses, they make the person feel alert and awake. In larger doses the person feels tense, panicky and restless. Users may have difficulty controlling their thoughts and may hallucinate and become suspicious and confused. The withdrawal reaction is typically associated with hunger and fatigue; it is usually mild.

• *Drugs that make the person hallucinate.* Many depressant and stimulant drugs can make a person hallucinate. Some drugs, such as LSD (or 'acid'), are specifically used for this experience. LSD can have an effect that lasts more than 12 hours. Some people can become very excited, confused and suspicious when taking these drugs. There is no withdrawal state.

Some people take many drugs at the same time, for example some of the above drugs with tobacco, alcohol or sleeping pills.

6.2.3 How are drugs used?

Drugs can be used in many ways. The common ways are:

• smoking – for cannabis, opium and cocaine and traditional drugs;

• drinking, chewing or eating – for pills, cannabis and traditional drugs;

• sniffing or snorting the drugs through the nose – for cocaine and glue;

• injecting – for heroin and cocaine. This is the most dangerous way of taking drugs because of the risk of infections and HIV/AIDS.

6.2.4 What does drug abuse do to the person?

Drug abuse causes enormous damage to the person and family.

• *Mental health problems.* Because drugs affect the brain, people who abuse drugs can feel depressed and tense. Some drugs can make the person suspicious and confused.

• *Physical health problems.* Problems can arise as a result of the way a drug is abused. Thus, smoking a drug can damage the breathing passages and lungs, while injecting a drug can cause infections (☛ Box 6.9).

• *Family problems.* Drug abuse often leads to fights and problems in the family.

• *Accidents.* Someone who abuses drugs may have accidents while intoxicated.

• *Social problems.* People who abuse drugs spend so much time taking them that they are usually not able to study, work or participate in everyday life.

• *Financial problems.* Drugs cost money. Because people who take drugs generally have little source of income, the drug abuse causes poverty.

Box 6.9. Drug abuse and life-threatening infections

Drugs like heroin are sometimes injected into the body. Because people who inject drugs may share needles and syringes, and because drug users are more likely to engage in unsafe sex, they are at risk of HIV infection. Another serious disease that is associated with the same routes of infection is hepatitis B.

You must educate people about the risks of these serious infections. Urge them never to share needles and syringes. Suggest using disposable syringes only. This will also reduce the risk of skin and body infections that can occur with dirty needles. Always give advice on safe sex. Suggest testing for HIV and hepatitis B after counselling. If the person is HIV positive, you will need to give advice on safe sex and other issues (see also WTIND and WWHND). If the person does not have either infection, recommend a hepatitis B vaccination. Encourage the person to switch from injection to smoking or other routes of drug use. Finally, of course, stopping taking the drug is the goal, although this may often not be possible at the start.

• *Legal problems*. Some people who abuse drugs may become involved in criminal activities in order to obtain the drug. In most societies, drug abuse itself is a crime and thus a person may be imprisoned if caught using drugs.

• *Death*. Drug abuse can kill people through overdose, serious infections and accidents.

6.2.5 Why do people use drugs at all?

Often drug abuse starts in youth. One of the main reasons for starting drug use is peer pressure (friends who are using drugs encourage the person to use them). Curiosity and easy availability are also important. A person may use drugs as a way of coping or dealing with stress, such as relationship conflicts and unemployment. Once the drug abuse has started, physical dependence caused is the main reason for continuing drug abuse.

The vicious cycle of drug abuse

(A) Drug use often begins when a person has friends who use drugs.
(B) He may first try drugs just as an experiment, which makes the person feel 'high' or 'stoned'.
(C) He enjoys it and uses the drug more and more, until he reaches a stage (D) when he feels sick every time he doesn't take the drug and he must take the drug regularly (E) to avoid feeling sick.

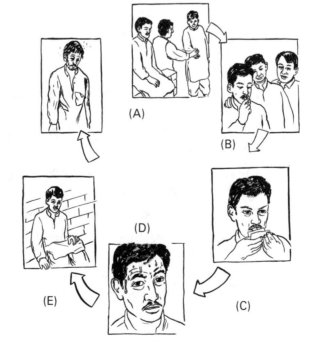

6.2.6 Why do drug users seek your help?

- Because of health problems due to the drug use.
- Because they have run out of drugs and are now suffering withdrawal symptoms.
- Because they are fed up with their habit and want help to stop.
- Because their family or the police have told them to seek your help.

6.2.7 When to suspect drug abuse

- If a young person develops problems in school or college, especially if he had no problems before.
- If a person starts neglecting his daily work or responsibilities.
- If a person drifts away from his old friends.
- If a person is repeatedly in trouble with the police.
- If a person appears confused during interview.
- If a person has mental or physical illnesses that are related to drug abuse, such as repeated accidents or skin infections on the arms, as a result of injecting.
- If a family member is worried about a change in his behaviour.

6.2.8 How to deal with this problem

Questions to ask the family or friends

- Have you noticed any change in his behaviour or friends? Since when?
- Do you suspect he is using drugs? Why?
- How do you feel about this? A compassionate attitude will be helpful for the drug user to stop her habit.

Questions to ask the person using drugs

- Which drugs are you using? How often do you take drugs? This will tell you about the type and frequency of drug abuse.
- How do you take the drugs? If by injection, ask: Do you share needles? If so, have you had an HIV test or hepatitis B test?
- Have you tried to stop the drugs on your own? What happened? People who have tried to stop may be more motivated to accept your help.
- How is the habit affecting your health? Your family life? Your work?
- Would you like to stop using the drugs? Why now? Being motivated is an important sign that the person may succeed in giving up the habit.
- Who are the people whom you trust and who would support you now? They may play an important role in helping the person stay off the drug.

Things to look for during the interview

Look for the following:

- signs of poor self-care;

- signs of injection use, such as marks or abscesses on the arms;

- signs that the person is intoxicated, such as looking drowsy or slurred speech;

- jaundice, which may be a sign of hepatitis B.

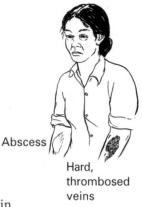

Abscess

Hard, thrombosed veins

Special interview suggestions

- Interview the person in private. Many drug users are taking the drug in secret and will not want to share their habit in front of their family.

- Even if you have strong views about drug abuse, you must not let them interfere with your role as a health worker.

What to do immediately

The physical health of your patient is an immediate concern. There are three situations in which a drug user can be in need of urgent medical help:

- *Intoxication.* This is when a person has used so much of the drug within a short period of time that he is very confused and may be unconscious. This is dangerous for people using heroin or opium because these drugs can suppress breathing.

- *Severe withdrawal reactions, such as confusion and fits.* Most withdrawal reactions, though, are milder and can be helped using simple medicines and reassurance.

- *Serious infections or injuries.*

If a person is not in need of urgent action, then the first goal of treatment is to establish rapport so that she can trust you. Explain that the physical dependence is making her take drugs repeatedly. With the permission of the drug user, counsel the family and involve them in the treatment plan. Where appropriate, also counsel the drug user about the risk of HIV and other infections (☛ Box 6.9).

For people who are willing to stop now:

- Set a definite date for stopping.

- The person should give himself at least one week to recover from the withdrawal reaction.

- Inform close family members or friends who can help during the withdrawal phase.

- If there is a risk of a withdrawal reaction, advise the person about the symptoms and how to control them. Use diazepam for sleep problems, antispasmodic medicines for diarrhoea and painkillers for aches and pains. If you feel unsure about the severity of the withdrawal, it is better to arrange for the person to go to hospital.

- In some countries, specific medicines are used to reduce the withdrawal symptoms of some drugs. The best examples are methadone and dextropropoxyphene, which are used for opium and heroin abuse. However, these drugs are usually available only through special clinics and it is best to refer people to such clinics.

- Relapse is common and often occurs because the person is not able to deal with life difficulties. Once drug use is stopped, discuss ways in which he could cope with life difficulties. Identify different things a person can do to reduce the risk of taking drugs such as:
  - Giving up friends who also take drugs.
  - Getting back to work or school.
  - Learning relaxation and problem-solving (☛ section 3.2).
  - Spending time doing other enjoyable activities.
  - Enjoying the increased money he will have.
  - Joining a community group that helps drug users (☛ Chapter 12).

For people who are not willing to stop now:

- Refer them to a community group that helps drug users.

- Consider ways of reducing the drug abuse, for example from smoking half a gram of heroin a day to a quarter of a gram.

- Move from more to less dangerous ways of using drugs, for example from injecting drugs to smoking them.

- Advise regarding reducing risk of infections from injections (Box 6.9).

- Point out the damage the drugs are causing.

- Always offer the person a chance to come back to talk to you.

For people who relapse:

- Explain how this is common. Find out why they relapsed and how they may prevent this from happening in the future.

- Give credit for whatever period of time they had managed to stay off the drugs.

- Start again as you would have the first time they came for help.

When to refer

Refer people to specialists when they:

- are abusing large amounts of drugs, such as more than a gram of heroin a day;

- are unable to stop the drugs despite your guidance;

- have developed severe physical or mental health problems due to the drug abuse;

- are injecting drugs and cannot stop this habit;

- also refer for methadone maintenance treatment, if this is available.

What to do later

Because giving up drugs is very hard and relapse is common, keep in regular touch with the person. Only when she has found new ways of dealing with stress and has become involved in new activities will the chances of relapse fall. In general, keep in touch for at least six months. In some countries, it is necessary for health workers to notify the legal authorities when they deal with a drug user. You will need to be aware of these rules and act appropriately.

Box 6.10. Things to remember when dealing with someone with a drug problem

- The commonest drugs that are abused are legal in most countries: tobacco and alcohol.
- Drug abuse is both a social and a health problem. It can cause serious health problems such as HIV/AIDS, especially in those injecting drugs.
- Completely stopping the drug abuse is the only solution.
- A single interview that combines advice and education can have a profound impact on people abusing drugs, even leading to them to change this behaviour.
- Advice on how to stop the drug abuse, treatment for withdrawal symptoms, counselling the family, regular follow-up and referral to community groups are the main treatments.

6.3 The person with a sleeping pill habit

Sleeping pills are medicines that are used to help a person sleep. The commonest are diazepam, nitrazepam, lorazepam, chlordiazepoxide and alprazolam (☛ Chapter 11 for trade names in your area). This section is about people who have become dependent on sleeping pills.

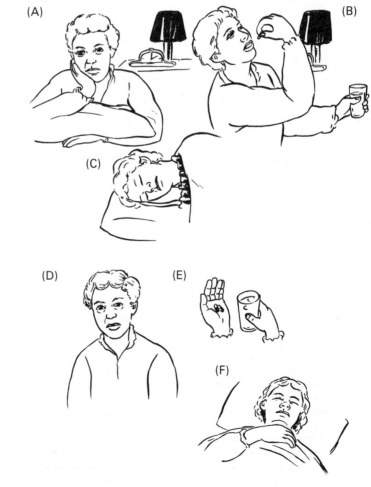

How a person becomes addicted to sleeping pills

(A) A person who cannot fall asleep may (B) start taking sleeping pills to sleep. (C) She will sleep much better for a few days, but as she continues taking the pill, (D) the effect it has on her sleep reduces and she has difficulty again. (E) She now needs more pills to fall asleep and (F) she can sleep only when she takes pills.

6.3.1 Why do people become dependent on sleeping pills?

Sleeping pills are one of the commonest types of medicine used in the world. They are in fact used for all types of mental health problems, but especially for sleep problems and anxiety. However, just like alcohol, sleeping pills can produce dependence. Once this happens, a person can no longer sleep or feel relaxed unless he is regularly taking sleeping pills. If the pill is stopped, a withdrawal reaction of sleep problems is felt and this leads the person to continue taking the pills.

6.3.2 When to suspect sleeping pill dependence

Dependence should be suspected with anyone who:

- has been taking sleeping pills for more than three months;

- insists that you should prescribe these medicines;

- needs more sleeping pills because of complaints of 'tension', for example, and sleep problems.

6.3.3 How to deal with this problem

Questions to ask the person who may be dependent on sleeping pills

- How long have you been taking these medicines? The longer the period, the greater the possibility of dependence.

- How often do you take them? If pills are taken during the day as well, then the person probably is dependent.

- In a day, how many tablets do you take? This will give you an estimate of the total amount of the medicine the person is taking each day.

- Do you drink alcohol? Some people with a sleeping pill dependence also have a drink problem.

What to do immediately

- Explain that when sleeping pills are used for a long time, they can produce a dependence problem in the same way as alcohol can.

- Explain that many of the person's complaints are the result of this dependence, rather than a sign that more sleeping pills are needed.

Box 6.11. A programme for withdrawal from sleeping pills

- Find out how much of the particular sleeping pill the person is taking each day. If the amount changes from day to day, take an average figure for the previous three days.
- Reduce the medicine immediately by a quarter. For example, if a person was taking four diazepam tablets a day, reduce it to three.
- The person should take this reduced amount for the next three or four days. After this, reduce again by quarter or a practical amount (for example, one tablet again).
- Continue in this manner until the person has been taken off the pills in about two weeks.
- If the person gets severe withdrawal symptoms, go back to the previous dose and wait for a week before starting the withdrawal again.

- With the person's understanding, you can now start her on a gradual withdrawal programme. This means reducing the medicine in small steps over a period of time so that the withdrawal symptoms are reduced. Typical withdrawal symptoms are tension, worry and sleep problems. Always warn people of the chance of withdrawal symptoms so that they are prepared for them. A withdrawal programme is described in Box 6.11.

- Some people will get their pills from other health workers if you are not prescribing them. If possible, be in touch with other local health workers and inform them of the need to avoid prescribing pills to these people.

When to refer

Refer anyone who is taking large amounts of sleeping pills. A person who is abusing many different types of drugs should also be referred.

Box 6.12. Things to remember when dealing with someone who is dependent on sleeping pills

- Sleeping pill dependence is one of the commonest problems with psychiatric medicines.
- Sleeping pills produce a similar effect on brain function as alcohol. When the two are taken together, their effect is even greater.
- Dependence on sleeping pills can lead to the same complaints that the person had before starting the pills, such as sleep problems and tension.
- Never prescribe sleeping pills for more than four weeks.
- The treatment is education and gradual reduction of the amount of sleeping pills the person is taking.

6.4 The person with a tobacco dependence

The leaf of the tobacco plant has been used as a drug for centuries. It can either be chewed (such as *gutka* in India) or smoked (in the form of cigarettes).

People start using tobacco for the same reasons as they start drinking. Peer pressure in school, being influenced by advertising by cigarette companies, and a belief that smoking is trendy or 'cool' are common reasons for starting smoking. Once smoking has begun, it quickly becomes a dependence because tobacco contains nicotine, a highly addictive drug. Nevertheless, many teenage smokers who are only experimenting will not become dependent on tobacco.

6.4.1 Why tobacco use is dangerous

Tobacco is an important cause of early death. Despite the enormous health damage, tobacco companies are aggressively marketing cigarettes, especially in developing countries. Women and youths are especially targeted; it is no surprise that, in many societies, the use of tobacco is rising the fastest in these groups.

The commonest diseases associated with tobacco use are:

- cancers of the breathing passages and lungs;

- heart attacks, strokes and high blood pressure;

- serious lung diseases such as chronic bronchitis and emphysema.

Smoking tobacco harms others who do not smoke, in these ways:

• The unborn child can be harmed when a mother smokes during pregnancy. The child may be born too early or too small.

• Passive smoking, when a non-smoker inhales the smoke created by a smoker, can cause the same diseases as actual smoking.

• Children who live in families where smoking occurs have a higher risk of suffering breathing diseases such as asthma.

6.4.2 When to ask about tobacco use

You should ask everyone who comes to see you about their tobacco use. This is because most tobacco-related diseases occur only after many years. Thus, teenagers who begin smoking regularly will show signs of disease only when they are in their 40s or 50s. By then, it is usually too late to prevent the disease. Suspect tobacco use:

• when you smell tobacco on the breath;

• when you notice yellow stained teeth or fingers;

• when you notice decayed teeth or a discoloured tongue;

• when you see a packet of cigarettes in the person's clothing;

• whenever a person has breathing or chest complaints.

6.4.3 How to deal with this problem

Questions to ask the person who uses tobacco

• How often do you chew tobacco/smoke a cigarette? This will give you an estimate of the severity of the dependence.

• How has the tobacco use affected your health? Ask specifically about breathing difficulties and repeated coughs.

• Do you drink alcohol? These problems may be linked, so that the person smokes while drinking.

• Would you like to stop? Many tobacco users would like to stop smoking and welcome any help or advice on how they can do so.

• Who else in the family uses tobacco? It is usually harder for someone to give up the habit if others in the home are also smoking. It may help to try and get all the smokers to kick the habit at the same time.

What to do immediately

Educate the person about the health risks of smoking or chewing tobacco.
  For people who are willing to stop now:

• Set a definite date to quit; this should be in the near future.

• Identify particular situations or times when the person smokes, such as with friends, in a bar, after a meal. Encourage her to find alternative things to do at these times, such as avoid the bar or friends who smoke, or chew a sweet after a meal.

• Reassure the person that giving up the dependence is difficult for all users but that nearly all people who want to quit can do so.

For people who relapse or do not want to stop immediately:

• Do not reject them.

• Continue to see them in the clinic to monitor their health. At each visit, discuss the smoking habit.

• Try to get the person to reduce the use, say from two packets a day to one. The positive effects on health this will produce may be a useful motivation for the person to give up altogether.

• If the person agrees to a reduction, help him plan how and when he will smoke (☞ Box 6.13). If he can reduce, his confidence will improve and help him stop later.

When to refer

Refer if you suspect cancers or heart disease caused by tobacco. Changes in the colour of the tongue or mouth, a persistent cough for more than a month, chest pain and difficulty breathing in long-term smokers are all signs that the person needs a medical examination.

Box 6.13. Ways to cut down on smoking

Here are some suggestions on how a person could cut down on smoking:
• Decide to smoke only once an hour. Then start increasing this time by half an hour.
• Make it hard to get a cigarette. Do not keep more than two packs at home at any time.
• Never buy more than one pack at a time.
• If you always smoke with tea or coffee, trying switching to some other drink.
• If you can quit even for one day, you can quit for another. Try it!
• Spend the money you save from smoking on something you like but haven't had money for in the past.
• Exercise and see how much better it feels when you are not smoking!
• If you break down and have a cigarette, it's OK! It was good that you tried and you can try again.
• Tell your friends you are going to quit.

Box 6.14. Things to remember when dealing with tobacco dependence

• Tobacco is an extremely harmful drug. Never ignore smoking dependence.
• Tobacco users rarely complain of their habit as a health problem. You should ask questions of all people regarding their use of tobacco.
• Educating people about the dangers of smoking may have a big impact on them give up the habit.

6.5 The person with a gambling habit

Gambling is when a person bets money on a game where the key to winning is mainly based on chance. Gambling occurs all over the world, even though it is illegal in many societies. Common examples of gambling including betting money on horse races, card games, sports, lotteries and gambling machines.

6.5.1 How does gambling become a habit?

Unlike drugs, gambling involves no external 'chemical' that can help explain why a person can become dependent. Gambling is seen as exciting and thrilling. The expectation of winning seems to be a major reason for gambling becoming a dependence problem. Most gamblers lose much more than they win and there is a desire to get back what they have lost. They may borrow or steal money to gamble. But the cycle of loss and gambling continues until the person is in deep financial trouble. When a person falls into this cycle, it is called pathological gambling.

6.5.2 Pathological gambling and health

Pathological gambling can affect health in many ways:

• Work is affected because a person has irregular hours and may sleep less because some gambling activities take place late at night.

• Because the gambler cannot think of anything other than gambling, she can become irritable, suffer poor concentration and become depressed.

• The gambler will have financial problems and may owe money to several people.

• Some gamblers will get involved in theft or other crime to raise money.

Gambling is often associated with other habits, such as smoking and drinking.

• Conflict with relatives is often the result of the gambler not giving enough time and attention to his family responsibilities.

• Gambling, drinking alcohol and smoking often go together. For example, gambling activities may be held in a bar.

6.5.3 When to suspect gambling is a problem

You should suspect a gambling problem when:

• a person has repeated problems with the police;

• a person you know has begun to show signs of increasing poverty;

• a person withdraws from old friends.

Whenever you see any person with a drinking problem, also ask about gambling.

6.5.4 How to deal with this problem

Questions to ask the person who may have a gambling problem

- Have you been gambling recently? What type of gambling do you do?
- Have you lost time from work due to gambling?
- How has gambling affected your home life?
- How do you feel about your gambling? Do you feel guilty?
- How do you find the money to gamble? How much do you owe others?
- Do you drink alcohol? If so, ask about problem drinking (☞ section 6.1).
- Have you thought about stopping gambling? Would you like to do so now?

What to do immediately

- Discuss the nature of the habit. Most gamblers do not even know that gambling can become a problem, just like other kinds of dependence. This awareness may motivate the person to consider stopping the habit.
- Discuss the negative effects of gambling on the person's life.
- If there are any other dependence problems, treat accordingly.

  If the person wishes to stop now, do the following:

- Identify other activities the person could do instead of gambling. These should be enjoyable to the person so that he is able to resist the urge to gamble.
- Identify the situations that make him want to gamble. For example, if he associates the urge to gamble with drinking in a bar, then he should avoid that bar. Similarly, he should avoid the friends he associates with gambling.
- Identify important people in his life who can understand his problem and support him during this difficult phase.
- Teach the person how to solve his problems (☞ section 3.2). For example, being in debt may be the most important problem he is facing. Identify all the people who are owed money and help the person develop a plan aimed at repaying his debts. This will help him gain in confidence that he will be able to resolve his difficulties. It will also help prevent him from gambling more in an effort to raise money to pay the debts.

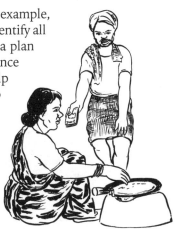

- It is helpful if a large share of the salary is given to the spouse, for example, on pay day, so that the month's income is not gambled away.
- In some places there are special groups that help people with gambling problems (such as Gamblers Anonymous). Refer the person to them.

If the person relapses or does not want to stop immediately:

• Do not reject the person.

• Ask the person to come and see you again.

• Always discuss the possibility of giving up at each visit.

• Attempt a reduction in gambling activity by reducing the amount of time spent gambling or setting an upper limit on the amount of money the person will gamble in a week.

Some gamblers can become depressed or anxious and may benefit from antidepressants (☞ Chapter 11).

Box 6.15. Things to remember when dealing with someone addicted to gambling

• Gambling can sometimes become an addiction and damage a person's mental and social health.
• Even though gamblers rarely come forward for treatment, many gamblers do recognise that they have a problem.
• Some gamblers may be depressed.
• Education about the nature of the problem, identifying different recreational activities and problem-solving are the best treatment.

Chapter 7

Problems arising from loss and violence

7.1 The person who has experienced a traumatic event

An incident that makes a person fear for his life or causes him extreme distress is a traumatic event. There are different types of traumatic events:

- *Personal trauma*. This is an incident that threatens a particular person, for example being raped, losing a loved one (bereavement), being a victim of crime or being involved in a road traffic accident.

- *War and terrorism*. The horror of war can be the cause of considerable trauma to both soldiers and civilians (☛ section 9.4).

- *Major disasters*. Disasters such as airplane crashes, fires and earthquakes can cause trauma to large numbers of people at the same time (☛ section 9.5).

The management of people affected by domestic violence, rape and bereavement are discussed later in this chapter.

The possible causes of post-traumatic stress disorder: crime; war; disasters.

7.1.1 How does trauma affect health?

Trauma can cause physical injuries such as a broken leg following an accident or a burn after an explosion. Such incidents can also produce a deep effect on a person's mental health. Even people who only saw what happened (such as someone walking down a street and seeing a terrible

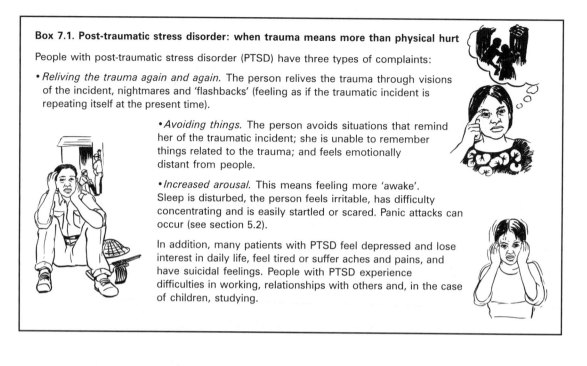

Box 7.1. Post-traumatic stress disorder: when trauma means more than physical hurt

People with post-traumatic stress disorder (PTSD) have three types of complaints:

• *Reliving the trauma again and again.* The person relives the trauma through visions of the incident, nightmares and 'flashbacks' (feeling as if the traumatic incident is repeating itself at the present time).

• *Avoiding things.* The person avoids situations that remind her of the traumatic incident; she is unable to remember things related to the trauma; and feels emotionally distant from people.

• *Increased arousal.* This means feeling more 'awake'. Sleep is disturbed, the person feels irritable, has difficulty concentrating and is easily startled or scared. Panic attacks can occur (see section 5.2).

In addition, many patients with PTSD feel depressed and lose interest in daily life, feel tired or suffer aches and pains, and have suicidal feelings. People with PTSD experience difficulties in working, relationships with others and, in the case of children, studying.

accident) can experience these mental health effects. Many people affected by trauma will experience emotional reactions. These can include a feeling of being numb or in a daze, fear, sleep difficulties, repeated thoughts of the event, irritability, nightmares and having difficulty concentrating. This is a normal response to a traumatic incident and lasts for a short period (typically two to four weeks). In a few people, however, these experiences continue for months or even years after the trauma. They begin to interfere with the person's daily life and may lead to new problems, such as alcohol misuse or problems in relationships with other people. This is a mental illness called post-traumatic stress disorder (or PTSD) (☛ Box 7.1).

7.1.2 Why do some victims of violence develop mental illness?

Events that lead to actual loss of life or events that were life-threatening are more likely to lead to PTSD. Man-made disasters such as terrorist violence may be more traumatic than natural disasters because they can seem so senseless. Survivors of traumatic events in which others died may also feel guilty or blame themselves for not having done enough to save the others. The greater the loss of social support and community bonds (as can happen in war), the greater is the risk of PTSD.

7.1.3 How to deal with this problem

Questions to ask the person who has experienced trauma

• What happened? Encourage the person to describe exactly what the traumatic event was. How did it start? What happened to you? Who else was present? What did you do immediately afterwards? These questions will help you get information on the incident. Talking about the incident can help the person feel better.

- How are you feeling now? The emotional response will depend on how much time has passed since the person experienced the trauma.

- Who can you share your feelings with? People with social support are likely to recover faster.

What to do immediately

- An important way of coping with traumatic events is sharing them with others. Encourage the person to talk about what happened.

- Reassure him that the emotional reactions are normal and are not a sign of going crazy.

- Encourage him to talk to others he trusts, including other survivors. Group discussions are helpful, especially when the traumatic event has affected many people, such as refugees escaping a war (☞ section 9.4).

- Encourage him not to avoid situations that remind him of the event.

- He should not be left alone for at least a few days. Make sure that he is staying with caring relatives or friends.

- For symptoms such as panic attacks, sleep problems and tiredness, follow the steps suggested elsewhere (☞ sections 5.2, 5.3, 5.4).

- If the person has severe difficulties, you can prescribe sleeping pills for up to four weeks.

- A course of antidepressants may also help some people who have experienced trauma (☞ Chapter 11).

When to refer

In some areas there are specialised services for people affected by trauma. This is more likely to be available when there is a war or civil unrest.

What to do later

Keep in touch with the person for as long as you, or she, feels it is of help. Initially, see her at least once a week for a month. If you see signs of gradual recovery, then you can be confident that she will make a full recovery. However, if symptoms seem to be getting worse, keep contact with her for a longer period, try a course of antidepressants, or refer.

Box 7.2. Things to remember when dealing with people who have experienced trauma

- Traumatic events include being a victim of violence or rape, being a victim of a criminal act, or being involved in war, terrorist violence or a major disaster.
- Some people can develop a mental illness called post-traumatic stress disorder (PTSD).
- The main features of PTSD are experiences of reliving the trauma, avoiding situations or places that bring back memories of trauma, and feeling fearful or aroused.
- Talking about the event and feelings is often of great help in recovery. Antidepressants can also help some people.

7.2 The woman who is being beaten or abused by her partner

Domestic violence is when one person in a family is violent towards another. Because the vast majority of victims are women, this section mainly deals with the specific issue of women being beaten by their male partner. The term 'male partner' includes both husbands as well as men who live with women in sexual or intimate relationships but who are not married to them. 'Abuse' is a term that recognises that it is not only physical violence that is harmful. Emotional abuse is not only more common, but can also be very damaging to women (Box 7.3).

7.2.1 Why is violence against women a health issue?

Violence against women is common. In some places one in three women are beaten by their husband. Violence occurs in all classes of society. It severely damages a woman's health. In the most extreme situations it can cause her death. Many victims seek help for the various health problems they suffer as a result of domestic violence. This is why violence against women is an important community health issue.

7.2.2 How do women suffering domestic violence present to health workers?

Women rarely complain of being beaten. The typical health problems that women do complain of are:

- those that are the direct result of violence, for example cuts, bruises and other injuries;
- those due to the fear and unhappiness of living with a violent man – the mental health damage caused by violence, most commonly depression and anxiety, is much less obvious to health workers than the physical damage;
- sexual problems, such as sexually transmitted diseases and miscarriages.

Box 7.3. The ways in which men can abuse women

By mocking, abusing and humiliating
For example, using foul language or verbally abusing the woman's relatives and friends.

By threatening
For example, threats of killing or harming the woman, but also threats of harming himself (e.g. through suicide) if the woman leaves.

By forcing her to have sex
Some people think that because a woman is married she must allow her husband to have sex whenever he wants. This is not true.

By controlling resources in the home
For example, denying the woman money, health care or the opportunity to work.

By forcing her to isolate herself
For example, denying the woman the chance to meet her friends or to leave the house.

By physical violence
This covers any physical act that hurts the woman, from slapping to hitting and kicking her. In more serious cases, the man may use a weapon or even try to kill the woman.

7.2.3 Why do some people beat or abuse their partners?

There are no simple answers to this question (☛ Box 7.4). Some men beat their wife because they believe this is an acceptable way of dealing with conflict. He may have seen his father behave in a similar way towards his mother. Violence becomes a way of keeping women 'in their place'. However, male domination cannot be the only reason, because violence is common even in societies where women have achieved considerable equality. In fact, men who beat their wives are generally not aggressive in relationships outside the family.

Violence, though mostly directed against women, can also be directed against other people in the family, such as children, elders and men. In homosexual relationships, men may be violent towards their male partner and in lesbian relationships women may be violent towards women. Thus, an important reason for violence may be related to the nature of the close emotional relationships between people who live in families. A key issue is that of 'power and control'. This

Box 7.5. Why do women stay in violent relationships?

Women do not leave their violent husband for many reasons:
- *No money, nowhere to go.* The woman is trapped by her money situation; if she leaves, she may have no home to go to and no money.
- *How will the children manage without a father?* If she has children, she may worry about their future.
- *What will he do if I go?* She may be scared of what he might do if she leaves. Some husbands threaten to kill their wife, or to kill themselves.
- *What will others think if I leave?* She may have little social support; some women find that their own families reject their complaints of violence.
- *Let me try to change to make things better.* Some women blame themselves for the violence. They may feel that they should try to change in order to make the situation better.
- *This is what marriage is about.* Some women may believe that violence is a 'normal' part of living with a man. This is especially so for women who have seen their own mothers or sisters being beaten.

---

means that if a person feels he has power or control over another, he is more likely to be violent towards that person.

You should not think that the abuser is a monster. He may be in need of help himself. The majority of women prefer to stay with their husband, even though he is violent (☞ Box 7.5). Thus, working with the abusive man may be an important part of helping the woman. If you have the attitude that the man is a monster, then it makes working with him difficult. This attitude may also make it hard for you to understand the woman's desire to continue living with him.

Some people say that some women 'deserve' it when they are beaten because they are 'loose' or flirtatious. There is no excuse of any sort for a man to abuse a woman.

Case 7.1. Nyasha's story: the cycle of violence

Nyasha married Tarisai when she was only 17 years old. Soon afterwards Tarisai began to shout at her. At first she was concerned because he had been so loving before they were married. The reasons for his anger were often small: one day it would be because the dinner was not tasty; another day just because he had had too much to drink and was unhappy at work. Nyasha spoke to her elder sister, who reassured her that a little anger was normal in every marriage. But the anger seemed to get worse with time. One day, Nyasha returned home later than usual from the market. Tarisai was very angry. He accused her of not being a good wife, and that he thought she was having an affair with another man. Nyasha apologised and said she was not having an affair. But this only made Tarisai more angry. He slapped her on the face. Nyasha was shocked. It was the first time he had slapped her. She ran to her room and cried. Tarisai said sorry. But it happened again. And again. The beatings became more regular. After a severe beating, Tarisai would cry and say sorry. He would threaten to kill himself if she left. The accusation and threats made her stop meeting her friends and she became isolated. She could no longer enjoy sex with him, which made him angry. One day, when Tarisai wanted sex, she refused. He became furious, again accusing her of having affairs. Then, he started beating her. Finally, he raped her. The next morning, Nyasha tried to kill herself by drinking poison. It was only when she went to the hospital that the health worker found out about the violence. In the meantime, 12 years had passed since Nyasha had married Tarisai.

7.2.4 How to identify domestic violence

Many health workers are unsure whether they should ask about violence because they feel there is little they can do about it. Some believe that violence is not a health issue. In fact, violence is as much a health issue as dirty drinking water. Simply pretending to be ignorant cannot in anyway be helpful to the woman. As a rule, if you feel that violence is occurring in a woman's home, always ask her a simple question about it. All women in the following groups should be screened for violence or abuse:

- any woman with chronic physical complaints, sleep problems, tiredness and so on;
- pregnant women;
- women who have unexplained injuries;
- women who have had a miscarriage or abortion;
- women who are suicidal or have attempted suicide;
- women who are disabled (mentally or physically);
- when a male partner is overly attentive or unwilling to leave the woman alone with you;
- women with gynaecological complaints.

7.2.5 How to deal with this problem

Questions to ask the woman

- Do you and your husband fight or argue? How often? About what? This is a relatively easy question since most husbands and wives argue.
- Has your husband ever hit you? Or threatened to hit you? A threat to hurt someone can be as terrifying as an actual hurt.
- If so, when was the first time? Since then, how often has he hit you? Has it been getting more frequent recently? Violence that is getting worse with time is likely to lead to serious harm unless quick action is taken.
- What is the worst injury you have suffered? Has he ever used a weapon or tried to kill you? Women who have suffered severe injuries such as fractures are at greater risk of physical injury in the future.
- How is this situation affecting your feelings? Ask questions regarding anxiety and depression (☞ Chapter 2). Ask specifically about suicidal thoughts.
- How are you coping with this violence? Have you told anyone else about it? Who? Identify the woman's social support and her ways of dealing with the violence. Check on the use of alcohol and sleeping pills.
- What about the children? If there are children caught in the violence, make arrangements to talk to them.
- What things have you thought of to change your situation? If the woman has considered separation, find out whom she has talked to. What are her concerns about separation? Whom would she go and stay with? This is especially important when there are no women's shelters in your area.
- Would your husband come to talk to me? In most cases he probably would not, but it does no harm to ask.

Questions to ask the family or friends

- What do you feel she should do? This will give you a sense of the views of the woman's close relatives. They often play an important role in influencing the decision taken by the woman.

- If she were to leave home, would she be welcome to stay with you? Or with someone else?

Special interview suggestions

- Look for signs of physical injury, such as bruises or cuts.

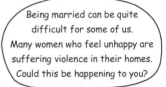

- Do not be afraid to ask. Most women are relieved when asked about violence because they are often scared or embarrassed to bring it up themselves. You can ask about it in different ways (see figures).

- Because violence is a subject that causes embarrassment, discuss it in private. If relatives or the husband seem unwilling to leave, you can say you need to 'examine' the woman and thus need to be alone with her.

- It is better that family members are not present during the interview until you have asked the woman about which relatives she feels safe with.

- Discussion of violence takes time. Do not be in a hurry to get the information.

- Do not take sides. Listen before you say anything on how to resolve the situation.

- Do not make judgements about whether she is right or wrong in deciding to stay with or separate from her husband.

- Do not be in a hurry to 'save' the woman from her situation.

- Do not be angry with the person who has been violent.

Being married can be quite difficult for some of us. Many women who feel unhappy are suffering violence in their homes. Could this be happening to you?

As you may know, it is not uncommon for a person to be emotionally, physically or sexually abused/harassed at some time in their lives. Has this ever happened to you?

Your symptoms are related to stress. Do you and you partner fight a lot? Have you ever been hurt by the fighting?

What to do immediately

- Clearly document the woman's history and any physical injuries. Record details such as exactly what the woman said her partner did (for example "Woman says partner hit her with a metal pan at least six times") and the nature of any injuries (for example "A bruise on the right shoulder area measuring about 2 cm by 3 cm"). These records may be important in the event of a police case.

- Many women develop negative feelings about themselves. Reassure the woman that she is not responsible for the violence.

- If the woman has symptoms of depression or post-traumatic stress disorder, treat appropriately (☞ Chapter 5 and section 7.1). If the depression is severe and not responding to counselling, try antidepressants (☞ Chapter 11).

- While you should not make decisions for the woman regarding whether she should continue living with her husband, you should share your concerns if the violence is severe and you feel that the woman's life is at risk.

- Involve important people in her life in planning for the future. This could include friends or relatives who have genuine concern for the woman.

- If the woman has legal problems, or wishes to make a police complaint, refer her to the appropriate authorities. It can help if you write a note describing the health issues, since the woman may not get a sensitive hearing from the police.

- If you know the legal situation for women who are victims of violence, then share this information with her. If you don't know this, consult a colleague or refer her to a woman's support group (☞ Chapter 12). For example, in some places judges can restrain a man from coming near the woman and force him to pay maintenance payments.

- Discuss what the woman will do if violence occurs again. The best immediate course of action is to recognise when a situation is becoming dangerous and leave the room immediately. For the longer term, help her plan her actions. Examples of how the woman can plan for her safety are:
  - consider where she could go for refuge, for example neighbours (she should make sure that this place will welcome her in an emergency);
  - if there are weapons in the house, hide them;
  - save money in case it is needed later;
  - leave copies of important documents, such as ration cards and marriage certificates, with others;
  - devise a code word she could use with children or relatives when she feels threatened and wants help.

- Give information regarding resources for women in your community (☞ Chapter 12).

- For more information on helping women, ☞ WWHND.

When to refer

- If the woman's life is at risk and she has nowhere to go, hospital may be the only safe shelter for her.

What to do later

- Try to involve the husband in marital counselling (☛ section 10.7).

- See the woman at regular intervals. If you are treating her for depression, then see her at least once a week.

- The difficulty in dealing with victims of violence is knowing what to do if the husband refuses to change and the woman cannot leave. Never give up on trying to work with the man (see below). Sometimes, the man may himself come to you for some different reason. Bring up the issue at this time. In the meantime, you can consider the following options for the woman:
  - make a police complaint (some men will back off when the police get involved);
  - share the news with the wider family and hoping that they will apply some pressure on the husband;
  - start planning for separation (examine the woman's concerns about separation and help her think of ways in which they can be overcome);
  - refer her to a woman's support group from whom she can seek advice.

7.2.6 Working with men who are violent

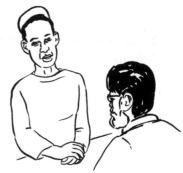

The greatest difficulty in helping women whose husbands are violent is that most men do not seek help for this problem. They may fear humiliation, police or legal action, or social stigma. These are some suggestions on how to work with violent men:

- It is important for you not to take sides in this situation and to try to help the man as well.

- There are also some situations where a man can become violent as a result of his mental health problems. The first is men who drink too much and become violent when they are drunk (☛ section 6.1). The second is men who are very suspicious that their partner is having an affair with another man and beat their wife to try to get her to confess to it. Of course, the affair is most often imaginary (☛ section 4.3).

- All violent men can benefit from advice on how to control and deal with their anger better. You should advise on how to manage anger (☛ Box 7.6).

- Preventing violence may mean helping to set up support groups for men who beat their wife, in the same way that Alcoholics Anonymous helps men with drinking problems (☛ section 10.1).

- Confidentiality is as important when working with partners as with separate individuals. Both partners must feel secure that their conversations with you will not be shared with the other partner.

Box 7.6. Anger management (advice for people who have difficulty controlling their temper)

- Anger is damaging to your health and to your life. Learning how to control it is an important way of improving your life.
- Anger can be controlled. Someone who says "I just cannot control what I do when I get angry" has not tried hard enough.
- The most important step in anger management is recognising the first signs of anger. These may be feeling hot in the head, having angry thoughts and feeling tense all over the body.
- As soon as the person notices any of these, he must immediately remove himself from the situation that is making him feel that way. For example, if he become furious while talking to his wife, he must leave the room they are in.
- He should wait until his mind feels calm and only then continue what he was doing. He should calmly think about what he wants to say to the person. After the anger has gone away, then he should plan to tell the person his thoughts with a view to reducing the conflict.

Managing one's anger

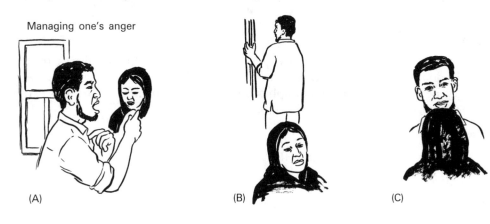

(A)   (B)   (C)

(A) Be aware of your feelings, of anger.
(B) Leave the room or place where you are beginning to feel angry.
(C) Return only when you feel calm and able to solve your difficulty without losing your temper.

Box 7.7. Things to remember when dealing with women who are being abused

- Abuse can be physical, sexual or emotional. Most victims of violence are women being abused by their male partner.
- Violence is common; suspect it in any woman with unexplained injuries or physical symptoms, sleep problems or suicidal feelings.
- Encourage the woman to share her experience with relatives or friends she trusts. Also encourage her to talk to a local women's support group.
- Try to work with the man; he is the cause of the problem.

7.3 The woman who has been raped or sexually assaulted

Rape is when a man forces a woman to have sex without her permission. In most countries rape refers to forced sex where there is penetration of the woman's sexual passage (her vagina) by the man's sexual organ (his penis). Sexual assault is a broader term that includes rape as well as other forms of sexual violence:

- touching or grabbing parts of her body;
- making sexually suggestive comments or movements;
- sexually attacking her in any way, whether or not there is sexual penetration.

  For sexual violence against children, ☞ section 8.4.

7.3.1 Why is rape a health issue?

Rape is one of the most terrifying experiences a person can experience. In some places, the woman experiences the double blow of suffering rape and then being discriminated against by members of her community. Because rape involves both physical violence and mental torture, it is extremely damaging to a woman's health. Rape can lead to:

- unwanted pregnancy;
- sexually transmitted diseases (including HIV/AIDS);
- physical injuries, such as bruises, tears, cuts or fractures;
- mental health problems, such as post-traumatic stress disorder and depression.

The health impact of rape

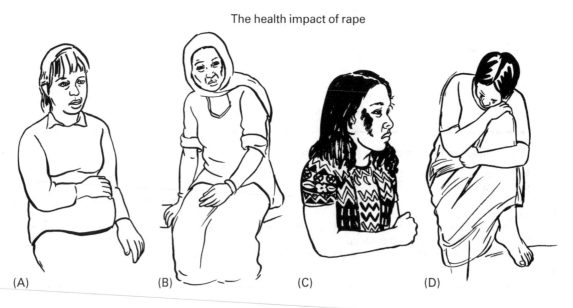

(A)   (B)   (C)   (D)

(A) Unwanted pregnancies.
(B) Sexually transmitted diseases such as HIV/AIDS.
(C) Physical injuries such as bruises, tears, cuts or fractures.
(D) Mental health problems such as PTSD and depression.

7.3.2 How do women react to being raped?

Some people argue that it is not possible for a man to rape a women unless she cooperates, for example by lying down and staying quiet during the rape. In fact, most women do put up resistance and many manage to escape the rapist in this manner. However, a rapist can overcome a woman by sheer physical strength. Sometimes, a woman is so scared that she fears resisting because the rapist might hurt her even more.

Typically, a woman goes through a series of emotional reactions as a result of being raped:

- Shock and anger are often the first reactions. The woman may be tearful, shaking with fear and anger, and unable to understand what she has just experienced.

- Some women may appear calm and controlled; this does not mean that they have coped well with the rape.

- In the days and weeks after a rape, the woman may blame herself, fear being killed or harmed, feel dirty, and have repeated thoughts of the rape, nightmares and sleep problems. Physical complaints such as aches and pains, loss of appetite and tiredness are also common.

- Later, the woman may develop a fear of people and of situations similar to those in which the rape occurred. She may have fear of or loss of interest in sex and repeated nightmares of the rape. This is similar to post-traumatic stress disorder (☛ section 7.1)

- In the end, the majority of women recover but not without having suffered ill effects for a long time. In a few women, though, frank depression can occur and will need treatment.

7.3.3 Who rapes a woman?

Most often the rapist is someone the woman knows. A woman can be raped in a number of situations:

- by a man whom she knows, such as an uncle or a neighbour or someone she works with;

- by her boyfriend (this is sometimes called 'date rape');

- by her husband (in many societies, having sex is considered a duty of a wife, but if she does not want sex and it is forced on her, it is sexual violence);

- by the police or soldiers (this happens especially when women are captured by soldiers or are police suspects for an offence – it is particularly terrifying because the woman is being raped by people who should be protecting her);

- by a complete stranger (this may happen on the streets on in the woman's house).

7.3.4 How to deal with this problem

Questions to ask the woman

- What happened? Get a detailed account of what happened. Did the rapist manage to have sexual intercourse? Did he hurt her physically? When did it happen?

- How are you feeling right now? If the woman says she is feeling in control, it does not mean that the rape was not a serious event.

- When was your last menstrual period? If the woman is in the risk period for pregnancy, and she is not using contraception, you may recommend emergency family planning methods (☛ WWHND).

- Have you told anyone about the rape? Who? What was their reaction? This will help you identify support the woman might need during this difficult period.

- If you suspect rape within marriage, the question could be worded like this: "Do you generally feel you have control over when and whether you have sex? Are there times when your partner has sex with you when you do not want to?"

Special interview suggestions

- A gynaecological examination is recommended if the rape occurred less than 24 hours earlier. The woman may be resistant to having such an examination. Reassure her that this is the main way in which a rape can be proved for legal purposes. The examination will include looking for injuries to the sexual organs or other body parts, and taking a smear of vaginal fluid to test for sperm.

- Rape is a very sensitive issue. Take time to discuss it. Discuss it in private. Reassure the woman about the confidentiality of her story. Do not ask for unnecessary details about the act. Do not challenge her story.

What to do immediately

- Reassure the woman that it is not her fault.

- Document her story in detail. Record who raped her, the circumstances and any injuries she reports. Findings of the physical and gynaecological examinations must also be recorded in detail.

- Encourage the woman to share her experience with a friend or relative. However, respect her wishes if she prefers to keep the experience a secret.

- Help her in making a decision about whether to report the rape to the police. Ideally, the event should be reported because the rapist is a threat to the entire community. The sense that justice may be done may help the woman regain confidence. It may also help reduce the risk of the rapist repeating this behaviour. However, factors such as the rapist being a close relative may make a woman hesitant to report the rape.

- Offer her treatment for emergency family planning, especially if the woman was raped during the fertile period of her menstrual cycle (☛ WWHND).

- Offer her treatment for sexually transmitted diseases. A simple regime is procaine penicillin (4.8 million units by intramuscular injection) and probenecid (1 g orally). This will treat gonorrhoea as well as syphilis. Test for penicillin sensitivity before using this medicine. If the woman is allergic, use another antibiotic such as erythromycin or tetracycline.

- Encourage the woman to spend a few days with someone she trusts. It is better if she is not alone for a while.
- Explain the psychological reactions to the rape so that the woman knows that the fearfulness, nightmares and sadness are typical reactions and not a sign that she is going crazy.
- If the woman has severe sleep problems or is very agitated, use a sleeping medicine such as lorazepam or diazepam for up to four weeks (☞ Chapter 11).
- Refer the woman to a support group that can advise her on her legal rights and share her concerns and worries (☞ Chapter 12).
- If the woman agrees, talk with the family. Some men reject their wife if she has been raped. Talk to the man and try to change this reaction by pointing out that rape is a crime and that it could have happened to any woman.
- If the woman has been raped by a relative or close friend, encourage her to share this with her family. If she is to grow out of her fear and prevent the rape from recurring, the rapist must be identified to others who know him.

When to refer

Refer if there is serious physical injury or the woman wants a documentation of her gynaecological health.

What to do later

- Review the woman in a week and counsel her regarding an HIV test. If positive, then it is likely that the woman was HIV positive before the rape. If the HIV test is negative, recommend the woman has protected sex with her regular partner for at least six months. Repeat the test in six months to be sure that she was not infected during the rape.
- Look for signs of depression or post-traumatic stress disorder. Both these conditions may be more apparent after the initial stage of shock passes.

Box 7.8. Things to remember when dealing with a woman who has been raped

- Rape is one of the most severe acts of violence that a woman can experience. It can affect her physical health, sexual health and mental health.
- Rape can lead to unwanted pregnancies, sexually transmitted diseases, including HIV infection, and serious injuries. Depression, suicidal feelings and post-traumatic stress disorder are the common mental health problems.
- The key issues for helping a rape victim are to ensure her physical health, document the rape carefully, provide advice on preventing pregnancy and sexually transmitted diseases, and counsel her on the mental health effects of the experience.
- Encourage the woman to file a police complaint along with the medical documents. A rapist who gets away once is more likely to strike again.

7.3.5 When men get raped

Men can also be victims of sexual assault and rape by other men. This is particularly so for young boys who are raped by older boys or male relatives, as well as in prisons and other situations where men live close to one another. Male rape is an even bigger secret than female rape. This is partly because male victims rarely seek help. Be especially aware of male rape when working in prisons (☛ section 9.3), army barracks, schools or if you are in any setting where men live together. Men who are raped can be helped in much the same way as women.

7.4 The person who has been bereaved

Bereavement (or grief) is the experience someone goes through when a loved one dies. Most people will experience bereavement at some point in their life. The death of someone we love is probably the most severe loss we have to cope with. This is why bereavement can become a mental health issue.

7.4.1 How does a person react to bereavement?

Bereavement is like a wound. Like a wound, it hurts. The person will need time to recover and to allow the wound to heal. And, like some wounds, bereavement can sometimes take longer to heal or become complicated. The stages of grief are set out in Box 7.9, but it is important to recognise that bereavement is an intensely personal experience: there is no right or wrong way to grieve. In some communities, bereavement can also be a collective experience involving many people grieving together. In such situations, the pain of loss can be shared with others.

7.4.2 When is a bereavement abnormal?

Sometimes, bereavement can become abnormal because it can last much too long or affect the person's life in a way that is damaging to her health. The following are some features that may indicate an abnormal bereavement:

- if the reaction lasts for more than six months;
- if the bereaved person becomes very depressed and suicidal;
- if the person withdraws from social interaction with others;
- if the person avoids people and things linked to the lost relative or friend.

    Abnormal bereavement is more likely to happen in the following situations:

- if the person has suffered multiple losses;
- if he lacks adequate social support;
- if he has lost a child, especially an only child;
- if an elderly person becomes bereaved due to the death of his spouse;

Box 7.9. The stages of grief

Typically, three stages are described in the human response to loss.

It cannot be true: the stage of denial
This happens in the days just after the loss. There is a feeling that the news is false, that the loved one cannot be dead. It is just not possible. This stage of shock is most obvious when the death was sudden. The bereaved person can feel numb, as if in an unreal, dream-like state. Activities such as the funeral can help the person distance himself from the loss.

I feel miserable: the stage of sadness
This stage usually begins once all the hectic activity surrounding the final rites and funeral are over and the bereaved person is back to his own usual life. The absence of the loved person is now noticed. Sadness and a feeling like searching for the missing person and imagining that she must still be alive are common experiences. Some people may even hear their name being called or have dreams about the lost person. Some may blame themselves for not having done enough to prevent the death, or get angry that the dead person left them. Crying, sleep problems, loss of interest in activities and meeting people, and even thoughts that life is not worth living can all be experienced in this stage.

It's time to move on: the stage of reorganisation
This is the final phase of bereavement. For most people it is the time when they accept the loss as part of life and get on with the rest of their own life. Coming to terms with loss is a gradual process. Most people will always think of the lost person now and again. What is important is that the sadness does not interfere with the ability to enjoy happy moments in life. The real sign that a person has moved on is when he begins to make plans for the future – a future without the loved person, but still a future with hope.

- if the death is sudden, for example in a road accident or suicide;

- if the person denies (or ignores) the loss for a long time.

7.4.3 How to deal with this problem

Questions to ask the bereaved

- What happened? Talking about the person's death may help reduce the feeling of shock.

- Who will you be spending the next few days with? Who can you talk to when you need someone?

- How are you feeling? Let the person share their feelings and thoughts. You will often find typical thoughts of shock and disbelief.

What to do immediately

- Reassure the person that experiences such as imagining that the lost relative is still alive, or searching for the relative, are normal and are not signs that she is going 'mad'. Educate her about the stages of grief so that she knows what to expect and is not worried about some of her feelings or thoughts.

- Encourage her to share her feelings with friends and relatives. As far as possible, she should not be alone for the first few days.

- If her community has rituals associated with death, encourage her to participate in them. These ceremonies can often make people feel supported by others. If she is religious, prayer may help her cope with the grief.

- A discussion of feelings of loss and sadness may be helpful a few days after the bereavement. The person may feel embarrassed to share some emotions, such as anger. Ask her about them to make her feel more confident that she can be frank and open with you.

- If she has suicidal ideas, treat as described elsewhere (☞ section 4.4). Special care must be taken with those who have been bereaved because of a suicide (☞ Box 7.10).

- Do not give simple reassurances such as "It's God's will" or "At least you have children". Grief is a universal human experience, and your ability to listen quietly and allow the sadness to be expressed is a treatment in itself.

- For sleep problems, you can give sleeping medicines. It is often important for the bereaved person to sleep well so that she does not feel tired in the daytime. Then she can make the necessary arrangements for the funeral and not feel overwhelmed by the work involved.

- Encourage a gradual return to daily life and work within three to six weeks. Work and other activities can themselves be helpful in raising spirits and helping people to reorganise their lives for the future.

> **Box 7.10. The needs of those bereaved through suicide**
>
> People who have been bereaved through suicide will need help to take the following:
> - get the suicide in perspective by talking about it;
> - deal with family problems caused by the suicide;
> - feel better about themselves (not to blame oneself);
> - obtain factual information about the suicide and its effects;
> - have a safe and private place to express feelings such as anger;
> - get advice on practical and social concerns;
> - deal with stigma and other people's reactions to suicide.

What to do if the bereavement is abnormal

- If the grief appears to be abnormal, you should consider counselling the person at least once a week. The counselling could include discussion about his relationship with the dead person (exploring both positive and negative feelings). Ask him to bring photographs or other items that remind him of the dead person, as this can help provide a focus for the discussion.

- If he shows signs of severe depression, treat with antidepressants (☞ Chapter 11).

Box 7.11. Things to remember when dealing with bereavement

- Bereavement is the normal human response to losing a loved one through death.
- Counsel the person about the loss and ask friends and relatives to provide support.
- If grief lasts more than six months, or leads to severe depression or suicidal ideas, then it is abnormal.
- Antidepressants may help if there are definite symptoms of depression and anxiety several months after the bereavement.

Chapter 8

Problems in childhood and adolescence

8.1 The child who is developing slowly

This section is about a child who is not developing at the rate at which most other children do. There is a great variation in physical and mental abilities among children (and adults!). Some children are better at sports than others. Some children are better in studies than others. Some children learn to walk later than others. When a child is slower in achieving important 'milestones' in development (☛ Box 8.1), then you should be concerned that the child may suffer from mental retardation (MR). This section deals with only some basic issues about mental retardation. For more details about specific care issues, ☛ DVC.

Box 8.1. The milestones of development

There are many milestones on the road from birth to becoming an adult. It is important to remember some important milestones that can be used to check whether a child is developing more slowly than expected. The milestones below can be used as a rough guide for detecting mental retardation.

Milestone	Age at which most children achieve this milestone	Suspect mental retardation if milestone is delayed beyond ...
Responds to name/voice	1–3 months	4th month
Smiles at others	1–4 months	6th month
Holds head steady	2–6 months	6th month
Sits without support	5–10 months	12th month
Stands without support	9–14 months	18th month
Walks well	10–20 months	20th month
Talks in 2–3-word sentences	16–30 months	3rd year
Eats/drinks by self	2–3 years	4th year
Can tell own name	2–3 years	4th year
Is toilet trained	3–4 years	4th year
Avoids simple hazards	3–4 years	4th year

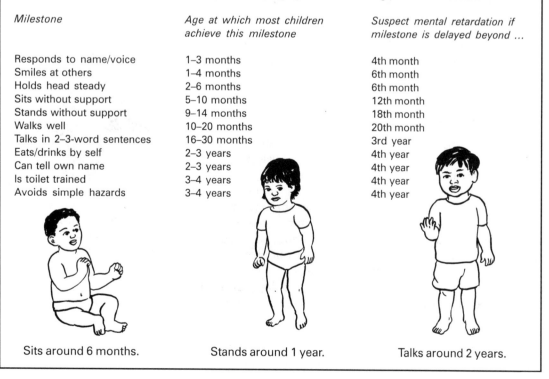

Sits around 6 months.　　　　Stands around 1 year.　　　　Talks around 2 years.

8.1.1 What is mental retardation (MR)?

Mental retardation means that mental functions are 'retarded' or, in other words, not as well developed as expected for the age of the child. Children with mental retardation have difficulty with learning new things. The disability may affect all aspects of a child's development, from learning how to sit and walk to learning how to talk and eat. Mental retardation is not an illness, but a condition present from an early stage of life (usually from birth) which lasts for the rest of the person's life. There is no cure or treatment for mental retardation. However, there is much that can be done to improve the quality of life for the child and family. Mental retardation can be mild, moderate or severe. The vast majority of children with mental retardation have the mild variety. You can identify the degree of mental retardation from a careful history of the child's development.

8.1.2 What causes mental retardation?

Mental retardation occurs because the brain is not developing properly. The development of the brain can be affected by many factors. The causes of mental retardation include:

- problems before the child is born, including poor nutrition for the mother, excess alcohol consumption by the mother and certain types of infections in the mother (in some parts of the world where there are low levels of iodine in the salt, the child may be born with a condition of low thyroid hormone function and mental retardation);

- problems during childbirth, such as prolonged labour or the umbilical cord becoming trapped around the baby's neck;

- problems in the first year of life, such as infections of the brain, severe and prolonged jaundice, uncontrolled convulsions, accidents and severe malnutrition;

- problems in the way the child is being looked after, such as poor stimulation, child abuse and emotional neglect;

- genetic conditions, such as Down's syndrome.

In most children with MR, we can never find out the exact cause.

8.1.3 When a child does not speak normally

Some children appear quite normal in terms of their development of movements, sitting, standing and other physical functions. However, they have problems mainly with talking and speech. Always check the hearing of these children, as hearing problems can cause delays in their language development. If their hearing is normal, it is possible that they may be suffering from mental retardation. Another possibility is a rare condition called autism. Children with autism also show other behaviour problems such as difficulties in making social relationships with other people. You should refer children with language delays to a child specialist because the correct diagnosis is often quite difficult to make.

Problems during childbirth and emotional neglect can cause mental retardation.

8.1.4 How does mental retardation affect the child?

Mental retardation affects a child's development in many respects:

- physical functions, for example the child's ability to walk and using his hands;
- self-care, for example the ability to feed, bathe and use the toilet independently;
- communication with others by talking and understanding what is being said;
- social functioning, such as playing with other children;
- mental illness (☞ Box 8.2);
- physical disabilities and diseases (the more severe the mental retardation, the greater will be the chance of physical health problems such as seizures and physical disabilities);
- family problems caused by guilt, unhappiness and anger about the child's mental retardation.

8.1.5 When should you suspect mental retardation?

Suspect mental retardation if a child:

- is delayed in achieving key milestones (☞ Box 8.1);
- has difficulties in school work and playing with other children;
- is not able to carry out instructions.

  Suspect mental retardation if an adolescent:

- has difficulties in social relationships with other adolescents;
- shows inappropriate sexual behaviour;
- is not able to learn at the same rate as other students in class.

  Suspect mental retardation if an adult:

- has difficulties in everyday functioning (e.g. cooking, cleaning);
- has problems in social adjustment (e.g. making friends, finding work).

Moderate to severe mental retardation is usually detected in a child under two years. When mental retardation is first detected in an adolescent or adult, it is usually mild. This is why it escaped being detected in childhood and showed up as a problem only when the person was faced with new responsibilities later in life.

Box 8.2. When mental retardation and mental illness occur together

Children with mental retardation are more vulnerable to mental illness. Children with mild mental retardation may become very aware of their limited abilities compared with other children and may show emotional and behavioural problems in the classroom (such as hyperactivity – see section 8.3). As they grow older, their difficulty in making friends may make them depressed and angry. Sexual problems may arise (see section 5.5). Children with more severe mental retardation often have brain damage, which can make them more vulnerable to psychoses. If a child with mental retardation shows a change in behaviour, you should suspect a mental illness.

8.1.6 How to deal with this problem

Questions to ask the parents

- Why are you concerned about your child's development? Get a clear story of which aspect of the child's development has led to the consultation.

- By what age did your child learn to hold her head steady? Sit with support? Stand with support? Walk by herself? Speak her first clear two-word sentence? These are the key milestones (☛ Box 8.1).

- Does your child have any difficulties with her hearing? Seeing things? Rule out any sensory problems before you consider the possibility of mental retardation.

- For older children, ask about self-care abilities, school performance and behaviour.

- Does your child have any medical problems, such as fits?

- What do you feel is the cause of the problems? Some parents may think that evil spirits or a curse has caused their child to become retarded.

- Were there any problems during the childbirth, for example prolonged labour? Did the child have any problems during the first month or so after she was born? For example, did she have a high fever or fits? Is there any family history of learning problems? These questions help to identify the cause of the mental retardation.

Questions to ask the child

Asking the child questions and examining his abilities requires some training and practice. The main tool in detecting mental retardation is a careful history from the parent about the child's development and abilities. If the child is old enough, you should ask about worries (such as relationships with friends, studies and school performance, and so on). Knowledge of the kinds of problems the child is facing may make you think of mental retardation as a cause of these problems. You will also be able to judge the child's verbal skills and get a sense of whether they are appropriate for his age.

Things to look for during the interview

- Note the child's level of attention and involvement with the interview. Children with mental retardation often have difficulty following the interview and their mind tends to wander. They may look like they are daydreaming or not paying attention. They may have difficulty understanding simple questions and may give inappropriate answers.

- Unusual physical findings are sometimes seen in children with mental retardation. These include a small or large head and physical disabilities. However, most children with mental retardation look just like any other child.

- Some children may have a specific genetic syndrome that, in addition to producing mental retardation, also causes specific physical features. The commonest of these syndromes is Down's syndrome, where a child has slanting eyes, low ears, a short neck and, typically, a single prominent crease across the palms.

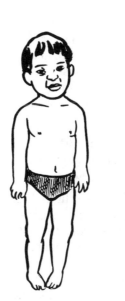

A child with Down's syndrome will have slanting eyes, low ears, a short neck and a single prominent crease across the palms.

Special interview suggestions

Just because a child has MR, it does not mean he is not able to understand what is being said about him. Do not make the mistake of behaving as if the child were not in the room at all. Treat all children, no matter how severe the MR, with dignity and respect.

What to do

The first and most important thing is to be absolutely sure that the child has mental retardation. The label of mental retardation has a serious impact because it means that the child has a problem that is not curable. It is a label that can cause great unhappiness and worry, so use it with care. Three useful strategies in being sure about the diagnoses are:

- In the interview, ask the child to do some simple verbal or written tests that you would expect a child of that age to be able to do easily. For example, ask a child who is three years old to tell you her name.

- For school-age children, ask for a teacher's report on school performance.

- Get a second opinion from a child or mental health specialist.

Once you are confident that the child has mental retardation, determine its severity. The abilities a child has will be an important indicator of how much progress he is likely to make in the years ahead (☛ DVC for more details). It is essential to educate the parents about what can be realistically expected of their child.

- Most children with mild mental retardation will be able to go to school. Many children may manage in a regular school, especially if the teachers are sensitive to their needs. Others may need special schooling. Most children will be able to care for themselves and be fairly independent. These children will mainly have difficulties in making friends as they grow older and in finding jobs. Routine jobs may be the ideal kind of employment for them.

- Most children with moderate mental retardation will need to be in special schools. They may need prompting and help with daily activities. For example, a child may learn to wash and go to the toilet on her own, but may need reminders and occasional checking. Most children will be dependent on their families for social interaction. Most will not be able to hold regular employment. However, some sort of sheltered employment in workshops may be possible (☞ Chapter 12 for your local resources). Sexual adjustment may become a problem in adulthood.

- Children with severe mental retardation are likely to need care for most of their lives. They may suffer from physical disabilities and medical problems. Bladder and bowel control may not be achieved until very late. Such children may not be able to cope even in special schools. Employment is not a realistic possibility.

If the child has a specific medical problem, such as low thyroid function, or fits, refer him for specialist advice. Other than these special (and rare) situations, there are no indications for the use of medicines for the treatment of mental retardation. Do not use 'brain tonics' or other medicines supposed to help 'mental function'. These are not only expensive but will not be of any help.

Reassure the family that even though their child has limited mental abilities, she will be able to achieve many milestones in life. They must be prepared to accept a delay in these milestones and be realistic in what they expect their child to achieve. Specifically explain that there are no cures, and that they should not waste money on false claims of cures.

Teach the parents how to help the child in daily activities such as toileting and feeding. Here are some general guidelines (☞ DVC for more details):

- Parents should be flexible in what they expect from their child.

- According to the degree of mental retardation and the child's age, parents should decide on what sorts of activities they want their child to learn. They should start with simple tasks and move to more complex activities only after the simpler ones have been achieved.

- Activities should be broken down into smaller parts. For example, having a bath can be broken down into holding the mug of water, holding the soap while the parent applies soap, the child soaping herself, pouring the water to wash away the soap and drying herself with a towel. Each of these parts may need to be learned separately before they can all be put together as a complete activity. The activity should be repeated for at least two weeks before the parents move on to teaching the next activity.

- The parents should stimulate the child even if they feel it is pointless. For example, they could talk to the child or read a book with him. They may need to use language that is more

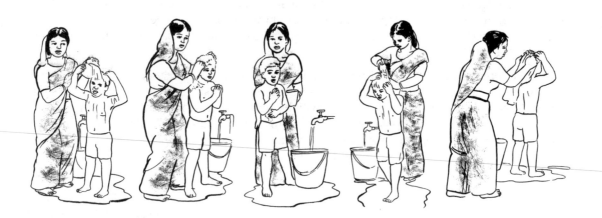

appropriate for younger children. As the child speaks more, the parents should keep raising the level of their own speech and story telling.

- Parents should use reward and praise whenever the child succeeds in any activity, however small.

- Parents should find activities that help them to spend time with the child and yet allow other household activities to be done. For example, the child could learn to help the mother in daily chores in the house.

- Social activities – such as learning to greet someone and say goodbye, to share toys and take turns, to ask for permission to use things that belong to others and to learn to deal appropriately with the opposite sex – are important aspects of the child's adjustment to living independently. Parents should be consistent when giving instructions, and be a role model to the child. They should explain clearly what they expect the child to do and why, and praise her when it is done the right way.

- Parents should not overprotect the child, but should let the child do whatever he can do on his own. This will make him more confident and self-reliant.

Never ignore the child's educational needs. Some parents simply feel like giving up on the child's education when they discover that the child has mental retardation. Stress to the parents their child needs education as much as any other child. Refer the family to local schools for children with special needs (☛ Chapter 12).

Provide information about any special schemes to help families with children with mental retardation through either financial or educational help.

Stay in regular touch with the family. Some families go through a lot of stress because of caring for a child with mental retardation, especially when it is severe. Caring can itself be a cause of stress and mental health problems (☛ section 9.10). Refer parents to support groups in your area (☛ section 10.1).

Finally, if you suspect child abuse or neglect, handle as described in section 8.4.

When to refer

Refer the child and family to a specialist if you suspect a condition such as low thyroid function or repeated convulsions is the cause of the mental retardation – early use of thyroid medicine or anticonvulsants can help prevent deterioration in mental abilities.

Box 8.3. Things to remember when dealing with mental retardation

- Delay in development is most often because of mental retardation. Mental retardation is not a disease, but a condition that lasts the entire lifetime of the person.
- The majority of children with mental retardation look like other children.
- Mental retardation is not curable but may be preventable. Ensuring healthy pregnancies, childbirth and early child care and development will help prevent the majority of cases (☛ section 10.2).
- Early detection is important because parent training may help improve the final outcome for the child.
- Mental retardation may not be detected until adolescence or even adulthood; usually, the mental retardation is mild in such situations.
- The parents will likely need information on how to care for the child and how to provide special education.
- Medicines have very little role to play in mental retardation except in the control of seizures and severe mental illnesses that can occur in some individuals.

If there is a child guidance clinic or mental health specialist in your area, refer any child you think has mental retardation for a further assessment. Mental retardation is a label the child will carry for life; be very careful about using it without a second opinion.

8.2 The child who has difficulties with studies

Children have problems with their studies for many reasons. For example, they may need to help their parents by working. The school may be in poor condition or the teacher may be poorly trained; this may make a child feel that education is of no use. There are also important child mental health problems that can make it more difficult to study. Helping children to stay in school is an important part of health promotion, since educated children grow up to be healthier adults.

8.2.1 What causes children to have difficulties with studies?

The common reasons can be found in the family, school or child. In the family, difficulties with studies may be caused by a lack of adequate parental care or even violence (☞ section 8.4); being a first-generation learner, which means that the child is growing up in a family where the adults have not been to school themselves, may also cause problems. Problems with the school may include poor classroom facilities, large class sizes, poorly trained teachers and the language of schooling (often a European language in many developing countries) not being the language the child speaks at home.

Reasons found in the child for difficulties with studies could include:

- mental retardation, because of the obvious difficulties in learning (☞ section 8.1);
- hyperactivity, because of the difficulties in concentration and attention (☞ section 8.3);
- depression, because the child feels unhappy and loses interest (☞ section 8.7);
- conduct disorder, because the child 'misbehaves' and gets in trouble (☞ section 8.5);
- child abuse, because the child is unhappy and distracted (☞ section 8.4);
- difficulties with hearing or vision;
- drug misuse, more particularly among adolescents (☞ section 6.2);
- dyslexia or specific learning disabilities (☞ Box 8.4).

8.2.2 How to deal with this problem

Questions to ask the parents and teachers

The child will usually be brought to you because she is doing badly in school and thus getting information from the teachers can be helpful. You will need to ask questions about common childhood mental health problems in the following manner:

- First ask questions about mental retardation. Particularly when mild mental retardation may go undetected until the child reaches school. A careful history of milestones may suggest that the child is mentally retarded (☞ section 8.1).

Box 8.4. What are specific learning disabilities?

Specific learning disability is a condition in which a child has a difficulty in a particular aspect of studies, for example a specific difficulty with reading, spelling, writing or mathematics. Dyslexia, the specific difficulty with reading, writing and spelling, is the most common type of specific learning disability. These children have normal intelligence. As a result of low awareness, many children with dyslexia are considered stupid or not to be trying hard enough by their teachers. The dyslexia makes lessons hard for the child to understand. The child loses concentration and becomes bored, unhappy and frustrated, and may misbehave in the class. Failure in examinations and loss of confidence are likely.

We do not know why some children have dyslexia; it is possible that there is a problem in the way the brain processes information. We do know, though, that dyslexia is common and that it is not the same as mental retardation. With special educational help, many children with dyslexia will do as well as other children. The kinds of problems that children with dyslexia can have are:

• difficulties with copying, spelling and writing;
• difficulties with understanding instructions;
• difficulties with numbers and mathematics;
• difficulties with reading;
• behaviour problems.

The vicious cycle of dyslexia

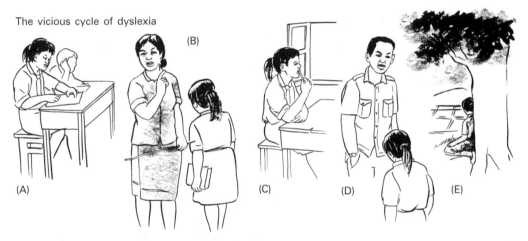

(A) Children with dyslexia have difficulty with their studies.
(B) This causes them to get in trouble with their teachers.
(C) This may make them lose interest in their studies and (D) they may land in even more trouble.
(E) They may eventually drop out of school.

• Ask about hearing and vision difficulties.

• Next consider hyperactivity. Ask questions about overactivity, difficulty in concentration and attention (☛ section 8.3).

If you are confident that the child is not mentally retarded, ask the following questions:

• What difficulty does your child have with studies? Does he make errors mainly with reading or spelling or writing? Does he have specific problems with mathematics? Does he have difficulty in understanding instructions? These are typically reported in children with dyslexia.

• Does your child have difficulty in telling right from left? Is she clumsy or poorly coordinated, for example in sports? Many children with dyslexia have these sorts of difficulties.

Finally, consider a family problem. Ask the parents about problems in the home, including violence and child abuse (☞ section 8.4).

Questions to ask the child

Interviewing children to identify dyslexia requires experience and skill. Ideally, you should refer the child to a specialist child guidance clinic for further tests. Explain to the parents why this is being done; they may become very worried about the 'testing'. If, however, you do not have a specialist clinic near you, you could ask the following questions to help detect dyslexia in the child:

- Why are you having difficulties with studies? The child's views are important; remember that the child is probably very worried about his difficulties.

- Are there some subjects that you find more enjoyable than others? For example, children with specific problems with numbers will not like mathematics.

- Do you have difficulty with reading or following what the teacher is saying?

- Do you have difficulty with spelling?

- Do you have difficulty with mathematics?

- Do you have difficulty with hearing what the teacher is saying? Or seeing what is written on the blackboard?

- How has this problem affected your life? How do your teachers and parents react to your difficulties?

Things to look for during the interview

Examine the child's hearing and vision. If the child can answer questions you are asking in a normal tone of voice, then her hearing is probably normal. Vision can be checked by asking the child to read something a short distance away, for example, the words on a poster on the clinic wall.

Specific signs of dyslexia can be of three types: academic, motor and language.

- *Academic signs.* Ask the child to write a few lines on any subject (for example, his family). Check what he has written for spelling errors such as reversal of letters or words that look like a mirror image of each other, such as 'b' and 'd' or 'no' and 'on'. The child may make spelling mistakes by omitting letters or putting the wrong letter in a word. The handwriting is often untidy. Difficulties in calculation can be tested by asking the child to repeat multiplication tables. Dyslexic children have difficulty in putting the order of multiplication correctly and get the results wrong.

- *Motor signs.* The child may be restless or overactive. She may appear distracted and forgetful. She may be clumsy. You can ask her to point out her right arm or left ear to check for right–left orientation. She may be unable to tie her shoelaces or button her shirt.

John has o funny tay boat Look how beg it is ! He can play with et.

Dyslexic handwriting

• *Language signs.* The child may have difficulty understanding instructions, reading a watch or telling a story.

What to do

• Parents are often frustrated because their child appears normal and yet is doing badly in school. They are worried that their child may be suffering from mental retardation. Reassure the parents that the child is suffering from a learning problem and is not to be blamed for poor performance in school. Ideally, you should refer the child for further testing before making any statement about the problem. Explain that the difficulty in studies may be due to a number of causes, of which dyslexia could be one.

• Remedial education is a special type of teaching method that helps children with dyslexia (and other problems) learn better. With this help, many children will be able to complete their schooling and many do quite well. Children with dyslexia do not need 'special' schools, which are mainly for children with mental retardation.

• Talk to the teacher about the child's needs. Explain that the child is not suffering from mental retardation. The school may be encouraged to exempt the child from some subjects or be more lenient in some aspects of marking (e.g. handwriting). (☞ section 10.3 for mental health promotion in schools.)

• If a child has mental retardation or hyperactivity, ☞ section 8.1 or 8.3, respectively.

• Counsel the child. She will probably be feeling angry and unhappy. Explain to her that she has a problem that is making it harder for her to cope with her studies. Reassure her that she is not 'stupid' and, with proper help, she will be able to do much better.

When to refer

Never label a child as mentally retarded or dyslexic unless you are confident about the diagnosis. This is especially true of mild mental retardation, which may appear just like dyslexia. Refer the child for assessment to an educational psychologist or a child specialist. They will also be able to give advice on remedial education facilities in your area (☞ also Chapter 12). Box 8.5 explains what to do if there are no specialist facilities to refer to.

Box 8.5. What to do when specialist help is not available

• Encourage the parents to spend time with the child, helping with homework and studies. Games like drawing and copying different shapes (e.g. a clock, a man) are useful exercises
• Test the child's ability to read, write and do number work of a class lower than the one he is presently in. In this manner, you can determine which class level the child should be placed in.
• Next, help the child master the level he is closest to.
• If mainstream schooling seems impossible, try to find a vocational school where the child can learn skills to improve future employment opportunities.

Box 8.6. Things to remember when dealing with children having difficulties with studies

- A child having difficulties with his studies may be suffering from a mental health problem. Mental retardation, hyperactivity, dyslexia, depression and child abuse can all lead to difficulties with studies.
- Dyslexia can cause a child of normal intelligence to do badly in school because she has a specific difficulty with reading, writing, spelling or mathematics.
- Dyslexia is an important cause of childhood misbehaviour and depression.
- Detecting dyslexia may need specialised tests.
- Children with dyslexia should continue in a regular school. Their teachers should know about the dyslexia and, if possible, special educational help should be provided.

8.3 The child who cannot sit still

Many children, especially those under the age of five years, find it hard to sit in one place for a long time. Being able to sit in one place reflects the ability of the mind to pay attention to a particular task, for example reading a book. As children grow older, the ability to pay attention is one of the essential needs for their education and discipline. If a child cannot pay attention, then he will not follow what is being taught in the classroom. He will become fidgety and restless. Similarly, if the child is not paying attention to what his parents want him to do, he is more likely to misbehave. Some children may become so restless that they may do dangerous things, for example jumping from heights. In such situations, the child may be suffering from an illness called attention deficit hyperactivity disorder (ADHD).

8.3.1 What is attention deficit hyperactivity disorder?

ADHD is an illness that is more common in boys. Children with ADHD will:

- be restless, for example being unable to sit in a chair through a full lesson;

- be fidgety, chattering and interrupting people;

- have difficulty concentrating or paying attention, for example being unable to complete homework;

- be easily distracted and not finish what they have started;

- be impulsive – suddenly doing things without thinking first;

- be unable to wait their turn in games or in talking to others;

- be extremely demanding of attention;

- have problems with learning and studies;

- be disorganised and untidy.

These behaviours are so extreme that they affect the child's life in many ways:

- At home he will be difficult to discipline and will irritate his parents with his impulsive behaviour and by not listening to them;

- At school he will do poorly in studies and irritate his teacher with his inability to sit quietly and by constantly interrupting the class;

- At play he will irritate his friends by not waiting his turn.

8.3.2 Why is ADHD an important problem?

Most children with ADHD are not recognised as suffering from an illness. Instead, they are labelled as being naughty and irresponsible. This makes them feel guilty and unhappy. They are denied proper treatment and, as a result do badly. Some children continue to have problems in adjusting to life even when they grow up. Some may develop conduct problems during their teenage years and start using drugs or alcohol. Later on, some become involved in antisocial activities. Recognising this illness can help parents and teachers understand why the child is behaving in this manner. Knowing what is wrong can help in providing effective treatments.

8.3.3 How to deal with this problem

Questions to ask the family

- What is the problem? Many parents are fed up with their child's behaviour. Ask the parents about specific details of what the child does.

- Does your child have difficulty paying attention to things, for example attention to what you have asked him to do? Does your child have difficulty staying put in one place, for example difficulty in sitting in one place till he finishes his dinner or studies?

- Have there been any complaints from school? In ADHD, the behavioural problem will be obvious in all aspects of a child's life. If the problem is only in school or in the home, then it may be related to a problem the child is facing in that particular environment, for example a learning problem that makes it more difficult for the child to follow the teacher, which in turn makes him restless only in school.

- Since when have you noticed this problem?

- What have you tried to do to reduce the problem? Ask about violence in the family. Many hyperactive children get beaten to stop their misbehaviour.

Questions to ask the child

- Have you been having any problems at home or school? Let the child give his point of view of the problem.

- Have you had difficulty following the teacher, for example do you have difficulty paying attention to what she says, or to your studies? Do you find it difficult to stay in one place for some time, for example sitting in your chair through an entire class?

- How about at home? Do you have problems concentrating on things at home, for example finishing your food or watching television?

- Do you get angry with others? Or unhappy?

- Do your parents get angry with you? Why? What do they do when they are angry?

Things to look for during the interview

A child with ADHD may be restless, fidgety, constantly trying to get up and walk around the room. She may interrupt what others are saying and talk out of turn.

What to do

- Explain to the family (with the child present) what the child's problem is. Simply understanding that a child has a health problem can help many parents and children feel more hopeful.

- Parents need advice on how to manage the behaviour at home (☛ Box 8.7).

- Send a note to the child's class teacher explaining the problem. You could discuss how to manage the child in the classroom with the teacher (☛ Box 8.8).

- Some children may benefit from a drug called methylphenidate. This medication should be given only by a child specialist or mental health specialist.

- Do not use sedative medicines; these will only make the child drowsy and worsen his ability to concentrate.

Box 8.7. Managing the hyperactive child: advice you can give parents

Parents should be advised to do the following:

- Give the child more help to remain calm and attentive at home and school.
- Avoid punishment; the child is not purposely behaving in this manner.
- When a child behaves badly, do not scold or hit him. You are giving the wrong kind of attention to the child and the behaviour will only get worse. Instead, try 'time out' (see Box 8.12) or ignore the behaviour or simply leave the room (see section 8.5).
- Give praise and reward when the child behaves in the right manner.
- Do not give too many commands at the same time because the child will not follow what you are expecting of him. For example, do not say "Have a bath and finish your studies". Instead, break this up into two commands; after the child has finished the first activity, give praise and then ask him to do the second.
- Reduce stimulation to the child; for example, give him one toy at a time.
- Keep a 'pride' file of the child's achievements; you can file drawings, certificates and other mementoes of the child's abilities.
- Be specific in what you want the child to do. For example, instead of telling a child who is about to eat "Be a good boy now", you could say "Please finish your food before you leave the table".
- Regular sport or physical activity is a useful way of allowing the child to release excess energy.
- Establish a regular routine for the child. Do not leave things for the child to decide. Put a time chart up on the wall so that the child knows what has to be done during the day.
- Listen to the child's feelings and thoughts. Many children with ADHD feel misunderstood and unhappy. Show the child that you know why he is having difficulties and that you want to help him get more in control of his life.
- Avoid taking him to crowded places like markets and weddings. If you do take him, be prepared to come back home if supervising him becomes difficult.
- Plan activities beforehand so as not to be surprised and upset by his behaviour.

Do not hit the child.

Instead, send the child to another part of the home where she will be alone for 5 to 10 minutes.

Box 8.8. Managing the hyperactive student: advice you can give teachers

Teachers should be advised to do the following:

- Make the student sit near the teacher's desk so that more attention can be given to his needs. Also, by sitting in the front of the class with the other students behind him, he will be less distracted.
- Surround the student with more responsible and respected students. Encourage one good role model student to be a friend.
- Avoid distractions; for example, do not place the student near the window or door.
- When giving instructions, look at the student. Ask him to repeat the instructions to make sure the

- Make instructions clear and concise. Try not to change routines day to day.
- Simplify complex directions. Avoid multiple commands. Break up tasks into smaller parts and give short rests in between.
- Make sure the student has understood your instructions. If you are not sure, repeat it in a calm manner. Shouting will not make it easier.
- Reassure the student that he can ask for help from others if he needs it.
- Make the student keep a homework book in which you can check whether the homework tasks have been written down before he goes home. This will also help improve communication between the teacher and parents.
- Allow the student more time in tests; for example, take his answer paper last.
- Monitor the student frequently during tasks.
- Never insult the student. Instead, calmly tell the student he has broken the class rules. Follow an established set of rules on discipline (for example, that he must leave the class for five minutes).
- Always praise and reward the student for every task successfully completed. Praising the effort is just as important as praising the achievement.

Section 10.3 gives guidance on mental health promotion in schools.

When to refer

It can be difficult to treat ADHD. If you have access to a specialist child or mental health service, then refer all children with this condition.

Box 8.9. Things to remember when dealing with a restless child

- Many children show restless behaviour and have a poor attention span, especially when they are toddlers. When this becomes severe, it affects the child at home, school and with friends. This is called attention deficit hyperactivity disorder (ADHD).
- ADHD is best treated by giving advice to parents and teachers on how to deal with the behaviour and taking steps to reduce the problems the child has because of his poor attention span.
- It is advisable to refer the child to a specialist when possible. There are medicines that can help many children with ADHD, but they should be given only by a specialist.

8.4 The child who has been abused

Child abuse is any action that can hurt a child's health or development. There are a number of ways in which children can be hurt.

- *Emotional abuse*. This is the commonest, but least reported, type of abuse. The child is neglected by not being given sufficient food or love and affection or medicines. Sometimes, just one child in the family is abused, while others are treated in a different manner. Verbal abuse by shouting, mocking and calling the child foul things is an example of emotional abuse.

- *Physical abuse*. Many parents use a slap occasionally to discipline their children. However, when the physical punishment is more severe and more frequent, it can cause great damage to a child's emotional health. Some children can also be hit so badly that they suffer broken bones or serious injury.

- *Sexual abuse*. This is the most troubling type of abuse. Here, an adult uses a child for his sexual pleasure. He may touch the child on the sexual organs, make the child touch his sexual organs, or even try to have sexual intercourse with the child.

8.4.1 Why do children get abused?

Both boys and girls can be abused. The commonest person to abuse a child is someone the child knows well, such as the father, brother, uncle, other male relative, family friend, housemaid, babysitter or neighbour. The adult takes advantage of his close relationship and control over the child. Families in which child abuse is taking place are often also families where there are other forms of violence (such as the father being violent towards the mother). Many abusers were abused themselves during their own childhood.

Less often, a child may be abused by a stranger. In some situations, children who are already vulnerable, such as those living on the streets, can be abused and used as sex workers by adults (☛ section 9.7). This is especially worrying in some parts of the world where tourism and rapid urban growth have led to a breakdown of the community networks that protected children. Most abusers are men. Some are immature, lonely, isolated men and may have a drink or drug problem, but most do not appear odd or behave in an unusual manner.

8.4.2 How are children affected by abuse?

This depends on the type and severity of abuse. For example, the occasional slap by a parent who is otherwise loving and supportive is unlikely to have any harmful effects. On the other hand, repeated physical abuse can lead to severe problems.

- *Physical health*. Injuries such as bruises or cuts, fractures, cigarette burns and, in severe cases, death can occur.

- *Sexual health*. Injuries to the sexual organs, pregnancy and sexually transmitted diseases are possible.

- *Mental health*. Abused children often show fear, aggression, poor concentration, depression and antisocial behaviour.

- *School performance*. Abused children may show a drop in their school performance.

8.4.3 When to suspect child abuse

Physical abuse

Suspect physical abuse when a child:

- appears fearful;
- withdraws from other children and does not want to play;
- is aggressive or bullies other children;
- runs away from home or school;
- is lying or stealing;
- performs poorly in school.

Sexual abuse

Suspect sexual abuse when a child:

- is withdrawn and appears sad;

- shows sexualised play or behaviour, such as touching and playing with her sexual parts in public;
- knows more about sex than you would expect;
- starts bed-wetting or soiling after having achieved control;
- performs poorly in school;
- is over-friendly with adults in a manner that was not usual for her;

- attempts suicide;
- is fearful of adults in her family for no clear reason;
- does not trust others;
- starts misusing alcohol or drugs;
- has repeated urine infections, pain while passing urine or other infections or inflammation of the sexual organs.

Emotional abuse

Suspect emotional abuse when a child:

- is not developing or growing properly (☛ section 8.1);
- is losing weight for no obvious medical reason;
- is constantly falling sick;
- has poor language development, that is, not speaking as well as he should;
- is passive and does not react like other children;
- has feeding problems;

- goes back to behaving like a younger child (e.g. when a six-year-old starts behaving like a three-year-old);

- tries to hurt himself;

- runs away from home;

- does not perform well in school;

- appears dull, with little energy; cries very little.

Note that the signs listed above are those that are typically associated with different types of abuse. However, there is overlap. For example, running away from home can be a sign of sexual abuse, while bed-wetting can be a sign of physical abuse.

8.4.4 How to deal with this problem

Questions to ask the family or friends

Few adults will openly report that they feel that a child they know is being abused. It is essential that, if you suspect child abuse, you ask the adult in a frank and open way.

- Do you suspect or know whether this child is being hurt in any way by someone? If there is a possibility, be more specific by asking about all three types of abuse. Do not skip asking about emotional abuse just because it seems less 'serious' than sexual or physical abuse.

- Who do you think is hurting the child? When did it start?

- Has the child been hurt physically? How seriously? What was done for this?

- Has the child been hurt sexually? How seriously? What was done for this?

- Have you shared this information with anyone else? Who?

- Have you told the person (the abuser) that you are concerned about what is going on? If so, what was his reaction?

- Who is the child's guardian? If it is the abuser, then ask who else could take responsibility for the child.

Questions to ask the child

- Sometimes children can get hurt by a grown-up person. Has anyone grown-up hurt you recently?

- If so, who was it? If the child is scared to answer, do not force her. Move on to the next question.

- How did he hurt you? How often?

- How do you feel about this?

- Have you told anyone else? Who? What did they say to you?

Special interview suggestions

- Interviewing children about the possibility of abuse is difficult. Ideally, get an experienced health worker to talk to the child. If possible, contact a child specialist or other health worker who has worked with abused children.

- Do not ask questions about abuse until you have established rapport with the child. If this means spending more time, then do so. Using toys can help the child relax.

- Speak to the child calmly. Make it clear that the child can ask questions about anything.

- Interview the child with the mother, or with another adult who is definitely not a suspect abuser and whom the child trusts.

- Do not make accusations or threats against anyone. You may frighten the child and make the adults suspicious of your intentions.

Things to look for during the interview

A child who has been abused is likely to be very sensitive to being examined physically. Respect the child's privacy. Explain what you are doing and why. Have a trusted family member present during the examination. Document the findings in detail. These may be needed in a police investigation. A thorough physical examination of the child should include:

- weight and height (to look for signs that the child is not growing properly);

- any injuries on the body;

- any injuries or inflammation of the sexual organs – always examine the anal region as well, especially for boys.

What to do immediately

- Your priority is the health and safety of the child. If you suspect the child's life is in danger, refer him immediately to a place of safety. This could be a family member, a nearby hospital or an organisation working with children.

- Explain to the adults concerned that child abuse is a serious criminal offence and that the abuser is liable for police action if a complaint is made. Carefully write down what was said during the interview. Consider whether informing the police would make the situation worse (for example, if the abuser is the only income earner in the family and he is taken to jail, how will the family survive?). Removing the child to a place of a safety (such as a relative's house) may provide a temporary solution. In some places health workers are required by law to inform the police of cases of child sexual abuse. In such places you must inform the police and let the legal process take its course.

I am very concerned about the safety of your child. Can you be sure that the abuse will not happen again at home?

- Talk to the family members who are available. Explain why you suspect abuse. Many parents are not aware that their actions can be so damaging to the child's health. Just telling them about the dangers of beating a child or neglecting her emotional needs may bring about a change in their behaviour. Often, a cycle of violence builds up in the home where parents beat their child, who, in turn, misbehaves even more, leading to more beatings.

Box 8.10. Helping the abused child

Help the child feel positive about himself
• Reassure the child that he is not responsible for the abuse.
• Give positive messages to the child about his behaviour and emotions.
• Suggest activities that the child enjoys, such as playing with friends.

Help the child to trust
• Be someone whom the child can talk to in confidence.
• Spend time alone with the child.
• Show love and affection, but remember to be careful about physical touching.

Help the child to identify and express emotions
• Play games that involve naming feelings and emotions.
• Read books that involve emotions.
• Talk about what emotions the child is experiencing and why.
• Teach the child ways of dealing with anger, such as playing with toys until she calms down.

Help the child make a safety plan
• If there is a local police number, write it down somewhere where the child will find it easily.
• Choose a friend or neighbour where the child can go for help.
• Help the child learn to say 'no' to the adult.

Healing messages for children
• I care about you.
• I respect you.
• You are lovable.
• You have strengths.
• It is a good thing you have told me; now we can make sure you will not be hurt again.
• Most adults would never hurt children.
• You can say no if you don't like the way someone touches you.

• If you suspect sexual abuse, then it is unlikely that the family will accept it easily, particularly if the abuser is someone close to the family. Do not accuse anyone. Instead, share your concerns openly with the family and stress that if the abuse continues, the child's health will be even more seriously affected.

• Teach the child how to ensure her safety. Explain that the abuse is not her fault and she should not feel guilty for having spoken out about it (☞ also Box 8.10). It is important to make sure this never happens again. Suggest the following to the child regarding how she may prevent abuse from recurring:
  • tell the abuser, in a firm manner, not to touch you;
  • run away from the abuser – go to another adult who can protect you.

• Put the family in touch with community supports. This could include child support groups, family violence groups, legal support, child protection agencies, the police or specialist health professionals (☞ Chapter 12).

Who do you trust? Could that person be someone who could help you when you feel you may be hurt?

When to refer

If the child abuse persists or is very serious, refer to a child specialist team and be sure to inform the police.

What to do later

Keep in close touch with the child and the family at regular intervals for at least six months. Very often the abuse stops once it has been openly discussed. If it does not, you may need to encourage the family to take action to stop it. Talk to the child each time; many children do recover from the trauma, but some children may develop mental health problems and may need specialist help from trained child health workers or counsellors.

Box 8.11. Things to remember when dealing with child abuse

- Child abuse is much commoner than is actually reported by children. This is because most children are too scared or embarrassed to tell an adult.
- The commonest type of abuser is someone whom the child knows – often a father, uncle, brother, domestic help or family friend.
- Boys can be abused as well as girls.
- Abuse can be physical, emotional or sexual. All three types of abuse can damage the physical and mental health of children.
- Most abusers will stop the abuse once they are found out. It is important for you to inform the parents immediately if you suspect abuse.
- Never doubt a child's claims that he is being abused. Take it seriously.

8.5 The child who behaves 'badly'

Most children will be disobedient or refuse to follow family rules at some time or another. Many children, especially those under the age of four years, will lose their temper and have tantrums if they do not get what they want. Most children will grow out of this phase. Many parents recognise that this behaviour is part of normal childhood and that a combination of love and discipline will bring the behaviour under control. Some parents, however, may become worried and may seek help. It is therefore useful to know when a child's misbehaviour becomes a health problem.

Children can behave badly in a number of ways: by getting into fights; by committing crimes; by abusing drugs.

8.5.1 When is misbehaviour a health problem?

A child's misbehaviour is a health problem if the problem:

- is present for a long time (more than six months);
- results in serious and repeated breaking of family or social rules, such as lying;
- is accompanied by serious aggression against others, such as hitting or abusing;
- is accompanied by potentially criminal acts, such as stealing;
- is accompanied by not attending school or poor school performance.

When a child's bad behaviour is very serious, it is referred to as a conduct disorder.

8.5.2 Why do children behave badly?

Many parents feel the main cause is that the child is 'bad'. This is never true. The main reason for conduct problems is the way a child has been taught about discipline by the parents. There are notable situations that lead to conduct problems:

- When there is violence in the family a child learns that this is a way in which adults deal with their anger and unhappiness. The child will do the same.
- When parents are not consistent in the way they discipline their child, the child is no longer sure whether the behaviour is right or wrong.
- When a child is neglected he may learn that the only way to get attention is to misbehave.
- When a child is using drugs, she may steal to get money to buy drugs.

Sometimes, children have conduct problems because of another mental health problem, such as hyperactivity (☛ section 8.3) or dyslexia (☛ section 8.2).

Case 8.1. How Salif went out of control
Salif was the sixth child in a family of eight children. His father worked far from their village. He would come home only for one month in the year, and when he did he was always tired and unhappy. He would drink a lot and fight with his mother. Salif had often seen his father beat his mother. When his father was around, he was very strict with the children. They would all be secretly happy when
their father went back to work. Their mother, who worked very hard at home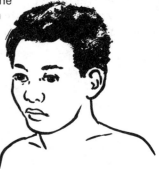
and in a nearby shop, had little time to discipline the children. Salif began
missing classes when he was nine. His teacher warned his mother that
Salif would be thrown out of school. His mother beat Salif badly; she
would then cry and say she was scared that if Salif got into mischief, his
father would blame her. Salif tried to understand, but was very angry with
his mother. He continued missing his classes and failed his examinations
that year. Things got worse when his father came home. One day Salif ran
away from home and spent a few nights with his friend. But he missed
home and came back, only to receive another beating. He started
spending more time out of the house and was regularly absent from
school. He would spend time with friends, smoking cigarettes and
stealing from shops. One day one of his friends suggested that they
smoke some heroin that he had obtained from a dealer passing through the village. Soon Salif became dependent on the drug and needed it every day. He stole money to support the habit until, one day, he was caught by the police. Salif was 16 years old when he was sent to a juvenile prison in a city far from the village.

8.5.3 How to deal with this problem

Questions to ask the family or friends

- What is the problem? Where, when and with whom does the bad behaviour occur? A parent may just say that the child is behaving badly. Find out what this means.

- Since when have you noticed this? How has it affected the family? The child's studies? The longer it has lasted, the more serious the problem is likely to be.

- Why do you think the child is behaving this way? What do you do when the child behaves like this? Find out how the parents discipline the child. Ask both parents this question separately, since this may reveal a different attitude or method of discipline.

- Do you hit the child? How often? With what? Violent discipline is likely to make the behaviour problem worse.

- What are you willing to do to change the situation? What would you like your child to do to change the situation?

Questions to ask the child

- Do you feel there is a problem with your behaviour? What is the problem? The child will have heard her parents complain about her. Now give her a chance to respond.

- Do you feel upset with your parents? Why? Finding out about difficulties from the child's viewpoint can help identify a solution.

- Have you been fighting with other children? Or getting in trouble at school?

- What are you willing to do to change the situation? What would you like your parents to do to change the situation?

These questions to the parents and the child will indicate how far they are prepared to go to achieve peace in the home.

Special interview suggestions

Most child behaviour problems are related to the family environment. Interview the child and family members together. Observe how they react to one another. You may notice anger between the parents and the child. When a parent is speaking, the child's facial expressions may tell you something about how he feels about what is being said. The child may be defiant or sad. Always talk to him as if his account is just as important as that of the parents.

What to do

- Reassure the family (in the presence of the child) that the behaviour problems are common and are not because the child is 'bad'.

- The main treatment is to explain the rules of disciplining children (☞ Box 8.12). Good behaviour should be praised or rewarded, while bad behaviour should be disciplined. The discipline must be clear and consistent so that all adults behave in the same way towards the child. 'Time out' (☛ Box 8.12) and denying privileges are the most effective ways of disciplining children; violence and abuse are the least effective ways. Discipline should be carried out immediately after bad behaviour.

- Discipline needs patience and time to work. Do not expect miracles. Discipline is especially difficult if there are other family problems, such as marital problems. If there are, you may need to work on these as well (☛ section 10.7).

- With the permission of the parents, share the problems with elders in the family or with friends. If the child's teachers are worried, talk to them about why the child is misbehaving.

- Do not use medicines even if you feel that the child needs to be 'calmed'.

- If the child has problems with learning or maintaining attention, think of the possibility of dyslexia or hyperactivity (☛ sections 8.2, 8.3).

- See the family every two weeks. At each meeting, review the child's behaviour. If there is no improvement, find out why not. Often, the reason is because the agreement made by the parents and child is not being observed.

How a behaviour contract can be negotiated. A health worker asks the son in a family what he wants his parents to allow him to do, and he is prepared to do for them. The health worker tells the family that it is important to know that their son will behave in a manner that he copies from them. Therefore, if they hit or shout at him, he will learn that this is how he should behave when he is angry. The health worker would finish by inviting the family to come again in two weeks to see how they have managed to follow the contract.

When to refer

Refer to a mental health or child specialist if:

• the child is at risk of harming others (or himself, such as through drug abuse);

• the child's family has severe problems, for example severe violence or abuse.

Box 8.12. Disciplining children: what's useful and what's not

As a health worker, you should be able to advise parents on how to discipline their children. Of course, this would also be helpful for your own role as a parent! The points below should be acceptable to most parents, especially if you explain how they may help improve a child's behaviour:

• Praise good behaviour. Say clearly what it is that you are praising and what you feel. For example, you may say "I see a whole page of homework done. I feel so happy". This helps the child to praise herself by thinking "I am capable".
• Be consistent. Stick to the rules you have made. Do not allow unacceptable behaviour one time, and then expect it to be controlled another time. If you don't like a behaviour, tell the child clearly why you don't like it and make sure that your rules apply each time the child misbehaves.
• Be sure that all adults treat the child the same way. A big problem is if the two parents treat the child's behaviour in different ways. The child will learn that if he misbehaves with one parent, the other will come to his rescue. The parents must share the same way of disciplining the child.
• Be clear. Explain why you are upset and why you are disciplining the child. Be specific in your commands. Commands should be one at a time. They should tell the child what to do rather than what not to do. For example, say "Please come home before 10 p.m." instead of "Don't come home late".
• Be calm. Do not lose your temper. If parents lose their temper, then it will be very hard for the child to learn how to deal with his own anger in a different way.
• Use 'time out'. This means that when a child misbehaves she is told to go away (for example to another room) and to come back only when she is calm, or after a fixed period of time (say, five minutes). It is important to talk to the child after the time out period and discuss why she misbehaved and what she feels about it. Time out must be coupled with 'time in'. This means playing with or listening to the child for some time every day.
• Deny privileges. For example, you can tell the child who is misbehaving that if he does not behave properly, he cannot watch the television on that day.
• Give short-term rewards. This can be done with 'when–then' statements, such as "When you have finished your food, then you can go out with your friends".
• Spend time with the child talking about her feelings and hopes and fears, and share your own with the child. Treat your child as a loved and trusted friend.
• Do not use violence under any circumstances. A slap, even in extreme circumstances, will not help change the problem in the long term.
• Establish a 'contract' with the child. A 'contract' of behaviour and discipline between the parents and child may help by clearly defining what is expected from the child and by getting both sides to agree to the plan. In return for good behaviour, the parents could agree to give a specified reward, while for bad behaviour a specific action would be taken. This sort of plan can also help establish who has kept to their side of the deal and who has not.
• The key to discipline is showing love and respect for your child.

Box 8.13. Things to remember when dealing with children who behave badly

• All children will behave badly at some time or another, especially when they are less than four years old. This is normal.
• When bad behaviour is present in older children for many months and is associated with breaking family or school rules by lying, stealing, bullying, fighting or not attending school, it is called conduct disorder.
• The commonest causes of conduct disorder are violence in the family and inconsistent parental discipline. Hyperactivity and dyslexia are other causes.
• Teaching simple rules of discipline and encouraging parent–child discussions are the key methods of dealing with conduct disorder. Medication has no role.

8.6 The child who wets the bed

Bed-wetting means urinating while sleeping in bed. All children wet the bed until they learn bladder control. Urinating in clothing in the daytime (enuresis) is a problem only when a child repeatedly does it after the age of three, and bed-wetting when asleep is a problem only after the age of five. Children with mental retardation may take longer to learn how to control their urine.

8.6.1 Why do children wet the bed?

The commonest cause is a delay in this area of development of the child. It does not mean that the child is mentally retarded. Some children simply take longer to learn how to control their urine than other children. Some children may start bed-wetting after having learned how to control their urine. This is often due to the child becoming upset about something, such as fights in the family or the arrival of a baby. Other, less common, reasons include urinary infections, child abuse, diabetes, physical problems in the urinary tract and some neurological problems.

8.6.2 What about daytime wetting (enuresis)?

Some children wet themselves in the daytime. If children wet themselves even after starting primary school, then it can cause problems because of shame and guilt. Common reasons for daytime wetting are not wanting to use the school toilets, urinary tract infections (especially in girls) and a problem related to schooling.

8.6.3 How to deal with this problem

Questions to ask the family or friends

- How old is the child? This is important to know if the bed-wetting is abnormal.

- Does it happen in the daytime as well?

- Has the child ever learned to control his urine? If not, then the problem is most likely due to a delay in development.

- If the child has ever learned to control his urine, when did you notice that he had started bed-wetting again? Was there any significant event in your family around that time, for example the birth of another child or some family problem?

- How do you feel about the bed-wetting? What have you said to the child? Angry parents who blame the child may make the problem much worse.

- How has the problem been handled so far?

Questions to ask the child

- How have things been recently? At home? At school? Start by asking general questions so as to give time for the child to feel more comfortable.

- Have you been worrying about anything of late? See if the child brings up the topic herself.

- Many children have difficulties with bed-wetting. Has this been a problem for you recently? You are now asking the question directly, but stating at the beginning that it is a common problem and something you are familiar with.

- Since when has this happened? Why do you feel it is happening? The child's views may point to the reason for being upset.

- Does it burn or hurt when you pass urine? This is to check for a urinary infection.

- How has this problem been affecting you? At home? At school?

- Has anyone hurt you recently? For example, by touching you in places where you feel they should not? Ask these questions if you suspect child abuse.

Special interview suggestions

Bed-wetting can be a very embarrassing topic for a child to talk about. By the time a child with bed-wetting is brought to see you, she will probably already know that she is doing something 'wrong'. She may feel ashamed and unhappy. Be sensitive to the child's feelings. Examine the child's lower back and walking to rule out rare diseases of the spine that may cause bed-wetting. Talk about bed-wetting in private, or with an adult relative who is sensitive. Ask for a urine examination for sugar and culture to check for diabetes and urinary tract infections.

What to do

Many families become very anxious about bed-wetting. Reassure them and explain that bed-wetting is common, that it is not a sign of mental retardation and that it is treatable. Parents should not blame the child for the bed-wetting. It is not the result of the child misbehaving.

If there is a urinary infection, treat with an antibiotic and advise the child to drink enough water. Remember to be sure that it is an infection before you give this advice because the same advice can make a child's problem worse if there is no infection!

For bed-wetting (i.e. night-time wetting), the parents should be told to try the following:

- Make sure that the child passes urine in the toilet just before bedtime.

- Give praise for nights when the child does not wet the bed, but do not get angry on nights that he does. Simply say that you are happy that he tried and that it will be better the next night. Use a star chart (see below).

- If bed-wetting persists, wake the child in the middle of the night to make him to go to the toilet.

- Encourage the child to learn how to 'hold' his urine in the daytime by increasing the amount of time spent between trips to the toilet.

Never scold a child who has wet his bed – children never wet their beds purposely; showing them love is an important part of helping stop the problem.

- Another exercise that can help the control over urine is making the child stop urinating before he has finished, then hold the urine for a few seconds, and start urinating again until he finishes. The more he can stop–start his urinating in this manner, the more control he will gain.

- Special 'buzzer' alarms are available in some places that can be attached to the bed sheets and make a loud noise the instant the bed is wet. This wakes the child before he completes urinating and the parent can then take the child to the toilet.

- If none of the advice above works, then you can try using imipramine (Chapter 11) in a dose of 25–50 mg two hours before bedtime. This medicine will help many children but the problem often comes back when the medicine is stopped. Thus, its real advantage is that by helping control the problem, it will boost the child's confidence. The medicine must be combined with all the other advice above. It can be used for up to six months.

- If there are any worries or stresses in the home, try to correct them.

  For daytime wetting, parents should be advised as follows:

- Reward the child with praise or other rewards for each day that goes off without wetting. An easy way to reward children is using a star chart. This is a sheet of paper which is stuck on the wall of the child's bedroom. Every day or night the child goes without wetting, she earns one star, which is stuck on the sheet. By prior agreement, after a certain number of stars are achieved, the child gets a reward (such as a toy or a special food).

- Get the child to go to the toilet regularly, say every two hours. This way, the bladder is always empty. Once this controls daytime wetting, gradually increase the time between trips to the toilet. If the child is in school, it helps to involve the teacher in this plan.

Review the child and parents until the problem is completely under control.

When to refer

Refer to a child specialist if:

- there is a physical cause such as diabetes or a neurological problem;
- there is severe family disturbance, especially if you suspect abuse;
- the problem persists despite your suggestions;
- the child has the problem beyond the age of 10 years.

8.6.4 Soiling clothes

Soiling means passing faeces or stools while dressed or in bed. This is abnormal if it happens beyond the age of four years. Some children know when to pass stools, but do it outside the toilet. There are two main causes of soiling; some children may suffer both. The first is severe constipation. The other is not learning how to use the toilet appropriately. This is often a part of a general refusal of a child to cooperate with parents. Advise the parents to ensure that the child's food has sufficient fluids, fruit, vegetables and fibre. Give stool softeners or laxatives if the stool is so hard that it causes pain on passing. Establish a regular routine for passing stools and praise the child each time a stool is passed in the toilet.

Box 8.14. Things to remember when dealing with bed-wetting

- Bed-wetting just once is not a cause for concern. It is only a concern when it occurs repeatedly after the age at which you expect the child to have learned to control urine (usually five years).
- Children with mental retardation may take longer to learn how to control their urine. However, just because a child wets the bed, it does not mean he is mentally retarded
- Bed-wetting is most commonly due to delay in development or a urinary tract infection. In either case, the outlook is good and all children will recover.
- Simple advice on how to control the bladder and passing urine at regular intervals can help most children.

8.7 The adolescent who is sad or complains of aches and pains

Adolescence covers the period between 10 and 19 years of age, between childhood and adulthood. It is a unique period for many reasons.

- Personalities mature in adolescence. Adolescents develop a clear idea about themselves, their likes and dislikes, their strengths and weaknesses.

- Their bodies change physically and they become sexually mature. This means they begin to be attracted, sexually, to others. And, of course, they become more sensitive to the attraction other people have towards them!

- This is the time when important decisions about education and career will be made.

    With all these great changes taking place, it is not surprising that some adolescents feel under stress.

8.7.1 Why do some adolescents feel sad?

Adolescents may become sad for many reasons:

- because their family lives are unhappy, for example because of violence, abuse and constant fights in the family;

- because they are frustrated with their school performance – failing in examinations or not doing as well as was expected;

- because they cannot be with someone they love – love affairs that are broken either by the parents or by the loved person;

- because they are suffering from physical pain or illness;

- because of abuse and violence;

- because they are suffering from severe depression or a psychotic illness;

- because they are abusing alcohol or drugs.

8.7.2 Depression in adolescents

Depression is a common problem in adolescents. It often presents with physical symptoms, frequently related to difficulties in schoolwork. Common features of teenage depression are:

- headaches and other aches and pains;
- difficulty in concentration;
- poor sleep;
- loss of appetite;
- withdrawing from family and friends;
- feeling bad about herself, for example feeling that she is not as attractive or intelligent as others;
- becoming moody and irritable, and getting into fights with family and friends;
- seeing life as being pointless;
- suicidal feelings;
- irritability.

    Depression can affect adolescents in many ways:

- poor school performance;
- poor relationships with friends and family;
- increased risk of harming themselves (even suicide);
- drug or alcohol misuse.

Case 8.2

Luisa was a 12-year-old girl who was one of the clever students in her class. However, recently she had become less friendly. While she once used to play games in the lunch break, she now spent her time sitting alone in the classroom. Her friends tried to get her involved, teasing her that she must be in love. But Luisa became even more distant from them. Finally, they gave up, thinking she was just being rude. The teacher became concerned when she failed in half her subjects. The teacher called the parents to discuss the poor results. The father did not come. Instead, the mother sat and listened quietly. She said she had no idea why Luisa was not doing well. She felt Luisa had become naughty and was not studying hard enough. But the head teacher noticed that Luisa's mother was distracted and unhappy. She asked whether there were any problems at home. Then, Luisa's mother broke down and cried. Her husband had left her some months ago, and he had now stopped sending money to feed her and Luisa. Luisa had become depressed because of these extreme difficulties in her home. The teacher then spoke to Luisa in private and with her mother to find out about her feelings and emotions. She suggested to Luisa that she could talk to the teacher regularly. Later, the teacher spoke to Luisa's friends and asked them to be gentle and sympathetic with Luisa. The teacher spoke to Luisa for 15 minutes every week to find out how she was feeling about her home situation and to help her organise her studies. Slowly, and with help from her friends, Luisa began to feel stronger and did better in school.

Case 8.3

Thomas was a 16-year-old boy who was in his final year of secondary school. This was an important year for him and his family. His family had spent a lot of money on his private schooling. They were all hoping that Thomas would go to medical school and become a doctor. But Thomas had always been an average student. He had never been interested in science subjects. Thomas studied hard for his examinations. But he started getting headaches and felt tired. He told his parents that his eyes hurt and he had difficulty reading his textbooks. His parents got his eyes checked, and they were normal. The headaches got worse and soon he started sleeping badly. Thomas did very badly in his examinations. His parents were angry and upset. Why was he not studying harder? They had him take private tuition. Thomas started feeling tired and having difficulty following his studies altogether. His parents were now very worried. Thomas was seen by a health worker, who recognised that he was under so much pressure to do well in his examinations that he had become stressed. She spoke to Thomas about this stress and what his own feelings about his future career were. He said he did not want to do medicine but would prefer some other field. The health worker spoke to the family and shared her concerns that Thomas was under stress. The parents spoke to Thomas about alternative careers. After all, Thomas was bright and if he was allowed to follow his own career choice, he might feel less pressured. He developed a closer relationship with his parents and began to feel much better.

8.7.3 How to deal with this problem

Questions to ask the parents

- Have you noticed any change in the adolescent's behaviour recently? What have you noticed?

- Why do you think this is happening? The parents' views may give a clue to the cause of the problem. For example, if a parent says that the adolescent is not studying hard enough, it could be that pressure for examination performance is a stress.

- Is there anything you have tried to make a difference? What do you think the adolescent should do to change the situation?

Questions to ask the adolescent

- How has your health been recently? Specifically ask about sleep, concentration and emotions.

- Have you been worried about anything recently? For example, about problems at home? Or with your studies? Or because of friends?

- Have you shared these worries or concerns with anyone else? Who? What was their suggestion? Find out about the adolescent's social supports.

- Have you felt like ending your life? Find out how often and since when. Thoughts that have been present for a period of time and that occur in the setting of a depressed mood should be taken more seriously.

- Has anyone hurt you recently? For example, hit you, or taken advantage of you sexually?

- Have you been drinking alcohol or taking drugs? If so, find out how much.

What to do

- Listen to the adolescent's account of his feelings and what he is worried about. Do not be in a hurry. If you do not have time immediately, then tell him to come back later, when you have more time.

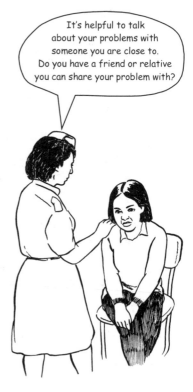

It's helpful to talk about your problems with someone you are close to. Do you have a friend or relative you can share your problem with?

- Help the adolescent to make the link between his feelings and the stressful situation he is facing. Often, understanding this link helps to make the symptoms less frightening.

- Suggest that you could talk to his parents (and teachers, if possible) and share his concerns with them. Often, the adolescent will not have been able to share his feelings with his parents and this will have made the problem even worse – he behaves in a sulky manner, his parents get fed up with him, and he feels even more unhappy. An open discussion of the problems with the family can help.

- Make practical suggestions. For example, if an adolescent has become stressed because he is having difficulties with a particular subject, write a note to his teacher explaining this. The teacher may help by giving the adolescent more time after regular school hours to help him make up for his difficulties.

- Teach the adolescent relaxation exercises (☞ section 3.2.3). This may help concentration. For other symptoms such as tiredness (☞ section 5.4) and sleep problems (☞ section 5.3), give advice as suggested elsewhere in the manual.

- Teach the adolescent problem-solving techniques to cope with the stresses he is facing (☞ Box 8.15, ☞ section 3.2.5).

- Advise him to avoid using alcohol or tobacco or drugs.

- Ask him to come back and see you regularly until he is feeling better. Improvement can be judged by the adolescent feeling more positive about his future, sharing his feelings with others, and better performance in school.

- If none of the above steps help, try using antidepressants (☞ Chapter 11).

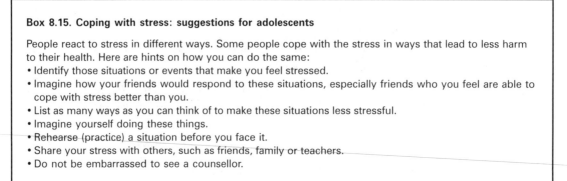

Box 8.15. Coping with stress: suggestions for adolescents

People react to stress in different ways. Some people cope with the stress in ways that lead to less harm to their health. Here are hints on how you can do the same:
- Identify those situations or events that make you feel stressed.
- Imagine how your friends would respond to these situations, especially friends who you feel are able to cope with stress better than you.
- List as many ways as you can think of to make these situations less stressful.
- Imagine yourself doing these things.
- Rehearse (practice) a situation before you face it.
- Share your stress with others, such as friends, family or teachers.
- Do not be embarrassed to see a counsellor.

Section 9.6 gives more information mental health promotion with adolescents.

When to refer

Refer if:

- there is no improvement despite your efforts;
- the adolescent has severe problems such as drug abuse, violence or mental illness.

Box 8.16. Things to remember when dealing with an adolescent who is sad

- Vague physical complaints in adolescents are most commonly related to stress and depression.
- Depression is a common health problem in adolescents.
- Working with families and teachers is an important way of helping adolescents, since stress in the family or in school are major causes of depression.
- Most adolescents with depression will get better. Talking and listening to their worries and feelings is the single most helpful treatment.

Part III
Integrating mental health

Earlier parts of this manual have described the types of mental disorders and their treatments. Part III now moves readers to particular settings of work. You may work in primary health care, with women's health issues, with prisoners or with teenagers. As a health worker, you may be called upon in times of emergency, such as war and disasters. The physical body and mind work very close together. If one is affected for any reason, often the other suffers too. Thus, mental health is an integral part of all health work. Caring for a person's mental health should be as natural a part of your daily responsibilities as looking after their physical health.

Chapter 9 discusses how mental health issues are integral to your work in all these varied settings. It examines the mental health issues relevant to different situations that you may find yourself in. It shows how mental health issues can be integrated into the other activities that you may perform as part of your regular duties. Paying attention to these issues will make your work more rewarding and the person who you are working with more satisfied.

General health workers play an important role in promoting health. Chapter 10 discusses how mental health matters can be promoted and advocated in the community. Health promotion can be seen as a way in which individuals and communities are empowered to increase their control over their resources and other factors that influence their health. Promoting positive attitudes towards mental health and advocating for the needs and rights of those with mental illness are important ways of ensuring the overall development of any community. The vulnerability of women and the poor are also considered as target groups for mental health promotion.

Chapter 9

Mental health in other contexts

9.1 Primary and general health care

Primary health care is the point in the health system to which a person first goes with a health complaint. In some places, a government primary health centre is the main primary care provider. In other places, private physicians and nursing homes are providing primary care. In many places, primary health care is provided by a combination of private and public health care providers. General health care refers to health care focusing on general health problems in adults. While this manual as a whole is concerned with the mental health issues relevant to the health worker based in a primary or general health care setting, this section provides a brief overview of the more broad issues.

9.1.1 Mental disorders in primary care

Any mental disorder may be seen in the primary care setting. However, there are two types of disorders that are especially common. These are depression and anxiety, and alcohol misuse (☞ Chapters 5 and 6). However, a person's complaints often do not offer clues to the underlying mental problem. Typically, the complaints are of physical symptoms, for which no medical explanation can be found. Box 9.1 sets out some guidelines on how the underlying mental problem can be detected in such cases.

Box 9.1. Medically unexplained symptoms: clues to identifying mental disorders in primary care

Suspect depression or anxiety in anyone with:

- physical symptoms that cannot be explained by a physical illness;
- multiple symptoms such as aches and pains in different regions of the body, tiredness, dizziness, sleep problems, palpitations, tingling numbness in the fingers;
- a history of complaints of more than three months;
- a history of problems at home, such as violence.

Ask about feelings and emotions to confirm the diagnosis (☞ Chapter 2).

Suspect alcohol misuse in anyone with:

- jaundice;
- blood in their vomit;
- frequent stomach upsets;
- injuries and accidents;
- sleep problems.

Ask about alcohol use to confirm the diagnosis (☞ section 6.1).

9.1.2 Primary mental health care

If we use a parallel from how we manage physical health problems, we can say that most mental health problems are like an upper respiratory tract infection – they are best treated by the primary health worker. Nonetheless, some severe types of respiratory problem, for example severe pneumonias, may need specialist care. In the same way, most cases of mental illness in primary care can be treated just as well by the primary health worker as by the specialist. The added advantage of receiving care in the primary health setting is that it is less expensive and is more acceptable to most people.

Ideally, you should ask anyone who comes to see you about their mental health. Simple questions such as the following can provide an indication about a person's mental health:

• How have you been feeling recently? I am asking not only about your physical health, but also your emotions and feelings.

• Have you been feeling under stress recently? If so, why? How is this affecting your health?

Most people will report no difficulty and you will not have used more than a couple of minutes of your time. For the few who do say they have problems, you can then ask more detailed questions to see whether there is a mental illness. Obviously, this will take more time, but you will also be helping the person get better. One of the most useful treatment skills in primary care settings is education about the symptoms (☞ section 3.2.5). Section 3.4 advises on when you would need to refer someone with a mental health problem for specialist care.

It is important not to think of mental health and physical health as separate spheres. In fact, mental and physical problems commonly occur together. Just because someone suffers from tuberculosis, it does not mean that he may not also suffer from alcohol abuse. Similarly, just because someone suffers from a mental disorder, it does not mean that she cannot get malaria. The reason to remember this is that once a person has a particular diagnosis, all his complaints are often attributed to that illness.

Case 9.1 describes a typical situation you might encounter in a primary care clinic.

Case 9.1
Faith was a 30-year-old married woman who attended an apostolic church. She complained of having dizziness and headaches for over a year, but no physical illness could be found. On enquiry, Faith admitted that she was thinking too much, sleeping badly and had had suicidal thoughts. She felt so tired that she could not do any housework. Her relationship with her husband had worsened. He was angry because she had not had a child, even though they had been married two years, and he was threatening to take another wife. She had lost her job three months previously and was very worried because, as a result of the way she was feeling, she thought she would not be able to look for another job. She was also complaining of feeling lonely.
The health worker helped Faith by:

• reassuring her that she was not suffering from a terminal or untreatable illness;

- explaining to her that she was thinking too much because of her job loss and marital problems, and this was why she was sleeping badly and feeling tired;
- identifying a problem and action list (problem-solving):
  - a depressive illness, for which she prescribed antidepressant treatments;
  - infertility, for which she referred Faith and her husband to a gynaecology clinic;
  - marital problems, for which she called the husband in for a joint interview;
  - unemployment, with regard to which she recommended postponing any action on job-hunting until Faith had sufficiently recovered from her depression;
  - loneliness, for which she advised attendance at her church and a chat with the pastor.

The health worker asked Faith to visit the clinic once a week. Faith felt much better after three weeks and she and her husband received counselling on how to improve their chances of having a baby. Once she was better, Faith found a job as a cleaner in a local restaurant. The health worker then saw Faith once a month for six months, after which follow-up and medicines were no longer needed.

9.1.3 Improving the system

Some health workers may be in a position from which they can play an important role in improving the overall primary health care system. For example, if a health worker is a member of a district health committee, his views may be sought on various policy issues. There are some specific steps that can improve primary mental health care:

- providing training in the diagnosis and treatment of common mental illnesses to health workers;

- placing at least one antidepressant, one antipsychotic and one anticonvulsant on the essential drugs list (☞ Chapter 11);

- providing clinics for follow-up for those with severe mental disorders (such clinics could be held during those times when fewer people arrive to see a doctor);

- increasing the number of social workers and psychologists in the health services, as these professionals are less expensive than a doctor and play an important role in mental health care;

- establishing a surveillance system where different mental disorders (☞ section 1.3) are counted and recorded in the case-notes of each patient.

9.2 Reproductive health

Reproductive health concerns physical, mental and social well-being in all matters relating to the reproductive system. In practice, a number of different subjects are included, such as gynaecological health, domestic violence, adolescent health, maternal health and HIV/AIDS. There are important mental health issues relevant to each of these. Many are considered elsewhere in this manual (e.g. ☞ sections 7.2 for domestic violence and 9.8 for HIV/AIDS). The broader issue of gender and mental health is discussed in section 10.9. Here the focus is on the mental health issues in relation to gynaecological morbidity and maternal health.

9.2.1 Gynaecological health and mental health

Three specific types of gynaecological problem are important from a mental health perspective:

- *Gynaecological complaints.* Gynaecological health complaints are common, particularly vaginal discharge and pain in the lower abdomen. Many women with such problems also suffer from tiredness and weakness, and depression and anxiety.

- *Menstrual complaints.* Some women complain of feeling unwell just before the monthly period. This is sometimes called the pre-menstrual syndrome. Women with this syndrome may complain of feeling irritable, depressed, lacking concentration, and tiredness. During the menopause, when menstrual periods stop in later life, some women complain of headaches, crying, irritability, anxiety, sleep problems, fatigue and lack of sexual feelings.

- *Following surgery on the gynaecological organs.* Women who have surgery such as family planning operations (e.g. tying of the Fallopian tubes) and operations on the womb (e.g. removal of the uterus) and breast (e.g. for breast cancer) may face mental health problems. Gynaecological surgery poses a unique stress for women because of the identification of the reproductive organs both with sexuality and with a woman's sense of feminine identity.

In practice, you should always ask women with gynaecological complaints about depression and anxiety. Counselling and antidepressants should be used as required.

9.2.2 Maternal health and mental health

Motherhood is one of the most enjoyable and rewarding periods in the life of a woman. Yet it is also a period of enormous change in the woman's body, relationships and work. For example, relationships with other children and the father may be affected. The workload may increase considerably with a new baby. These changes can affect emotions. Mental health issues are important in two specific maternal health situations.

- *Depression after childbirth.* Women are vulnerable to depression during the period immediately after childbirth. An unhappy marriage, domestic violence, problems with breast-feeding, death or sickness of the newborn baby and, in some communities, the birth of a girl are all known to make depression more likely. On the other hand, a planned pregnancy and support from close family members protect mothers from postnatal depression. Postnatal depression can last up to 12 months. The babies may suffer from neglect and their growth and development may be affected (☛ section 4.6 for details)

- *Abortion and pregnancy loss.* Losing a pregnancy due to abortion or miscarriage can lead to depression. The woman may feel guilty about having had an abortion. There may be a loss of self-esteem resulting from the woman's inability to rely on her body and give birth. Feelings of loss, sadness, emptiness, anger, inadequacy, blame and jealousy are feelings sometimes experienced after the loss of a pregnancy.

Health workers in maternal health settings, such as midwives and antenatal clinic staff, can play an important role in preventing depression associated with pregnancy loss and childbirth. Counselling may be given especially to those women at particular risk of becoming depressed, for example those whose babies have died or who have miscarried, whose marriages are unhappy and who have little support from other family members. The focus of counselling is twofold:

• to empower the mother to cope with the pregnancy loss or with caring for her newborn baby, by giving advice on breast-feeding and baby care, and advising her of the need for adequate rest and nutrition (for the mother) and the benefit of sharing her feelings with close relatives;

• to inform both parents together about the need for shared responsibilities in parenting, which is especially important in those communities where men do not traditionally contribute to parenting, seeing this as a woman's job. Fathers need education that parenting is not only a shared responsibility, but a joyful experience as well.

Sometimes the counselling may be extended to other members of the family, especially where there is a joint family system. Encourage senior members to help the mother by reducing her workload, and educate those who have negative views about having a baby girl. Finally, you must encourage all couples to discuss and plan pregnancies. Planned pregnancies help to ensure better maternal physical and mental health.

9.3 Health of prisoners

9.3.1 Mental illness and crime

Certain kinds of mental illness may influence sufferers' behaviour in such a way that they do things that break the law. These are typical examples:

• Violent behaviour can occur in people who are suffering from severe mental disorders. For example, during a psychotic phase, they may wander in public places, shouting at people. Rarely, the mentally ill person may threaten or attack someone.

• Stealing is a crime associated with people who abuse drugs or alcohol. The reason is simple: these people are stealing in order to get money to pay for their drug habit. In adolescents, stealing may be the result of conduct problems.

• Dangerous driving is associated with drinking too much alcohol and severe mental disorders.

However, if we look at the issue of mental illness and crime by asking the question "Do most people who commit crimes suffer from a mental illness?", the answer is no. Thus, it is important that you do not treat people with mental illness as if they are potentially violent or likely to break the law. The vast majority of people with mental illness are not violent.

9.3.2 The mental health of prisoners

The mental health of prisoners is important for two reasons:

• Some people with mental illness get involved in criminal activities and end up in prison.

• Being in prison can be a stressful experience. The isolation, loss of freedom and anxiety can, in some people, lead to mental illness. Drug use and violence may occur in some prisons. Thus, being in a prison can cause mental illness.

The types of mental illnesses that are relatively common in prisons are:

- psychotic disorders, especially in people who are behaving in an odd way, speaking to imaginary people or themselves, restless or agitated;

- withdrawal reactions in people with drink or drug problems, very soon after being put in prison;

- depression and anxiety, which are likely to be the result of imprisonment (suicides can occur even in the most highly guarded environment such as a prison).

9.3.3 Caring for the mental health of prisoners

In general, prisons are harsh places, where discipline and routine are the essence of daily life. After all, they are places to which people are sent as punishment. It may be difficult to be sympathetic to someone who, for example, may have hurt another person very badly. Health workers, however, must consciously avoid making judgements such as whether a person is guilty or not guilty, good or bad. One useful skill is that of "empathy", which means the ability to put yourself in the other person's situation and try to feel the way he does. You will find that many crimes are committed by people who feel they have no options left in their lives – perhaps they have been pushed into a corner by poverty. This, of course, does not justify the crime, but it can help you understand the prisoner as a vulnerable human being.

You can help improve the mental health of prisoners by:

- *Individual counselling*. The key elements are:
  - Listen: allow the prisoner to share feelings and use this discussion to assess whether he is suffering from a psychotic illness.
  - Discuss practical needs: for example, a prisoner may be desperate to meet his family and this may be making him very unhappy. Simply arranging a family visit may do wonders for his mental health.
  - Problem-solving skills (☞ section 3.2.5).

- *Peer support*. Prison health workers often get to know which prisoners are reliable, sympathetic and have the skills needed to help others. You can use such people to act as counsellors or friends to support other prisoners in need of help.

- *Groups*. Suggest to the prison authorities the need for group meetings of prisoners where common concerns can be discussed (☞ section 10.1).

- *Treatment for specific mental illnesses*. Specific symptoms are likely to include:
  - withdrawal reactions from alcohol or drugs (☞ Chapter 6);
  - violent or agitated or confused behaviour (☞ sections 4.1 and 4.2);
  - suicidal behaviour or thoughts (☞ section 4.4).

9.3.4 Improving the system

It is often difficult to work with prisoners because the entire prison system can be unsympathetic towards the emotional needs of the inmates. Working in prisons can also be stressful, leading to emotional problems for wardens, guards and others. You can play a useful role in improving the quality of life within prisons, and this will ultimately benefit the mental health of all those who live or work there. Activities that enable frank discussion of issues between prisoners and the prison staff can help remove suspicions. Regular group meetings and the involvement of non-governmental organisations that are concerned about mental health issues or the rights of prisoners can be beneficial. Efforts to help both prisoners and staff deal with stress through meditation or relaxation training (☛ section 3.2.3) can also help in sharing skills and raising morale.

9.4 Refugees

Thousands of people are displaced from their homes as they attempt to flee war, persecution or famine. We call them refugees: people who have been forced to leave their homes in an attempt to save their own lives. Wars and terrorism, riots and civil unrest are tragically evident in many regions of the world. As technology advances, so have the killing machines and arms trade become more lethal and brutal. Commonly, it is civilians, especially women and children, who bear the worst injuries. Yet the refugees are probably the lucky ones. Those who are left behind are exposed to the horrors of modern warfare and the inhumanity of the aggressors. Women are raped, men murdered and entire villages and communities destroyed. It is this lack of humanity, the complete loss of faith, and the terror of seeing people hurt that cause the mental health consequences of war.

9.4.1 Meet basic needs first

Providing safety and basic needs such as water and food are the most important interventions to support the mental health of refugees and those living in war zones. As time passes, it is important for people to lead as much of a normal life as possible. Assigning responsibilities and specific roles to individuals will mean that the relief work can be managed by the refugees themselves. This will reduce feelings of dependence and helplessness.

9.4.2 The mental health of refugees

There are many reasons why the mental health of refugees may suffer:

- *Grief and mourning*. The loss of all personal belongings, including the family home, and income is a terrible blow to people, particularly those who are already poor. Grief is made worse by the senselessness of the events.

- *Being exposed to horrific violence*. Many refugees will have witnessed or suffered terrible experiences.

- *Physical injury and illness*. These may well have consequences for mental health.

- *Living in an environment with no community networks*. Refugee camps are often sad places, with overcrowding and poor sanitation. People from different communities may find themselves living together.

Most refugees will learn to cope with the stress. They will find ways of seeking support from others and keeping themselves occupied. However, you should be aware that signs of mental disturbance can be expected in some people. The commonest mental illnesses are depression and post-traumatic stress disorder (☛ section 7.1). Typically, the person may complain of sleep difficulties, nightmares, feeling scared, tiredness, losing interest in daily activities and feeling suicidal. Less often, some people may become very disturbed, talking irrationally and behaving in an odd manner. These people may need to be cared for in a medical facility.

9.4.3 Children involved in war

The stress of conflict can be a cause of great stress to a child. Children are often the worst victims of war, not only because they may lose their parents and families but also because they may be used as agents of war. Child soldiers may not only face severe physical injuries and death, but also perpetrate violence on others. Such experiences may make them violent persons when they grow up.

When exposed to violence, some children become withdrawn, complain of nightmares, headaches and other body aches, and behave as if they are much younger than they actually are (☛ section 8.4).

9.4.4 Mental health promotion in a refugee camp

A health worker could do much to promote mental health in a refugee camp.

- *Hand over responsibilities*. One of the most disturbing experiences of being a refugee is the sense of helplessness. From being responsible and able to make decisions in response to their needs, refugees find themselves entirely dependent on relief workers and that their circumstances are beyond their control. Handing back responsibilities means assigning specific tasks to individuals. Identify the strengths of each individual and then assign appropriate tasks.

- *Organise group activities*. Refugees can work in a variety of group activities such as helping to prepare food and caring for sick people. Support groups can help identify and solve common problems (☛ section 10.1). Children should be given an opportunity to restore some semblance of normal life by going to classes and playing in groups.

- *Counsel the individual.* Some refugees may need specific help, for example a woman who has lost all her children or was violently raped. Counselling means listening to people's experiences, meeting them regularly, providing simple practical help and advice, and problem-solving (☛ section 3.2.5).

- *Provide medicines*. Sometimes a person may be found to be very depressed. Using antidepressant medicines may be helpful in these situations. At other times, a person may be behaving in a disturbed manner. Appropriate use of sleeping medicines or tranquillisers for short periods may help in calming the person (☛ Chapter 11).

9.5 Disasters

Disasters are events where groups of people are affected by a life-threatening situation. Disasters can be man-made, such as building collapses and war, or natural, such as earthquakes and landslides. The impact of disasters is greatest on communities in developing countries because they generally have few reserves and resources to begin with. Also, many developing countries have no planned strategies for dealing with disasters. As a result, when disasters occur, the poorest suffer the most.

The most important aspect of disaster relief is to provide for the basic needs of those affected, which include food, drinking water, shelter and emergency medical aid for injuries.

9.5.1 Disasters and mental health

Consider some of these experiences which are associated with disasters:

- your life is threatened;

- close members of your family have suffered serious injury or have died;

- your home has been destroyed (you and your family are homeless);

- your physical health is affected because of lack of drinking water and food.

Such experiences can have a serious effect on mental health. Indeed, many people in disaster situations suffer mental health problems. The most common problems are depression, anxiety and post-traumatic stress disorder. Feelings of hopelessness, fear, suicidal thoughts and loss of interest in life are the early signs of mental distress.

9.5.2 Integrating mental health with disaster relief

Disasters demand a holistic approach to health. In providing for basic needs, the relief worker is also providing an important mental health intervention. Counselling will help victims cope better with their situation. Counselling a disaster victim should include:

- finding out about where other members of the family are – often families are separated as a result of a disaster and putting families together can be an very important task;

- asking about what the person needs – practical help, for example information on how to rebuild a home, may be the most important thing;

- asking about what the person remembers of the events of the disaster – discussing and sharing the traumatic experience can help reduce the sense of isolation and loneliness;

- problem-solving – the person may feel overwhelmed by the scale of problems she is facing, and helping her select the main problems and then work out ways of tackling them (☞ section 3.2.5) can be an important empowering experience;

Do you know where the rest of your family are?

- providing treatment for mental disorders, such as depression.

Many different agencies come together to work in areas affected by disaster. It is important for you to be aware of the different facilities being offered by them. You may find that there are specific facilities being organised for mental health care. If this is the case, then you may consider referring individuals who are very depressed or suicidal to them. Finally, remember that working with disaster victims (and victims of violence and war) can itself be stressful; look after your own mental health as well (☞ section 9.11).

9.6 Adolescent health

9.6.1 Growing up should be fun

Adolescence is a special period in anyone's life. It is that period when children begin to feel grown up, and when they begin to see themselves as unique and special individuals. They want to have friends. They need to study because they will face important examinations. In particular, adolescence is that exciting period when people first begin to feel sexually attracted to others. Adolescence begins around the age of 11 or 12 and continues until about 19 or 20 years.

Adolescent health has become an important issue. If we can ensure good health for our young people, then the future of our communities is secure. Because so much is happening to the bodies and lives of young people, it is also the time when there is a greater chance of stress and difficulties. An important reason for our concern for the health of young people is their emerging sexual maturity. Promoting sexual knowledge and common sense among young people is an important way of preventing HIV/AIDS and other sexually transmitted diseases.

9.6.2 Mental health issues

There are three important mental health issues that are associated with growing up:

- *Becoming depressed.* Common reasons for depression include fights within the family, difficulties with studies, and problems in relationships with friends (☛ section 8.7).

- *Abusing drugs and alcohol.* Many young people try smoking, drinking alcohol and taking drugs such as cannabis (hashish, marijuana). The danger is that what may have begun as an experiment can turn into a habit (☛ section 10.5).

- *Developing schizophrenia.* This is much less common than the first two problems. However, it is important to keep in mind because schizophrenia, a severe mental disorder, often begins in adolescence, especially in boys. If parents tell you that their son has gradually become more withdrawn from his friends and family, behaves in an odd manner and says odd things, think of schizophrenia.

Depression   Drug abuse   Schizophrenia

The main mental health problems faced by adolescents

9.6.3 Integrating mental health with education

In many schools, sex education is now provided to teach adolescents how to make sensible decisions about their sexual behaviour. Such programmes will benefit from the inclusion of a mental health component. The issues that need to be covered in such an intervention are:

- *Thinking positively*. Self-esteem means how much a person values herself. If she feels good about herself, her self-esteem is high. If she is miserable and unhappy, her self-esteem will be low. When she feels good about herself, she will accept challenges, have self-confidence and enjoy friendships. The key to promoting self-esteem is to help people learn to accept themselves by identifying their strengths and weaknesses. Adolescents need to understand the importance of setting realistic goals, of learning to trust and develop close friendships with peers, and of taking pride in their achievements, however small. A common reason for low self-esteem in adolescents is their perception of their physical appearance. This is because a particular kind of appearance is marketed as being beautiful by the fashion industry. Counter this prejudice by highlighting the role of the complete individual, by focusing on personalities who have contributed to society in ways other than their physical appearance alone.

- *Learning to say no*. This message is an important part of sexual health promotion, but it applies just as well to helping young people learn how to deal with the desire to use tobacco, alcohol or drugs (☞ section 10.5).

- *Talking to friends*. Sharing is the best way of dealing with stress. Sometimes not having any friends to talk to is a problem in itself. This is best dealt with in individual counselling, where problem-solving (☞ section 3.2.5) is used to identify ways to make new friendships.

- *Planning ahead*. Planning ahead, especially in the crucial years of school, ensures that studying for examinations does not cause stress. Using timetables is a simple way of planning ahead.

9.6.4 The provision of school-based counselling

School-based counselling is a way of providing guidance to adolescents on matters that concern them. The specific issues you may need to cover will vary from one adolescent to another. The following are some general principles that you can follow:

- *Listen*. Allow time to listen to the young person's worries and problems.

- *Ask*. Ask specifically about mood and suicidal feelings, and about the use of alcohol or drugs.

- *Problem-solving*. Remember that most mental problems in adolescents are linked to real problems they are facing.

- *Involve the family*. Teach parents and adolescents about the need to talk to one another, to be flexible in what is expected from each other and to be able to negotiate and compromise. These are especially important in resolving family conflict (☞ section 8.5 for an example of a behaviour contract).

I want to share with you all something which happened to me last week.

- *Offer practical help*. If you discover, for example, that the key problem is that the young person is having difficulties with mathematics or that he is being bullied, then you may offer to take this issue up with the school authorities.

- *Peer groups*. Groups of adolescents can meet regularly and discuss shared concerns, such as studies, stress, friendships and so on (☞ section 10.1).

9.7 Homeless people and street children

In many cities, men, women and children sleep on the streets and have no shelter. The main reason for people being homeless is poverty. Poor people, in search of jobs and a better future, leave their rural homes and migrate to cities. Here they are lost in a strange world full of people, busy roads and expensive housing. The
only jobs they can find are as unskilled labourers. There are limited opportunities to find a safe shelter.

9.7.1 Homelessness and mental health

Homelessness can be an extremely unhappy experience. Typical stressors associated with homelessness include lack of security, no protection from bad weather and poor nutrition. When homelessness occurs in the midst of great wealth, as in many cities, anger and resentment can arise. As a result, the homeless can suffer mental health problems. Especially important mental health problems are depression and drug abuse (alcohol, tobacco, sniffing glue).

Mental health problems can often be the cause of homelessness. The most important cause in adults is a severe mental disorder. People with schizophrenia, in particular, may be discharged from hospital without any planning, or may be abandoned by their families. The stress of being homeless is much worse since their ability to deal with everyday problems is already much reduced because of the illness. These people may end up in prison because they are found wandering in a manner that the police find threatening.

Provision for their basic needs, in particular food and shelter, will undoubtedly have a positive effect on the mental health of homeless people. You should look out for alcohol abuse and severe mental disorders; providing treatment for these can produce dramatic improvements in the person's sense of well-being. Individual counselling can help, especially if you have built up a trusting relationship with the homeless persons. This involves regularly visiting the places where they spend time and providing sensitive care for their health concerns. The key to counselling is problem-solving (☞ section 3.2.5); finding solutions to problems such as lack of secure employment, poor physical health and lack of shelter will help improve mental health.

9.7.2 Street children

Children live on the streets of cities mainly because of the poverty in their own homes. Violence and abuse also lead children to run away from home. However, street life can be cruel. Street children have to work, often in dangerous conditions, as labourers, servants and sex workers. They may become members of criminal gangs and end up in prison.

Street children suffer from a variety of physical health problems, such as skin infections and diarrhoea, caused by poor hygiene and malnutrition. These often go untreated because there is no one to take the children to a health centre. Children living on the streets miss out on the two most important parts of childhood: growing up in a safe and loving family environment, and being able to go to school and get an education.

Street children are more vulnerable to mental health problems because of the stresses they faced that led them to leave their own home, and because of the stresses they face living on the streets. Street children often come from homes where they may not have had adequate food or attention to their emotional development.

They may have faced neglect and abuse (☞ section 8.4). Unhappy experiences in childhood may have an effect on mental health later in life. Some children may become loners and isolated, engaging in antisocial activities. Others become unhappy, miserable and suicidal.

The most important way to help street children is to give them what all children need for healthy emotional development: love and attention. This is best done by providing an educational opportunity. Informal schools can provide children with an hour or two a day of rediscovering their lost childhood. Street children who are abusing drugs need special help. There are some special issues when working with street children that you must be aware of. Some children may resent attention and reject offers of help. They may be suspicious of adults who take advantage of them. Provide whatever help the child needs and concentrate on building a trusting relationship. The opposite problem may also occur: some street children become so attached to you that they relate to you as if you were a parent. You should not encourage an unhealthy dependency.

Any relationship with a child that begins to acquire a sexual character must be avoided. The best way of dealing with this is to be sensitive to any feelings of sexual attraction to the child, or to any evidence of sexual approaches in the child's behaviour. You should explain to the child that there is a need to reduce the close relationship because of the risk of sexual involvement. You could entrust the care of the child to another colleague but must try to do so in a way that does not make the child feel betrayed. Remember that the child may already have been abused and neglected in the past.

9.8 HIV/AIDS

AIDS is a disease that is caused by HIV, the human immunodeficiency virus, which destroys those cells in the blood that are responsible for protecting the body from infections and cancers. Because we do not have any curative treatments for AIDS at present, it is a disease that will eventually kill most of its sufferers. The disease can take many years to run its course. In some parts of the world AIDS has become the most important cause of death. The epidemic of AIDS is worst in developing countries, where people with the disease die much faster because they have much less access to the care and medicines needed to maintain their health.

9.8.1 Why should mental health be affected?

AIDS can affect mental health in many ways.

- *Pain.* Many diseases associated with AIDS cause severe pain. Pain, in turn, can make a person miserable.

- *Disability.* People who feel so weak and tired that they are unable to function at work or at home can feel helpless and angry.

- *Fear of dying.* The person may be scared of death. She may be worried for the future of her family, particularly her spouse, who may also be infected.

- *Expense.* The medicines for HIV infection are very expensive; most families cannot afford them and those that can must bear considerable financial hardship.

- *Resentment of others in the family.* People who cannot contribute to the family and, instead, need constant help and support may be seen as a burden. The spouse may be angry that the person has been sexually unfaithful and brought the disease on himself and exposed her to the disease too.

- *Stigma and discrimination.* There is much misunderstanding of HIV infection and discrimination against those infected.

- *Direct involvement of the brain.* The brain can be affected by HIV or other diseases such as dementia. This can lead to seizures and severe mental disorders.

9.8.2 Integrating mental health with health care for those who are HIV positive

Mental health can be affected at two different times: when people are first faced with the news that they have AIDS; and later, when the reality and implications of suffering and dying begin to sink in.

In the first instance, many people will react with shock and disbelief. Thoughts such as "It can't be true" may come to mind. People may feel sad and angry. They may go into a depression some weeks after diagnosis. This early reaction to finding out about the sickness can be reduced by a sensitive way of sharing the information. During later stages of the disease, counselling must be combined with other steps that may help promote the person's mental health, for example:

What worries do you have about dying?

- providing good pain relief;

- providing treatment for infections or other physical health problems;

- giving practical hints to improve mobility and function in the home;

- supporting and counselling the family and carers (☞ section 9.10);

Box 9.2. Caring for the terminally ill

People who are suffering from a terminal illness such as cancer or AIDS can suffer mental health problems for many reasons, such as pain, fear of dying and sadness at leaving behind loved ones. You can help promote mental health by:
- establishing a good relationship with the person by visiting regularly;
- talking about what dying means to the person (what are her worries and how can they be best tackled now?);
- involving the family, especially close relatives, in sharing concerns (family disputes that may have not been resolved for a long time could be tackled);
- advising the person to close unfinished business, such as financial or legal matters;
- ensuring that the person understands the nature of the illness and is getting the best possible treatment available, especially for pain relief;
- giving antidepressants or other medicines if there is depression or another mental illness;
- with children, trying to get the family to meet a wish that the child has;
- caring for the carer (see section 9.10).

• ensuring that good and affordable health care is available.

Some people who are HIV positive may need drug treatments for a mental disorder. Depression is not a natural result of AIDS, although it can make the suffering much worse. Treating it with antidepressants can give relief and help the person cope better with the sickness (☛ Chapter 11).

Psychoses in people with AIDS are often the result of an infection in the brain. Treating the symptoms of the psychosis with a major tranquilliser (☛ section 4.3) should be combined with treating the infection. Ideally, these problems should be treated in a specialised clinic.

9.9 The health of the elderly

In most countries, as physical health improves, people are living longer. In some countries, the average number of years that a person may expect to live is now well over 60. It means a longer life to share, learn, experience and contribute. However, it is also true that, as people grow older, so too do their bodies and minds become more vulnerable to certain health problems. Social life changes. People retire from regular work and earn less than they used to. Their daily routine changes. Their children become adults and may leave the home and start their own family. For most elderly people old age is a positive and rewarding period. It is a period in which to enjoy grandchildren. It is a time to read books or do things that could not be done during working years. It is a period to spend time with friends.

9.9.1 The mental health problems faced by the elderly

In some situations, however, the elderly can suffer mental illnesses. There are many reasons for these problems.

• *Loneliness.* In many places, joint family systems are giving way to smaller families. More and more elderly people are living alone with little support from their children. Loneliness is an especial difficulty when an elderly person loses a spouse (☛ section 7.4).

• *Physical health.* Some elderly people develop physical health problems that cause disability. Examples include arthritis, and heart and lung diseases. These problems limit what the person can do and make him increasingly dependent on others.

• *Brain diseases.* Some types of brain disease, especially dementia (☛ section 4.7) and stroke, are commoner in elderly people. By affecting the brain, they can lead to mental illness.

• *Financial difficulties.* Elderly people generally do not work. They are therefore reliant on pensions and savings, which, in a world of rising costs, may be inadequate.

All the types of mental health problems that are seen in younger adults can also occur in the elderly. However, there are three types of problem that you should be especially aware of.

• Depression is, by far, the commonest mental illness in older people (☛ section 4.4).

• Dementia, which is a brain disease, typically begins with memory problems. However, it is most commonly noticed when behaviour problems begin (☛ section 4.7).

• Delirium or confusion usually occurs as a result of medical problems or medicines (☛ section 4.2).

9.9.2 Caring for the elderly

Most elderly people live healthy lives and are mentally able. If an elderly person appears withdrawn or has memory problems, always make sure she is not depressed or suffering from dementia. Keeping regular contact with elderly people provides an excellent opportunity to support them and to detect mental problems early on. Remember when giving any medicine to an elderly person that they need about half the dose that you would prescribe to a younger adult. Too much medicine may cause confusion (☞ section 4.2). Update the resources section of the manual (☞ Chapter 12) to record old age homes and other services geared for the elderly. These can be valuable when you need to provide an elderly person with shelter or to reduce the impact of loneliness.

9.10 Caring for carers

This section is about the mental health needs of people who care for others with chronic or terminal illnesses. Most carers are women: wives, daughters, mothers, daughters-in-law. Caring is associated with stresses that can affect health. Yet carers' health problems often go unnoticed because of the presence of a sick person in the home.

9.10.1 The stresses of caring

Caring for a sick person can have a variety of consequences for carers.

- *Physical burden*. When the sick person is unable to look after basic needs, such as toileting and feeding, caring requires much physical exertion.

- *Emotional burden*. Seeing a loved one suffer is not be easy for any carer, especially when the illness begins to get worse.

- *The difficulty of dealing with symptoms of mental disorders*. Caring for a mentally ill person poses special challenges. Three types of symptoms are especially distressing. Aggressive and agitated behaviour can be seen in psychoses and dementias. The sick person may hit out or abuse the carer, who is only trying to help her with daily activities. Memory loss in dementia is another painful symptom for carers; it can be very distressing when the spouse you have lived with for 40 years no longer recognises you. The third symptom is suicide attempts or threats.

- *Sickness in the carer*. Carers can themselves suffer from health problems. In AIDS the spouse who is caring for the sick person may also be HIV positive. Many sick people are of older age and so are their carers.

- *Expense*. As a sickness gets chronic, expenses rise. Money for other household things, such as food, may become less.

- *Loss of other activities*. Carers may have to push aside their own interests and perhaps give up work.

- *Loss of social contact*. When someone is sick, the home environment changes so that visitors may stop coming for social visits.

- *Grief*. This will follow when the person who has been sick dies.

9.10.2 The mental health of carers

Carers can experience all types of distressing emotions:

- anger at the sick person for having made life difficult;

- guilt because of negative thoughts about the sick person;

- sadness to see a loved one suffer;

- fear of catching the disease from the sick person;

- hopelessness about the future for the sick person and themselves;

- frustration at finding that, no matter what they do, the sickness remains.

These emotions are common in all carers, especially during the earlier days of caring. However, most carers cope admirably well in the long term. Love for the sick person, receiving practical help from others, talking about feelings with friends and family, and finding time to enjoy personal pleasures are some of the ways in which carers cope. Some, however, do not cope as well. Their negative feelings can get worse with time and the carer may begin to feel depressed and anxious (☛ section 4.4).

9.10.3 Promoting the mental health of carers

The first step is to recognise a carer who is at risk of suffering mental health problems and may benefit from your support. Carers who are elderly, isolated and or suffering from physical health problems themselves are more likely to suffer from the stresses of caring. You must act to promote mental health before the carer becomes depressed. Whenever you visit the sick person, take a few minutes to talk to the carer about her own health. Do this in private, away from the sick person. Most carers would not be frank about their negative feelings in front of the person they are caring for. Keeping in regular touch with the sick person and the carer is the best way of promoting their mental health.

9.10.4 Helping a carer in distress

Helping a carer in distress requires patience and empathy, that is, the ability to put yourself in the carer's situation and imagine what it must feel like.

- Listen to the carer's experiences. Many carers will display an outward picture of strength, even when they are feeling sad. Always ask about feelings of sadness.

- Counsel for grief. Often, the carer is faced with the imminent death of the sick person. Preparing carers for death and counselling them for grief (☛ section 7.4) is an important task.

- Treat depression using both antidepressants (☛ Chapter 11) and problem-solving techniques (☛ section 3.2).

- Provide information on support groups (☛ section 10.1) and help put the carer in touch with other carers.

- Involve other members of the family. Speak to them and share your concerns about the stress on the carer. Suggest ways in which caring could be shared.

I think it would be very helpful for you to find ways to share the work of looking after your sick mother.

- Practical advice can be of great help. Carers often struggle with the tasks of feeding, bathing and toileting the sick person, and other daily activities. Simple hints and suggestions on how this could be made easier will make life a lot easier for the carer (☞ section 4.7).

9.11 The mental health of health workers

Just as health workers can suffer colds and infections, they may also suffer mental health problems. There are many reasons for this. One, of course, is that health workers are human beings themselves, with worries and concerns like any other person. In addition, while spending most of their time caring for other people, health workers may ignore their own problems or feelings.

The kind of work which a health worker does or the setting in which she works may pose special stresses. These are some examples of such situations:

- when the health worker is also a victim, for example, in a disaster or war situation – despite being a victim, the health worker may be required to ignore her own needs in order to counsel other people who have been affected;

- when the health worker is faced with very sick patients, for example those working in terminal care, or where many people are sick (for example, because of HIV/AIDS) – each time a person dies, the health worker may feel sadness;

- when the health worker faces a traumatic history – health workers who deal with the victims, or the perpetrators, of violence (such as in prisons, or working with rape victims) can develop strong emotional reactions to their clients.

If your mental health is not good, then this will not only affect your own well-being but also your ability to work properly. Therefore, it is important for you to be aware of your own mental health and seek help from someone else if you are concerned. Sometimes you may feel that admitting to feeling under stress at work is a sign of weakness or lack of commitment to work. This is not true.

If a health worker approaches you for help, it is extremely important to observe the rules of confidentiality, just as you should with anyone else.

9.11.1 Looking after yourself

It is useful to plan how you might look after yourself when working in a situation that is known to be stressful. This can be seen as a kind of immunisation to prevent mental health problems later on. The kinds of activities you may do to look after your mental health can be practised by any health worker.

- *Relaxation and meditation.* Relaxation exercises (☛ section 3.2.3) can be very helpful in dealing with stress when practised daily. These exercises are very similar to meditation techniques such as yoga and prayer.

- *Creative and fun activities.* Always set aside some time each day for activities that you find interesting or fun, but which are not related to work. Spending 'fun' time with the family or friends, reading a book, gardening, sewing or taking a walk are examples of simple activities you might enjoy. Creative activities may include writing a poem or story or doing a drawing.

- *Improving your surroundings.* If your work surroundings are dirty, this is bound to have an effect on your mental health. Tidying up, fixing broken windows or chairs, putting colourful drawings or posters on the walls, trying to cut down on noise and allowing as much natural light into the rooms as possible can help improve your work environment, and your mental health. This is best achieved by working together with all the other people who share your work setting.

- *Sharing and socialising.* There is no substitute for sharing and talking to others to improve your mental health. Take time to talk to your spouse or friend about your day at work. Listen to your colleagues' experiences so you might support them in their difficult moments, and learn from them.

- *Forming a support group.* This is a very useful way of helping yourself and your colleagues. A support group consists of people who share something in common, in this case the fact that they are all health workers. The group should meet regularly to discuss shared concerns and problems (☛ section 10.1 for details on support groups).

9.11.2 When to seek professional help

There are two situations in which it would be essential for you to seek professional help.

- *Suicidal feelings.* We all experience feelings of hopelessness or wishing to end our lives at some time. It is very helpful to talk about these feelings, however embarrassing they may seem, with someone you trust. If you find that you are making plans on how to end your life or that the suicidal feelings are present all the time, then you should seek professional help from another health worker.

- *Problems with drink or drugs.* Health workers are at higher risk of developing dependence problems, especially with sleeping pills (☛ section 6.3), because they have easy access to them. If you find yourself concerned that you are abusing drugs or alcohol, or close relatives or friends express concern to you about your habit, you should seek professional help.

Seek help from someone who is senior to you and whom you feel comfortable with sharing personal health problems.

Chapter 10

Mental health promotion and advocacy

10.1 Support groups for mental health

Support groups are groups of people who meet regularly to share and discuss issues of common interest. Members of a support group share some characteristic with each other. Two types of support group are relevant to mental health:

- groups of people suffering from the same type of mental health problem, the best example of which is Alcoholics Anonymous, where people with drinking problems meet regularly;

- groups consisting of people who care for those who suffer from a particular type of mental health problem – examples include groups of family members caring for people with dementia, severe mental disorders and mental retardation.

10.1.1 How do support groups work?

Support groups provide an opportunity for participants to share their feelings, problems, ideas and information with others who have a similar experience. Box 10.1 answers some common questions about them. The groups work by providing:

- practical hints – for example, a mother of a mentally retarded child sharing how she manages her child's temper tantrums, or a person with a drinking problem sharing how he resists the urge to drink whenever he passes by the local bar;

- information – for example, a brother of a person with schizophrenia sharing some news he has read about new medical treatments for the illness, or the daughter of someone with dementia sharing information about a new day-care home for elderly people;

- an opportunity to help each other – for example, when two parents of people with severely retarded children decide to babysit each other's children for a day each week, to allow both parents a day to get on with other chores, or when two people with schizophrenia who feel lonely decide to get together and go to the cinema;

- the sense that "I am not alone" in my suffering;

- a space to share sensitive and distressing feelings about the mental illness in a group of people who can understand the reasons for such feelings.

Ultimately, a support group works by providing mutual support. This means each member of the group is both being supported by others and providing support to others. This is an empowering feeling, quite unlike that of being a patient in a medical clinic.

Box 10.1. Some common questions about support groups

How many members can take part?
There is no perfect number. Most groups start off very small. If the group gets too large, then it is obviously helping many people. Smaller groups can then be worked out based on factors such as area of residence or age of the participants.

Where should the group meet?
Anywhere convenient with enough space and privacy. Ideally, the meeting place should be the same each time. Some groups may move around by taking place in the homes of different members on different occasions.

How often should the group meet?
The group itself should decide on how frequently it will meet. To make it easy to remember, it helps to have a specific way of remembering the day of the meeting, such as the first Saturday of every month.

How much will it cost?
It should not cost anything to be a member of a support group. The only expenses may be those required to host the group (for example, tea and biscuits) and these can be contributed by all members.

How long will the group last?
As long as its members feel that it should go on. Successful groups have no time limit. For example, Alcoholics Anonymous groups run for an indefinite period of time. Participants may change over time; some may stop attending, while new members may join.

10.1.2 Setting up a support group

Support groups are not easy to get going. They need, first and foremost, a group of people who are interested and committed to the idea. Not everyone is interested in support groups. Some people are not comfortable sharing personal feelings. They may not see the point of regularly meeting others with a similar problem. You can play three important roles in helping set up support groups in your community.

• Put people who share a common problem in touch with one another. Many families facing a mental health problem are embarrassed and keep it quiet from others. You may know of a number of families in the community with, say, a mentally retarded child. You could introduce one family to another and thus help in setting up an informal, small support group. It is important that you discuss this with each family before informing any outsider about their problem. Another way of bringing people together is putting up information on the proposed group in a public place, for example a poster in the health centre. You can fix a meeting and simply tell all the people who may be eligible to participate in the group to attend that meeting to find out more about the group.

• Help provide a space for meetings. Ideally, support groups should meet in the homes of the members. However, this may not always be possible. In these situations, you may be able to offer a room in the clinic during hours when it is not too busy. Members could then meet in a safe place and combine their participation in the support group with a consultation with you if they so wished.

• Facilitate the group. The idea of self-help groups is not familiar to many people. You can play a guiding role in helping getting a group going by participating in the first few meetings.

10.1.3 The first meeting

The first meeting is an important time to set the agenda for the group. What sorts of activities will the group get involved in? How often would it meet? (☛ Box 10.1.) The next important issue is selecting a group leader who can encourage participation by other members. Often the person who took the lead role in helping set up the group becomes the group leader. You could sometimes play the role of group leader for the first few meetings. Once members are comfortable in running the group themselves, one of the members can be selected by the group to be the leader. The leadership position may change with time.

I want to share with you some information I have just received about medicine for schizophrenia.

10.1.4 The role of the group leader

The group leader can facilitate meetings in the following ways:

• by welcoming all members (and at the first meeting by asking everyone to introduce themselves and to say what they hope will be achieved in the group);

• by sharing information that is relevant to the members of the group;

• by asking members to share their concerns on any relevant issue (members may respond by providing information, sharing their own experiences and expressing support – the discussion between members forms the core activity of the group);

• by summing up at the end, to ensure that the group discussions come to some kind of sensible conclusion (and also at this time getting agreement on the date and time of the next meeting).

10.1.5 Basic rules of groups

There are some basic rules in every group:

• What goes on must be kept confidential.

• Everyone should be prepared to listen to others and, when they feel comfortable, to share their own experiences.

• No one should make judgements or criticise others.

• Everyone must respect every other member's situation. What is right for one person does not have to be right for the others.

10.1.6 Keeping the group going

Group members should review, regularly, how the group is getting on. You may attend occasional meetings of the group to provide information and advice on how to keep the group going. Common difficulties that may occur in keeping groups going are an inconvenient meeting place, a lack of time to attend the groups, finding the discussions unhelpful and feeling marginalised in the group. Identifying these difficulties are important if solutions are to help the support group work properly.

10.2 The prevention of mental retardation

Mental retardation (☛ section 8.1) is a condition that will last the lifetime of the affected child. If we can prevent mental retardation, we will have provided the child with better overall health and life opportunities. You can do much to help prevent mental retardation. The single most important preventive steps are to provide good-quality care for mothers, before and during childbirth, and good-quality child health care thereafter.

10.2.1 Before the child is born

The key when the mother is pregnant is to take care of the mother and know when to refer. Taking care of the mother involves the following:

- Try to make sure mothers get enough to eat and sufficient rest.

- Monitor the progress of the pregnancy regularly; if there is evidence of poor growth of the baby (for example, less than expected increase in weight or abdominal size in the mother), refer her to a gynaecologist.

- Advise adolescents to avoid pregnancy (until the woman is at least 18 years old).

- If the mother is seriously ill during pregnancy, especially in the first three months, refer her to a gynaecologist.

- If the mother is over 40 years of age, discuss the risk of mental retardation (which is increased in the babies of older mothers). If the mother is concerned, refer her to a gynaecologist.

- If the mother is drinking alcohol, educate her about the need not to abuse it; heavy drinking during pregnancy can lead to mental retardation in the child.

- Treat high blood pressure or fits in mothers urgently. Refer for specialist care any mother who is semiconscious or confused or has vaginal bleeding.

- Avoid giving pregnant women drugs and X-rays unless absolutely necessary. Also, pregnant women should not work with toxic substances.

- Pregnant women should be advised to avoid carrying heavy loads and accident-prone activities such as walking on slippery ground.

- Immunise mothers against measles and tetanus. Do not let them come into contact with people with German measles, mumps or chickenpox during pregnancy.

- If there is a family history of mental retardation, refer the mother for counselling; some conditions do run in families and can be detected through specialised tests. There is also a higher risk if the parents are related to one another.

10.2.2 At the time of childbirth

Childbirth is a crucial time at which to prevent brain damage, which can lead to mental retardation. These are some of the strategies that can ensure a safe childbirth:

- Avoid prematurity. If the mother starts showing signs of labour too early, advise bed rest and refer to a specialist.

- Provide good maternal care. Among the commonest reasons for mental retardation are prolonged labour and too rapid labour, for example by asking the woman to push too early (☛ WTIND and WWHND).

- Only skilled people should conduct deliveries.

- Be familiar with all the emergency measures of childbirth. Learn what to do if the baby is born blue and limp and does not breathe right away, or has the cord wrapped around the neck. If the birth cry is delayed, give oxygen and seek help.

- If it becomes apparent that the baby is in an abnormal position (e.g. breech presentation), refer.

10.2.3 After childbirth

Children who are born healthy will become retarded only if they suffer a serious infection of the brain, or their brain is affected by lack of food or injuries. These can all be prevented.

- Ensure that all babies are breast-fed; in the first four months of life breast-feeding should be exclusive, as this prevents infections and ensures adequate nutrition.

- Ensure proper immunisations for diphtheria, polio, tetanus, tuberculosis, measles and whooping cough.

- Educate the family about nutrition; babies who are not growing properly need immediate attention.

- Ensure early control of any high fever with cold sponging and paracetamol.

- Treat repeated seizures with anticonvulsant medicines. Refer to a child specialist.

- If the child does not grow well and has abnormal physical signs such as puffy eyes or jaundice, or shows breathing or feeding difficulties, refer to a child specialist.

- Advise on parenting issues, such as playing with children, spending quality time with them, not neglecting or abusing them, keeping down family size, and ensuring a safe home to prevent accidental injuries or poisoning.

10.2.4 Early intervention for babies at high risk

A few babies will have conditions that may result in developmental delay, for example prematurity, low birth weight, convulsions, jaundice and meningitis, lack of oxygen at birth and genetic disorders such as Down's syndrome. Early intervention programmes are important for these babies.

The brain needs activity, exercise and excitement to grow well. A child who is slower in learning to use her body and mind needs extra help. Early intervention programmes work with a baby or child and family to prevent or minimise developmental delays. The aims of early intervention are:

- to improve the development of the child;

- to help the child to function as independently as possible;

- to decrease the effects of handicap as much as possible;

- to give information to the parents about the child's disability and teach them skills to manage the disability;

- to help parents to accept the child's disability and improve family functioning.

These are a few principles for an early intervention programme:

- determine what developmental stage the child is at, by observing what the child can and cannot do;

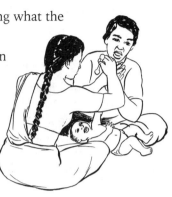

- decide what are the next steps forward so that the child can learn new target skills in the same order as a normal child;

- divide each skill into small steps;

- choose activities that parents can do to teach the child the skill;

- encourage parents to provide practice through repetition of the play and stimulation activities every day;

Some general guidelines for parents that are vital for making the stimulation programme work are:

- use praise abundantly;

- talk a lot to the child about what you are doing;

- guide the child's movements with your hands, gradually decreasing support as the child is able to complete the activity on his own;

- use a mirror to increase the child's awareness of his body;

- teach by encouraging imitation;

- make learning fun by trying new things;

- involve other children, as they can be the best teachers.

Early intervention can be carried out by parents in the child's home, using locally available toys and aids, during the child's daily activities. The younger the child is when the stimulation programme is started, the greater are the chances of the child achieving her developmental milestones. There are several excellent early intervention programmes readily available (for details, ☛ DVC).

10.3 Mental health promotion in schools

Schools provide many opportunities for children. In addition to education, there are opportunities to learn how to make friends, play sports, participate in group activities and be rewarded for performing well. Most children cope well with school life. However, some struggle from the start, while others who seemed to be doing well start failing in later years. A school mental health programme aims to do two important things:

- to identify and help those children who are having difficulties coping with school life, whether it is studies or social activities in school;

- to ensure that the overall school environment provides a safe and supportive atmosphere for children to learn and grow.

This section deals specifically with school mental health for primary and secondary school years (for adolescents, ☞ section 9.6).

Some health workers provide a regular school health programme. Expanding the scope of such programmes provides the easiest way of promoting school mental health. Working in partnership with teachers is crucial, since most interventions will need to be delivered by the teacher. Also, the teacher is often the first person to notice that a child is having difficulties or might have a problem.

10.3.1 Promoting school mental health

To promote mental health within a school, you should visit regularly, say once a month, on a particular day. The teachers can then refer those children they are concerned about to you for an assessment. Educate children about the need to get their vision and hearing checked if they have any problems. The commonest school problems in these years are to do with classroom behaviour and studies. You can ask the teachers if any children have difficulties and then follow the guidelines described in sections 8.2 and 8.5. Two issues are particularly relevant to the creation of an environment that will promote the mental health of all schoolchildren, bullying and building self-esteem.

Bullying

Bullying is aggression by some students against others. It can range from teasing to physical violence. Often, older students are the main culprits and younger students are the victims. Those who are shy and less likely to fight back are often targeted by bullies. Children who have some type of disability, for example stammering, are also picked on. Children who are bullied may become quiet, lack confidence and have few friends. Some may even try to end their life. A school where bullying is a problem often has other problems too. Tackling bullying will help both individual children and the entire school system. The key strategy in tackling bullying is to encourage the school to have a policy on the issue. Students should be encouraged to share experiences of being bullied and firm action must be taken against those who continue to bully others despite warnings. Any child who is complaining of being bullied must be taken seriously; dismissing them as 'weak' is wrong. Those who bully may also be unhappy students; counsel them before threatening them with stern action.

Building self-esteem

All children can benefit from activities that help build self-esteem (☞ Box 10.2). Teachers should be encouraged to include activities for building self-esteem into their classroom. You can play an important role by informing teachers of the potential benefits of such activities for child mental health. In turn, these will improve academic performance and reduce behaviour problems and conflicts in the class. These activities can also be used with children who have been abused or who are out of school.

Box 10.2. Building self-esteem in children – 'Let's feel better about ourselves'

Building a sense of security
Children need to feel safe and know what is expected of them. To promote this:
• have clear classroom rules and limits – rules can include the need to raise a hand before speaking in class, to ensure that everyone gets a chance to be heard, and the need to be polite, to ensure that everyone feels welcome and supported in this class;
• discuss the rules and the advantages of having them;
• place the rules prominently in the classroom and follow a pre-dictable routine;
• ensure that there is no bullying in the class.

Today's homework is to write one page about the things you like about yourself.

Building a sense of identity
This means knowing one's strengths and weaknesses and feeling unique. To build a child's sense of identity:
• encourage 'all about me' activities (collages, pictures and reports) to help children to get to know more about themselves;
• include homework assignments where children need to interact with other family members.

Enhance a sense of belonging
It is important for children to feel they belong to a larger group.
• Allow opportunities for group work, where children help each other to present joint assignments.
• Discuss how to deal with conflict by stating accepted behaviour and limits.
• Help them develop tolerance towards those from different back-grounds.
• Point out their strengths constantly.

Build children's sense of purpose
Children need clearly defined goals towards which they are working. To promote this:
• convey reasonable expectations of all children;
• help children set their own daily or weekly targets and monitor progress;
• praise even the smallest progress in achieving these targets;
• display all students' work prominently;
• praise more effectively and efficiently – try to say exactly what the student is doing that you like, for example "John, you are working quietly and doing your own work", which is more descriptive than "Good work John";
• be constructive – suggest what can be done rather than what has not been done.

10.3.2 *When a child drops out of school*

In many places dropping out of school is a major problem. There are, of course, many reasons for children leaving school, such as poverty and poor school facilities. Not completing school could have a negative influence on physical and mental health when the child grows up. Thus, making efforts to keep children in school is a key mental health promotion activity. Tackling school drop-out requires cooperation between school authorities, health workers and social workers based in the community. Ideally, a child surveillance team should be formed which includes these people. A health worker's role in that team is to identify and

manage any health problems. Reducing school drop-out could involve some of the following activities:

- A warning system should be developed whereby children who drop out are referred to the child surveillance team.

- The reasons need to be identified for any child dropping out. This could involve home visits to speak to the child and family. Family-based issues that can cause school drop-out include lack of proper parental guidance and lack of interest in a child's education, especially the education of girls. The teacher would provide information on the child's behaviour and learning abilities. Some mental health problems, in particular a learning problem (☞ section 8.2), hyperactivity (☞ section 8.3) and child abuse (☞ section 8.4), can lead to children struggling with studies and leaving school.

- Interventions should be made to get children back to school. These could include:
  - raising parental awareness about their child's education;
  - improving communication between parents and teachers;
  - providing educational assessments for children with learning problems;
  - liaising with school teachers when punishment, bullying or other school factors are identified as a cause;
  - providing individual counselling to children who have emotional reasons for avoiding school.

- Follow-up evaluation is required for all children referred to the team. This is essential to ensure that children have returned to school and their problems are being adequately addressed.

    ☞ section 10.5.3 for advice on the prevention of alcohol and tobacco misuse in schools.

10.4 The early identification of mental illness

10.4.1 Detecting the onset of a new mental illness

Often there is considerable delay before a person with mental illness is brought to you. There are three important reasons for this:

- Many mental disorders start very slowly. For example, depression and schizophrenia take weeks to develop, so that there is no real sense of a sudden worsening of health.

- Some people feel embarrassed about mental illness and try to keep the person with the illness hidden from others.

- Some families take mentally ill relatives to religious or spiritual healers because they feel the illness is the result of a curse or black magic.

Just as with physical health problems, the earlier you identify and treat mental illnesses, the better the outcome. You must be alert for the early signs of mental illness in everyone who comes to see you. At the same time, you must also educate community leaders about these signs, so that people who may not be consulting you can also be identified.

Opportunities for early identification may arise in a number of situations. For example, when someone sees you in the clinic for any health problem, you could ask, "How are things at home? How are the others at home doing?" Remember that you need to ask since most people will not openly volunteer information because of ignorance or embarrassment.

These are some of the early signs of mental illness:

- unusual or odd behaviour, such as a person talking to herself or laughing for no reason;

- becoming withdrawn, losing interest in daily activities;

- a sudden change in mood, so that the person has become unnaturally cheerful and full of energy or is spending too much money;

- a person claiming to be possessed by evil spirits;

- a person threatening to kill herself;

- a child who is doing poorly in school;

- someone who is using increasing amounts of alcohol.

The provision of telephone hotlines as a way of reaching out to people in distress is becoming popular in some places. These hotlines allow people who are feeling depressed or worried to call a trained counsellor for advice and guidance (☛ Chapter 12 for recording resources in your area, and also section 2.9.3 on how to assess someone over the telephone).

10.4.2 Relapse prevention

Unfortunately, many people with mental illnesses tend to stop their medicines too early, which often leads to relapse. You must ensure that those who are suffering from mental disorders receive and continue treatment as required. Educate the person, and his family, about the benefits of taking treatment, the time taken for some medicines to act and the possible side-effects and how these can be reduced. If someone with a severe mental disorder fails to come to the clinic for a regular review, a home visit and assessment may help prevent a relapse. If someone is insistent that she does not want any more medicines, frequent visits will help to detect any signs of relapse.

10.5 Preventing alcohol and tobacco abuse

Alcohol and tobacco abuse together account for the most important causes of preventable deaths and disability in the world. It is important to distinguish between alcohol on the one hand, and hard drugs and tobacco on the other. If consumed within limits and with common sense, alcohol does no damage to health; on the other hand, tobacco and hard drugs are dangerous irrespective of the amounts in which they are used. Thus, the prevention of alcohol abuse may focus on strategies to educate people about 'sensible' drinking (in a similar way as to sensible sexual behaviour). On the other hand, strategies for combating tobacco or hard drug abuse should focus on complete abstinence. "Just say no" is the slogan of choice for these substances.

10.5.1 Prevention in the clinic

The simplest strategy is to ask everyone two simple questions:

- Do you drink alcohol? If so, have you been concerned about the amount you drink?

• Do you smoke or chew tobacco?

Based on what the person says, educate him about the dangers of abuse and the need to reduce or stop drinking and to completely give up tobacco. There is no better prevention technique than this (for more details, ☞ Chapter 6).

10.5.2 Prevention in the community

It is important that you are familiar with the law in your country regarding alcohol and tobacco. For example, in some countries bars are not allowed to stay open beyond a certain time and children are not allowed to purchase tobacco or alcohol. If you know of potential offenders, you could approach either community leaders or the police to ensure the law is enforced. You could ask bar owners to insist that customers do not drink and drive home, or teach them ways of politely, but firmly, refusing to serve alcohol to someone who is clearly drunk.

Tobacco advertising is banned in many countries

Encouraging the formation of self-help groups like Alcoholics Anonymous in the community can help peole with a drinking problem. Ensuring that closed areas, such as clinics and schools, are designated "no smoking" reduces both tobacco use and the dangers posed by passive smoking.

10.5.3 Prevention in schools and colleges

Adolescence is the time when many people first try smoking or drinking. This is the most important time to provide education on how to avoid smoking and prevent drinking problems. These are some messages you can use in schools and colleges:

• It is not 'cool' to drink alcohol or smoke cigarettes. Do you think smelling of stale smoke or drink is 'sexy'?

• Smoking and drinking before the age of 18 (or 21 in some countries) is a crime, just like stealing.

• Advertisements that show beautiful and athletic people smoking and drinking are selling a lie. In fact, those who smoke or drink are much sicker than others and look much worse.

• You can have fun and party without drugs or alcohol. Having a good time means enjoying friendships and activities without the need to take any substances.

• If you know someone who is smoking or drinking, be a friend and suggest to them they should stop.

• You will use up all your money on alcohol or tobacco; imagine what you could do with that money if you stopped.

• Why do you need a drug to be yourself? Stop, and you will really be yourself.

10.6 Promoting the rights of people with a mental illness

Literally, stigma means a physical mark on the body. This is what was done to people with mental illness in some societies, as a way of marking them as being different. Today, people with mental illness are excluded or marked out from society in more subtle ways. It is useful to remember that society has stigmatised many types of illnesses, from leprosy to AIDS. Just as health workers have tried to challenge stigma associated with these illnesses, so too must they strive to challenge discrimination against the mentally ill.

The key to challenging discrimination is to understand why it occurs. Of course, sometimes mentally ill people do behave differently: a depressed person may appear withdrawn, while a psychotic person may be aggressive. However, the main reason for discrimination is ignorance. Not knowing the facts about mental illness makes people fear the mentally ill. Some answers to common questions about mental illness are presented in Box 10.3.

Challenging stigma requires that you are clear in your own mind about the facts. Extending the hand of friendship, support and understanding establishes a role model for others in the community. Never use slang words to describe the mentally ill (such as 'psycho' or 'loony'). Such words are disrespectful and increase discrimination.

You need to combat stigma at several levels of the community, by doing the following:

- Place posters (☛ Box 10.4) and other information materials in public spaces (such as clinics and schools).

- Sensitise key people in the community, such as village heads, other health workers, police officers, potential employers and community leaders, to mental illness issues.

- Encourage employers to give opportunities to people recovering from mental illness.

- Encourage the police to take into account mental illness by referring someone who is behaving inappropriately for medical care rather than putting him in prison.

- Encourage relatives to permit the mentally ill person to participate in activities like any other member of the family and to ensure that she gets adequate medical care.

- Encourage doctors to take the health complaints of people with mental illness as seriously as they would with any other patient.

10.6.1 Human rights and mental illness

In the past, people with mental illnesses were locked up, chained to walls and treated as if they did not deserve any dignity or compassion. Even though these terrible scenes are rarely seen today, the human rights of mentally ill people continue to be abused in many parts of the world. Many people with a mental

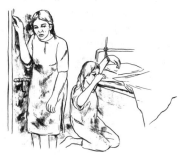

Box 10.3. Some common questions about mental illness: myths and facts

illness continue to be denied their freedom and appropriate health care. Many continue to be locked up, either in prisons or in mental hospitals, where they may be treated in a cruel manner. In particular, they are often denied access to medical care, which is what is most needed during the acute phases of their illness. Many spend years in mental hospitals because their relatives have abandoned them. Some mental hospitals are poorly staffed and are instead run almost as prisons, where the aim is not to treat and rehabilitate the sick but to keep them locked away from society. Cruel practices, such as beating, tying up the person or giving shock therapy without anaesthesia, continue to be practised. The human rights of mentally ill people can also be violated in their own homes.

Identifying human right violations is an important task for health workers. Your aim must be to educate families and those working in mental hospitals (Box 10.4 gives examples of some slogans

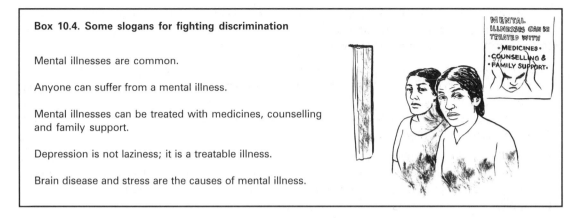

Box 10.4. Some slogans for fighting discrimination

Mental illnesses are common.

Anyone can suffer from a mental illness.

Mental illnesses can be treated with medicines, counselling and family support.

Depression is not laziness; it is a treatable illness.

Brain disease and stress are the causes of mental illness.

with which to fight discrimination against people with a mental illness). If efforts to change their behaviour through education fail, you may need to take stronger action by informing non-governmental organisations, the police or lawyers about human rights abuses.

10.7 Relationships in distress

People who have relationships that are affectionate and supportive generally enjoy good mental health. The most important relationships in our lives are the ones we have with our spouses or partners, with our parents and our children, and with our close friends. For most of us, these close relationships provide us with joy and pleasure. When we feel worried, they provide us with support and hope. However, relationships can also become unhappy. When they run into trouble, we can become sad and angry. This is why helping relationships in distress is an important way of promoting mental health. If you can advise people to boil drinking water to avoid diarrhoeal diseases, then, in the same way, resolving problems within relationships can help prevent mental health problems in those affected.

10.7.1 Why relationships break down

Sometimes there is unhappiness in the relationship for a long time. Sometimes a relationship is thrown into crisis suddenly by an event such as the death of a child or the loss of a job. There are many common reasons why relationships run into difficulties.

- *Major life events*. Both happy and unpleasant events can cause relationship difficulties. For example, babies generally bring pleasure and joy to parents and families. However, they can also lead to a mother and father becoming less affectionate towards one another. Babies mean hard work too, and resentment may build up if the mother feels she is not getting enough support. On the other hand, the husband may feel he is not getting enough time with his wife. Unpleasant events, such as losing a job, can place great stress on people, which then causes distress in their relationships with others. The unemployed person's self-esteem is affected, which makes him feel sad and irritable. The partner may resent the fact that she is having to support the entire family.

- *Money problems.* Shortage of money means that many of the things families would like to do may not be possible. Resentment about who spends how much money and who earns the money can lead to conflicts and arguments between family members.

- *Violence.* Violence is difficult to deal with. The most common victims of violence in relationships are wives. Children can also be abused by their parents, and elders by their children. Emotional violence, such as threats and verbal abuses, can hurt a relationship just as much as physical violence. Sexual violence, such as forcing your wife to have sex, can do terrible damage to the relationship (☛ sections 7.2, 7.3).

- *Falling in love with someone else.* Marriage is meant to be a lifelong relationship, but unfortunately this is not always the case. Having a love affair with someone outside the marriage is often the result of an unhappy marital relationship, and usually makes the marital relationship even unhappier.

- *Sexual difficulties.* This is a sensitive and important aspect of marital relationships. Relationships where both partners are sexually satisfied tend to be happy ones. Sexual satisfaction does not mean that the level of sexual activity is high; it simply means that both partners enjoy having sex as often as they do. The problem arises when one partner is less keen on sex than the other, or when one partner finds sex less satisfying. The real difficulty about sexual problems is that sexuality is such a private area that most people feel embarassed to discuss it with anyone else.

- *Sickness and illnesses.* Sickness, both physical and mental, can affect any relationship, especially when present for a long time. Sickness may mean that the person is not able to work or participate in the activities that make a relationship satisfying. Caring for a sick person can lead to resentment and anger.

- *Alcoholism.* People with a drinking problem can be abusive and violent, especially when drunk. Drinking problems often lead to money problems and sexual difficulties.

10.7.2. How to help rebuild relationships

You can play an important role in helping rebuild relationships. The key is to remember that an unhappy relationship can cause a health problem, or make it worse. Recognising a relationship in distress is the first step to helping rebuild it. In a small community, simply being aware and listening to the community gossip about problems in particular families can give you an idea about who has relationship difficulties. More often, however, you will need to ask about relationships. People who are at risk of facing problems are:

You have health problems because you are unhappy in your marriage. I would like you both to tell me what you think the problems are.

- those with mental health and drinking problems;

- those with unexplained injuries or accidents;

- those with a long-term sickness in their family;

- families who have faced a major life event, such as the loss of a job or arrival of a baby.

There are three steps in helping rebuild relationships:

- understanding the problem;

- establishing ground rules;

- improving communication.

Understanding the problem

Talk to both partners together about their difficulties. If this is not possible, speak to both separately, but make it clear that, if they are interested in stopping the relationship from getting worse, they will need to see you together. Often, a frank discussion about what is bothering each partner can itself lead to suggestions on how to improve the relationship. Simply sharing feelings can be very helpful in rebuilding trust and hope. You may also suggest actions, for example if there is sickness in one partner, or advice on getting a job.

Establishing ground rules

The basic ground rule is that each partner must not abuse or hit the other. Then, they could suggest some other rules they wish their partner to follow. By discussion with you, both partners agree on a set of rules that will govern the way their relationship is to be rebuilt. For example, the wife may suggest that her husband should reduce his drinking so that he drinks only once a week. In return, the husband may say that his wife should not nag him about his friends. These rules are then monitored regularly to see how the couple are progressing. If things are going well, the rules may gradually become part of their daily lives.

Improving communication

This is the key to rebuilding relationships. If people talk about and share problems, they are more likely to trust each other and come up with solutions. Communication can be improved by asking partners to spend some time, say half an hour, each day talking to each other about their day. Here are some simple ways of improving communication between partners:

- speaking about what made them happy and what made them sad that day;

- sharing each other's activities, for example household chores and looking after children, as this can build emotional bonds;

- finding a common and trusted third person to talk to, such as some other family member or friend;

- creating time to enjoy activities that the partners shared during happier times;

- exploring, when you have gained trust, whether there are any sexual problems (☞ section 5.5).

10.7.3 Knowing when to separate

Sometimes a relationship is so unhappy that separating may be the best solution. An unhappy relationship can be much worse for the entire family than separation. The kinds of situations where separating is probably best include:

- when violence in the relationship remains a problem or is getting worse;

- when one partner is having another relationship or affair and has no intention of changing this behaviour;

- when both partners want to separate;

- when, despite help, the relationship remains deeply unhappy.

You can help by supporting both people in making the right decisions about how to part (for example, sharing parenting responsibilities for children) and the need to avoid costly, and unpleasant, legal fights. After the separation, you could play a role in counselling the couple, or more particularly the person who has been left alone, in coming to terms with their new life and instilling hope for a happier future.

10.8 Poverty and mental health

Poverty is linked to poor mental health. This should not be surprising, since there are many stresses associated with being poor. Some of the factors that may lead to mental illness in a person living in deprived circumstances are:

- *Urban migration and disintegration of rural communities*. People who have migrated to urban areas often live in slums, with few social networks. For those left behind, usually women, children and the elderly, the loss of a productive member of the household may lead to loneliness.

- *Material stressors*. The poor have fewer material resources and are more likely to suffer the physical hardships associated with poverty. Thus, access to clean water, food and banking credit are restricted.

- *Squalid and unhygienic living conditions*. Living in such environments leads to stress and unhappiness.

- *Lack of education and employment opportunities*. The poor have less access to affordable, quality education and, subsequently, to employment. The lack of education limits the ability of the person to find a way out of poverty, which leads to a loss of hope and despair for the future.

- *Inadequate access to good health care*. The poor have less access to appropriate health care. Thus, poor people with mental illness are less likely to receive the right treatment.

- *Higher burden of physical ill health*. The poor suffer a greater burden of physical disease. Mental illness occurs more often in those who suffer a physical disease.

Mental illness, in turn, can worsen a person's economic circumstances in a number of ways:

- Mental disorders affect the ability of a person to function at work (as well as at home).

- Owing to the inappropriate treatment of mental disorders, many people seek multiple sources of health care and, consequently, spend more money on their health.

- Increased expenditure on sustaining a habit such as alcohol or drug dependence can impoverish addicts and their families.

- The stigma associated with mental illness limits opportunities for employment.

- Some mental disorders, such as substance misuse, learning disabilities and schizophrenia, affect the ability of the person to complete their education and, therefore, limit the economic opportunities available in the future.

Thus, people living in poverty are more likely to suffer mental illness, and mental illness is more likely to worsen poverty. Across the world, especially in poor countries, globalisation and economic reform are leading to enormous changes in daily life. These policies are influencing the health prospects of every citizen in a number of different ways. The cost of health care is getting higher as government subsidies are withdrawn. User fees mean that public health care is no longer free and private health care is getting more expensive all the time. Medicines are getting more expensive. New international laws that govern the way medicines are manufactured and sold in the world will mean a rise in the cost of most new medicines. But perhaps the greatest risk posed by economic reforms to health is that it is worsening inequalities within every community. The richest few in every society are getting much richer, while the poor majority get poorer. This inequality poses a grave challenge for the future harmony of our societies and the health of the millions who belong to the less well-off sections.

10.8.1 Mental health promotion among the poor

When faced with the problems of poverty, people may tend to think of mental health issues as being irrelevant. Some people assume that depression and other mental health problems are the result of 'materialism' and 'excess', and that mental health problems are either a luxury for the poor or are the natural result of their poverty. These beliefs are wrong. Mental illnesses are not only more common in the poor, but they also have a greater impact on their health and ability to work. Mental health problems are not the natural result of poverty; the fact is that most poor people cope and stay in good mental health. Thus, mental health problems must be seen as illnesses associated with poverty. In much the same way as you would give antibiotics for the treatment of tuberculosis, a disease associated with poverty, you should be able to provide treatment for depression and other mental health problems associated with poverty.

Promoting mental health among the poor focuses on these initiatives:

- *The provision of basic services in the community*. Individuals who live in a community that is clean are more likely to be in better health. If, for example, you were playing an active role in improving sanitation in the community to reduce diarrhoeal diseases, this action would also help promote mental health.

- *Promoting community networks and harmony*. You may be especially well placed to provide social networks at an individual level. For example, you may know of an elderly person who is living alone and is very unhappy. Nearby is a family comprising a single mother and two young children; she is finding it hard to cope with work and care for the children. You could suggest to these different people the possibility of supporting each other. For example, the elderly person may mind the children in the day, and the single mother may provide friendship and shared meals.

- *Reduce levels of violence*. Crime and violence are more common when there is greater inequality or when a community is divided along religious or ethnic lines. In such situations you should collaborate closely with other community leaders and opinion makers on the need to build social harmony. This may involve:
  - boycotting all forms of political action that divides people into groups;
  - advocating equal treatment of all members of the community with the police, health and legal systems;
  - identifying those politicians who are committed to a reduction in violence as the favoured candidates in local elections;
  - sensitising police to dealing with complaints of violence in families.

- *Improving economic opportunities for the community*. You may not have much scope to influence the provision of new jobs or economic opportunities directly. However, keeping yourself well informed of welfare and employment schemes or programmes will allow you to provide that information to those who might need it. For example, debt may be tackled by providing access to small-scale loans through micro-credit schemes. You could encourage the local councillors or women's groups to set up similar schemes. Your position as a health worker means that your suggestions may be taken seriously.

- *Providing effective care in the health centre.* Be competent in detecting and treating common mental health problems. Never dismiss these as the natural consequence of poverty. Instead, treating mental illness will not only make people feel better, but will also provide them with the necessary strengths in thinking and feeling to come up with solutions for their problems.

10.9 Gender and mental health

Gender inequality is a term used to describe the different way in which men's and women's position, roles, rights and powers in a community are practised. In other sections of this manual, you will have read about some of the more serious consequences of the weaker position of women in our society, such as the fact that they may be victims of domestic violence and rape. These are examples of how gender inequality influences the personal relationship between a man and a woman. This chapter considers the influence of gender inequality on the way society and the health system interact with mental health issues in women.

10.9.1 Gender inequality and mental health

There are three issues to consider when we think about women and mental health.

- *Are women more likely to suffer mental health problems?* This depends on the kind of mental illness. Women are more likely to suffer depression and anxiety. However, severe mental disorders are equally common in both sexes, and dependence problems, such as alcohol abuse, are much commoner in men.

- *Why do women suffer mental health problems?* Stresses in life are known to make a person more likely to become depressed. Gender inequality leads to considerable stresses on women's lives. Thus, a woman may work as hard as a man, but her work is likely to be less rewarded financially. She may not be entitled to 'relaxation' time or time for herself because her work is not valued. Also, at home she may face pressure to produce children.

- *What happens to women who suffer mental health problems?* Women with any health problem are less likely to receive the same quality of health care as men. Women's complaints are taken less seriously by relatives and health workers. Women who are depressed often do not get the right treatment for their problems; instead they are prescribed sleeping pills and vitamins. Mentally handicapped girls are less likely to be sent to special schools. Whereas a mentally ill man may get married, mentally ill women are often left alone. Mentally ill women may be severely

condemned for any behaviour that could be perceived as a violation of feminine nature, such as lack of attention towards the preparation of food or neglect of children. Mental illness in women may be seen as a disgrace to the family. Many mentally ill women receive little social support. Married mentally ill women are more likely to be sent back to their parental home, deserted or divorced.

10.9.2 Promoting mental health for women

The promotion of gender equality, by empowering women to take decisions that influence their lives and educating men about the need for equal rights, is the most important way of promoting women's mental health. In this task, you need to be an activist and advocate for women's rights. In many places, women's groups are actively working towards greater recognition of women's rights. Participating in these activities is an important contribution a health worker can make towards promoting better health for women.

Some people argue that, by saying that women are more likely to suffer depression, there is a danger that real social problems are being perceived as health problems. Thus, if a woman is being beaten by her husband and becomes depressed, then the real problem is the violence in her home, which is directly responsible for her depression. While this is true, you must also be concerned about the woman's current health. Thus, if a woman's arm was broken by a violent husband, you would first try to treat the fracture. In the same way, treating the depression can help by improving the woman's concentration, sleep, feelings of self-esteem and energy levels. This, in turn, can help in trying to find a solution for the problems at home that are causing stress.

You must be constantly aware of the powerful role played by gender inequality in the health of women. There are many ways in which you can help reduce the impact of this inequality on women's mental health.

- Whenever a woman consults, in particular a woman who consults repeatedly for minor health problems, spare some time to find out about her domestic situation and other stresses. Allow women an opportunity to speak about their feelings and problems.

- If you feel comfortable (and if you have obtained the woman's permission), speak to the husband or other family members and educate them about the difficulties the woman is facing and how it is affecting her health. You can also provide specific suggestions to improve relationships (☞ section 10.7).

- Sensitise your colleagues in the clinic about gender inequality in the way health care is provided. Be sure that you and your colleagues treat health complaints in men and women with equal concern.

- When you know that a particular woman suffers from a severe mental disorder, pay special attention to her needs by ensuring that she sees you regularly. If she is not brought to the health centre, arrange to see her at her home. Counsel her family members to remove any doubts they may have about the illness.

- When you know that a woman is living in a home where she is suffering a great deal of stress, make an effort to ask her if, and how, this is affecting her health. If you find she is suffering mental health problems, counsel her and try to work with her on her problem-solving skills (☞ section 3.2).

- If women's groups are active in your community, take the initiative to participate in their meetings and discuss mental health problems as an area of concern for women (☞ Chapter 12).

- Facilitate the formation of self-help or support groups for women with mental health problems(☞ section 10.1).

Part IV
Localising this manual
for your area

The earlier sections of the manual have described the clinical approach to mental health problems from a general health worker's perspective. You will have often found cross-references to Part IV of the manual. Part IV allows readers to record information that is specific to their area of work. Two chapters are included.

Chapter 11 provides a quick reference guide to different medicines for mental illnesses and space for you to write the local brand names and costs of these medicines.

Chapter 12 suggests how you might record information on resources in your local area that may be useful in helping people with mental illness.

The Glossary of technical terms has space in which you can note the word for particular items in your own language.

Chapter 11

Medicines for mental illness

11.1 Choosing the right medicine: cost and efficacy

Throughout the world the cost of health care is rising. Particularly in developing countries, this means making hard choices about which medicines to prescribe. Many newer medicines are protected by international patent laws. This means that only one company is allowed to produce that medicine for a certain period of time. These medicines are almost always much more expensive than older medicines. When making a decision on whether to use an older, cheaper medicine or a newer, more expensive medicine, you must consider these issues:

• the cost of the medicine;

• the efficacy of the medicine (i.e. how good it is);

• the side-effects;

• the income bracket of the family.

Thus, a newer medicine, which may be no better than an older medicine in reducing the symptoms of a mental illness, may have lesser side-effects. This could be very important for some people. For example, older antipsychotic medicines produce more stiffness and restlessness than newer ones. A person taking an older medicine may feel so restless that he cannot work and, therefore, cannot earn any money. On the other hand, a person taking a newer antipsychotic may spend more money on the medicines, but because she can work she can more readily afford the treatment than would have been the case with the older medicine.

In choosing medicines, the following situations may arise:

• The older, cheaper medicine is more effective or just as good as than the newer, expensive medicine and there are no differences in side-effects. Recommend the older, cheaper medicine. A good example from drugs for mental illnesses are the choice between amitriptyline and nortriptyline, two tricyclic antidepressants. Whereas the former is cheaper than the latter, they are equally effective and have similar side-effects. Therefore, you should choose amitriptyline. Many of the newest psychiatric medicines are no different from the ones produced a few years earlier in terms of both side-effects and efficacy. Do not recommend them.

• The older, cheaper medicine is just as good as than the newer, expensive medicine, but there is a greater risk of side-effects with the older medicine. A good example of such a choice is that between older antidepressants, such as amitriptyline, and newer antidepressants, such as fluoxetine. The former is just as good as the latter but has more side-effects. More people using the former will drop out of treatment because of the side-effects. Another example of such a choice is that between older antipsychotic drugs, such as haloperidol, and newer antipsychotic drugs, such as risperidone. Two options are available to you. For those patients who can afford the newer medicine, you can offer both options and explain the pros and cons of each. Let the person make the choice. If, on the other hand, the person is from a poorer family, recommend the older medicine. Monitor the person's progress; if severe side-effects appear, switch to the newer medicine.

• The newer, more expensive medicine is more effective than the older medicine. In this situation, you should ideally recommend the newer medicine. However, if the person cannot afford the new medicine, the older medicine may be given a trial. If it works well, there is no need for change. If it does not work well, then the newer medicine may be the only choice left. An example of such a choice is between older antipsychotic drugs and newer ones. Thus, risperidone may produce better results in people with schizophrenia than chlorpromazine.

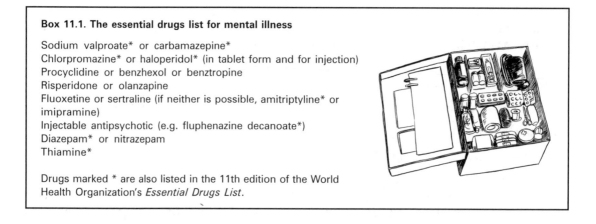

Box 11.1. The essential drugs list for mental illness

Sodium valproate* or carbamazepine*
Chlorpromazine* or haloperidol* (in tablet form and for injection)
Procyclidine or benzhexol or benztropine
Risperidone or olanzapine
Fluoxetine or sertraline (if neither is possible, amitriptyline* or imipramine)
Injectable antipsychotic (e.g. fluphenazine decanoate*)
Diazepam* or nitrazepam
Thiamine*

Drugs marked * are also listed in the 11th edition of the World Health Organization's *Essential Drugs List*.

11.2 A quick reference guide to medicines for mental illnesses

You should enter the local trade names and costs of the medicines in the second column of the tables. The list of medicines in each class of drugs is not exhaustive. Only the most commonly-used or well recognised drugs are included. However, blank rows are left at the end of each class of medicines for you to enter any other medicines available in your region. Box 11.1 lists the drugs that are essential to have available for the treatment of mental illness.

Table 11.1. Antipsychotic medicines for severe mental disorders and people who are confused, agitated or aggressive

Medication	Local trade names and cost	Special uses	Dosage	Side-effects
Low-potency drugs: these drugs have a lower risk of side-effects				
Chlorpromazine		Helps sleep and is useful given at night for people with a psychosis *and* sleep problems	Start with 25 mg at night; increase up to 200 mg twice daily	Stiffness, dryness of mouth, restlessness, drowsiness, dizziness, weight gain, sudden jerky movements
High-potency older antipsychotics: these drugs have a higher risk of side-effects				
Trifluoperazine		Useful for severe agitation and is less sedative	Start with 5 mg at night; increase up to 10 mg twice daily	Same as with chlorpromazine
Haloperidol		Same as with trifluoperazine	Start with 5 mg at night; increase up to 10 mg twice daily	Same as with chlorpromazine
Loxapine		Same as with trifluoperazine	Start with 20 mg at night, increase up to 100 mg twice daily	Same as with chlorpromazine
Pimozide		Can be used for monosymptomatic delusional hypochondriasis	Start with 2 mg at night; increase up to 8 mg at night	Same as with chlorpromazine and ECG abnormalities

Table continues over

Table 11.1. Antipsychotic medicines, *continued*

Medication	Local trade names and cost	Special uses	Dosage	Side-effects
High-potency newer antipsychotics: these drugs are effective and may have a lower risk of side-effects				
Risperidone		Potent drug, fewer side-effects	Start with 2 mg at night; increase up to 6 mg	Drowsiness, restlessness, agitation
Olanzapine		Same as with risperidone	Start with 2.5 mg at night; increase up to 20 mg	Drowsiness, weight gain
Clozapine		Potent drug, useful for people who do not respond to other medicines; *should be used only in consultation with a specialist*	Start with 50 mg at night; increase in steps of 50 mg every 2–3 days up to 200–300 mg twice daily	Drop in white blood cell count can cause fatal infections; drowsiness; weight gain; increased salivation Monitor blood count weekly
Injectable (depot) antipsychotics: always give a test dose (the lowest dose of the range) before starting regular treatment				
Flupenthixol decanoate		Given as deep intramuscular injections for the long-term treatment of schizophrenia	12.5–200 mg every 4 weeks	Same as with chlorpromazine
Fluphenazine decanoate		Same as with flupenthixol decanoate	6.25–75 mg every 4 weeks	Same as with chlorpromazine
Haloperidol decanoate		Same as with flupenthixol decanoate	12.5–100 mg every 4 weeks	Same as with chlorpromazine
Zuclopenthixol decanoate		Same as with flupenthixol decanoate	100–400 mg every 1–2 weeks	Same as with chlorpromazine

Table 11.2. Antidepressant medicines, for common mental disorders (panic attacks, depression, anxiety, obsessive–compulsive disorders, medically unexplained physical symptoms)

Medication	Trade names and cost	Uses	Dosage	Side-effects
Older, cheaper tricyclic antidepressants: these drugs are cheaper but have more side-effects; they all take at least 2 weeks to have an effect				
Amitriptyline		Common mental disorders	Start with 25 mg at night; increase in steps up to a minimum of 75 mg and a maximum of 150 mg at night	Drowsiness, dry mouth, dizziness, weight gain, blurred vision, constipation
Imipramine		Same as with amitriptyline, but is also useful for bed-wetting in children	Same as with amitriptyline	Same as with amitriptyline but is less sedative
Clomipramine		Same as with amitriptyline but is also useful for obsessive–compulsive disorder	Same as with amitriptyline	Same as with amitriptyline
Desipramine		Same as with amitriptyline	Same as with amitriptyline	Same as with amitriptyline but less drowsiness
Nortriptyline		Same as with amitriptyline	Start with 20 mg once a day; increase up to 100 mg	Same as with amitriptyline but less dizziness and drowsiness

Table continues over

Table 11.2. Antidepressant medicines, *continued*

Medication	Trade names and cost	Uses	Dosage	Side-effects
Newer, more expensive, antidepressants (selective serotonin reuptake inhibitors and related classes): these drugs are more expensive but have fewer side-effects; they take at least 2 weeks to have an effect				
Fluoxetine		Common mental disorders	Start with 20 mg in the morning; increase up to 60 mg in the morning	Nervousness, insomnia, fatigue, nausea, diarrhoea, loss of appetite, sexual impairment
Sertraline		Same as with fluoxetine	Start with 50 mg in the morning; increase up to 200 mg in the morning	Same as with fluoxetine
Fluvoxamine		Same as with fluoxetine	Start with 100 mg in the morning; increase up to 300 mg a day	Same as with fluoxetine
Paroxetine		Same as with fluoxetine	Start with 20 mg in the morning; increase up to 60 mg in the morning	Same as with fluoxetine Extrapyrimidal side-effects
Venlafaxine		Same as with fluoxetine	Start with 37.5 mg twice daily; increase up to 150 mg twice daily	Nausea, drowsiness, dizziness, headaches, dry mouth, raised blood pressure, fits

Table 11.3. Anti-anxiety and sleeping medicines, for short-term use for anxiety problems and sleep difficulties (these medicines must not be used for more than four weeks at a time to avoid dependence)

Medication	Trade names and cost	Uses	Dosage	Side-effects
Diazepam		For anxiety and difficulty sleeping, alcohol withdrawal	Start with 5 mg at night; increase up to 10 mg twice daily	Drowsiness, dizziness, dependence (if used for long periods), suppression of breathing (in overdose)
Lorazepam		Same as with diazepam but also useful for the control of acute mania	Start with 1 mg at night; increase up to 4 mg	Same as with diazepam
Nitrazepam		Same as with diazepam	Start with 5 mg at night; increase up to 10 mg	Same as with diazepam
Chlordiazepoxide		Same as with diazepam but especially useful for alcohol withdrawal	For alcohol withdrawal, see section 6.1	Same as with diazepam
Clonazepam		Same as with diazepam but also useful for epilepsy	Start with 0.5 mg at night; increase up to 2 mg twice daily	Same as with diazepam
Alprazolam		Same as with diazepam	Start with 0.25 mg; increase up to 1 mg twice daily	Same as with diazepam
Oxazepam		Same as with diazepam	Start with 7.5 mg at night; increase up to 40 mg twice daily	Same as with diazepam
Triazolam		Same as with diazepam	Start with 0.125 mg at night; increase up to 0.25 mg at night	Same as with diazepam

Table 11.4. Medicine for manic–depressive disorder (mood stabilisers)

Medication	Trade names and cost	Uses	Dosage	Side-effects
Lithium carbonate		For the control of manic–depressive disorder; avoid if serum levels cannot be obtained or when the person is taking diuretics	400–1200 mg a day given as a single dose; serum levels must be 0.6–1.2 mmol/l	Nausea, diarrhoea, weight gain, increased thirst, interactions with non-steroidal anti-inflammatory drugs. Note that lithium can be very dangerous if taken in excess
Sodium valproate		Same as with lithium but also useful for epilepsy	Start with 200 mg twice daily; increase in steps up to 600 mg twice daily	Nausea, drowsiness, diarrhoea, weight gain, tremor, jaundice, liver failure, pancreatitis
Carbamazepine		Same as with lithium but also useful for epilepsy	Start with 200 mg a day; increase over 2 weeks to 800 mg a day. Serum levels should be in the range 8–12 mg/l	Nausea, difficulty walking, constipation, sedation, serious allergic reactions, hyponatraemia. Note that a sudden fall in blood count can occur

Table 11.5. Anticonvulsant medicines, for the control of epilepsy

Medication	Trade names and cost	Uses	Dosage[1]	Side-effects
Phenobarbitone		For all types of epilepsy in adults	Start with 60 mg at night; increase up to 120 mg at night	Drowsiness, restlessness, confusion
Primidone		For all types of epilepsy in adults	Start with 125 mg at night; increase in steps up to 500 mg twice daily	Drowsiness, restlessness, confusion
Phenytoin		For all types of epilepsy in adults	Start with 150 mg once daily; increase up to 600 mg daily	Nausea, tremor, confusion, dizziness, headache
Sodium valproate		For all types of epilepsy in adults	Start with 200 mg twice daily; increase in steps up to 800 mg twice daily	Nausea, drowsiness, diarrhoea, weight gain, tremor
Carbamazepine		For all types of epilepsy in adults	Start with 200 mg/day; increase over 2 weeks to a maximum of 1000 mg a day	Nausea, difficulty walking, constipation, sedation. Note that sudden fall in blood count can occur

Table 11.6. Other medicine used for mental illness

Medication	Trade names and cost	Uses	Dosage	Side-effects
Propanalol		For severe physical symptoms of anxiety	Start with 20 mg twice daily; increase up to 40 mg twice daily	Heart failure, asthma, fatigue, nausea
Procyclidine		For the side-effects of antipsychotic drugs	2.5 mg twice daily; increase up to 5 mg three times daily	Dry mouth, constipation blurred vision, urinary retention, confusion
Benzhexol		Same as with procyclidine	1 mg once daily; increase up to 2.5 mg three times daily	Same as with procyclidine
Benztropine		Same as with procyclidine	0.5 mg at night; increase up to 2 mg at night	Same as with procyclidine
Thiamine		For drinking problems and alcohol withdrawal	20–50 mg three times daily	Rarely reported

11.3 Cautions when using medicines for mental illness

- Many medicines interact with alcohol. In particular, medicines that cause sedation will worsen the drowsiness felt after drinking alcohol.

- The doses given in the tables are for adults. Use a third to a half of these doses for people over the age of 60 and for children aged under 16 years.

- Many psychiatric medicines produce drowsiness, weight gain and sexual problems. Be aware of these. Advise people taking them to diet and exercise regularly to control weight gain. Drowsiness is often temporary and goes away as medication continues. Sexual problems may be tackled as described in section 5.5.

- Avoid the following drugs during pregnancy: lithium, carbamazepine, valproate, clonazepam and other anti-anxiety medicines, older antidepressants and all antipsychotic medicines.

- There are a few other medicines that may be used for mental disorders that are not included in the tables. These include medicines such as methylphenidate for children with hyperactivity, disulfiram for alcohol dependence, vigabatrin for epilepsy, and methadone for heroin dependence. These medicines must not be started (and preferably not even be monitored) by general physicians or community health workers. They should be used, as far as possible, only by specialists.

Chapter 12

Resources in your area

Enter information on the availability of various types of resources in your region in the tables below.

12.1 Resources for children

These may include: children's homes; juvenile homes; child telephone helplines; child abuse agencies; organisations working with street children; child protection agencies; agencies specifically working on children's issues such as Save the Children; rehabilitation workshops and special schools for children with mental retardation.

Name and contact person	Services offered	Address; telephone

12.2 Resources for the elderly

These may include: residential homes for the elderly; government agencies providing welfare and financial assistance to elders; local chapters of Alzheimer's Disease International, HelpAge and other agencies specifically working on issues that affect elderly people.

Name and contact person	Services offered	Address; telephone

12.3 Resources for drug and alcohol problems

These may include: local chapters of Alcoholics Anonymous and other agencies working with drinking problems; agencies working with the families of persons with dependence problems; health facilities specialising in drug and alcohol dependence.

Name and contact person	Services offered	Address; telephone

12.4 Resources for women and domestic violence

These may include: women's organisations; family violence units in the police and other government agencies; lawyers, social workers and counsellors sensitive to women's violence issues; residential shelters for women; women's health clinics.

Name and contact person	Services offered	Address; telephone

12.5 Resources for families of the mentally ill

These may include support groups and organisations working with the families of those who suffer from any type of mental illness, or more specifically, mental retardation, dementias in older people, drinking and drug problems, and severe mental disorders.

Name and contact person	Services offered	Address; telephone

12.6 Mental health professionals

These may include psychiatrists, psychologists and other mental health professionals. Make sure you have information on private and public health care. In particular, record information on the nearest psychiatric hospital facility and emergency clinic to which to refer very sick people.

Name and contact person	Services offered	Address; telephone

12.7 Telephone helplines

Record the telephone numbers for different services, such as suicide prevention, women in distress, and so on.

Telephone number	For what problems

Appendix. Flow charts for clinical problem-solving

These flow charts may be photocopied and pasted on your clinic or office wall for quick reference. Flow charts are presented for the clinical approach to the broad categories of clinical problems that form the bases of the clinical chapters (Part II).

Behaviours that cause concern

Typical presentations:

- aggressive behaviour;
- confused behaviour;
- agitated behaviour;
- bizarre or unusual behaviour.

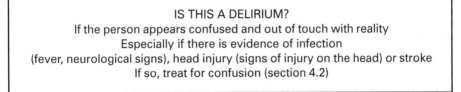

```
┌──────────────────────────────────────────────────────────────────┐
│                      IS THIS A DELIRIUM?                           │
│       If the person appears confused and out of touch with reality │
│              Especially if there is evidence of infection          │
│ (fever, neurological signs), head injury (signs of injury on the   │
│                      head) or stroke                               │
│              If so, treat for confusion (section 4.2)              │
└──────────────────────────────────────────────────────────────────┘
                                 │
                                 ▼
┌──────────────────────────────────────────────────────────────────┐
│      ASK ABOUT ALCOHOL OR DRUG WITHDRAWAL OR INTOXICATION          │
│   such as history of problem drinking or drug abuse, smell of      │
│                          alcohol                                   │
│  If so, treat for alcohol or drug dependence (sections 6.1, 6.2)   │
└──────────────────────────────────────────────────────────────────┘
                                 │
                                 ▼
┌──────────────────────────────────────────────────────────────────┐
│                  ASK ABOUT PSYCHOTIC SYMPTOMS                      │
│              such as hallucinations and delusions                  │
│              If so, treat for psychosis (section 4.3)              │
└──────────────────────────────────────────────────────────────────┘
                                 │
                                 ▼
┌──────────────────────────────────────────────────────────────────┐
│                ASK ABOUT RECENT DEPRESSED MOOD                     │
│      such as suicidal ideas, loss of weight and poor sleep         │
│        If so, treat as for suicidal behaviour (section 4.4)        │
└──────────────────────────────────────────────────────────────────┘
                                 │
                                 ▼
┌──────────────────────────────────────────────────────────────────┐
│                 ASK ABOUT RECENT TRAGIC EVENTS                     │
│                 such as sudden loss or violence                    │
│          If so, treat as for bereavement (section 7.4)             │
│          or post traumatic mental illness (Chapter 7)              │
└──────────────────────────────────────────────────────────────────┘
```

Symptoms that are medically unexplained

Such symptoms include:

- aches and pains;
- tiredness;
- palpitations;
- dizziness;
- bowel complaints (constipation/loose motions);
- sudden loss of motor function;
- chest pains;
- difficulty breathing.

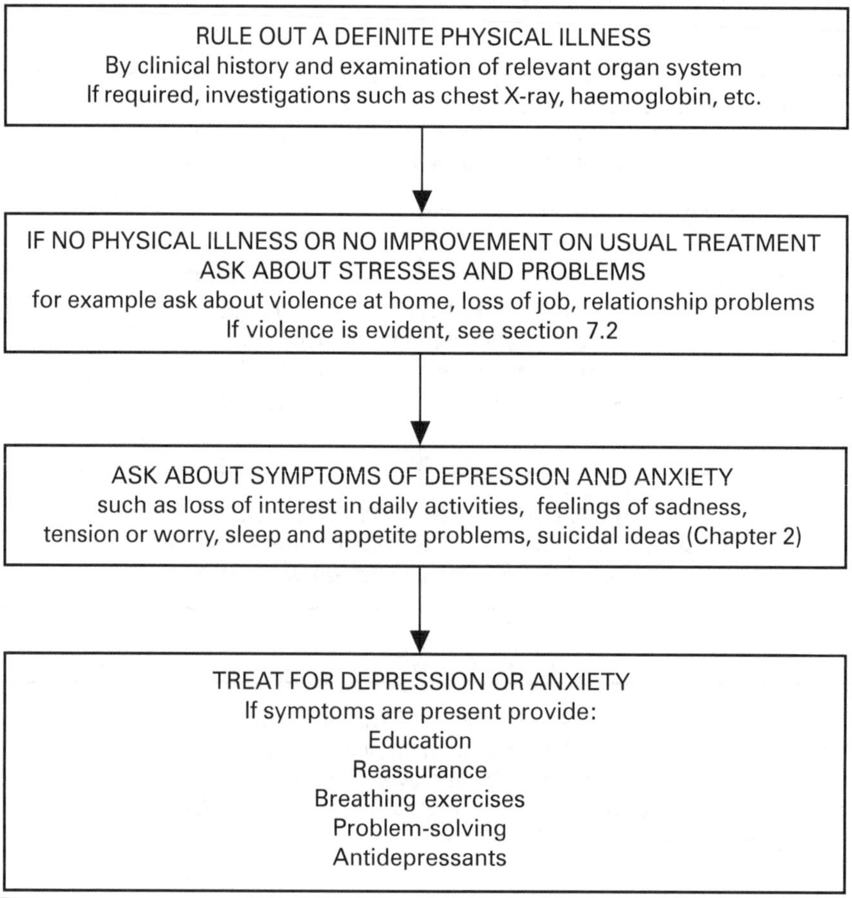

RULE OUT A DEFINITE PHYSICAL ILLNESS
By clinical history and examination of relevant organ system
If required, investigations such as chest X-ray, haemoglobin, etc.

↓

**IF NO PHYSICAL ILLNESS OR NO IMPROVEMENT ON USUAL TREATMENT
ASK ABOUT STRESSES AND PROBLEMS**
for example ask about violence at home, loss of job, relationship problems
If violence is evident, see section 7.2

↓

ASK ABOUT SYMPTOMS OF DEPRESSION AND ANXIETY
such as loss of interest in daily activities, feelings of sadness,
tension or worry, sleep and appetite problems, suicidal ideas (Chapter 2)

↓

TREAT FOR DEPRESSION OR ANXIETY
If symptoms are present provide:
Education
Reassurance
Breathing exercises
Problem-solving
Antidepressants

Habits that cause health problems

Suspect alcohol/drug dependence in the following situations:

• poor physical health;

• stomach or liver disease (alcohol);

• skin infections (intravenous drug abuse);

• repeated sexually transmitted diseases;

• repeated accidents and unexplained injuries;

• frequent absence from work.

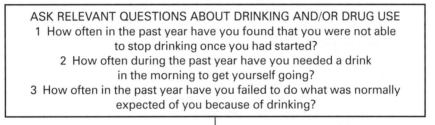

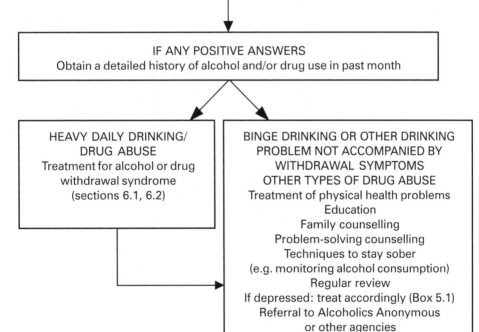

Children with mental health problems

Typical presentations would be:

- not achieving the expected milestones, e.g. speaking, walking;

- not doing well in school;

- being naughty and undisciplined;

- being withdrawn and quiet.

```
┌─────────────────────────────────────────────────────────┐
│        TAKE A CAREFUL HISTORY OF DEVELOPMENT              │
│         See section 8.1 for important milestones          │
│      If delay: consider mental retardation (section 8.1)  │
└─────────────────────────────────────────────────────────┘
                            │
                            ▼
┌─────────────────────────────────────────────────────────┐
│             ASK ABOUT SCHOOL PERFORMANCE                  │
│  If normal development, but poor school behaviour and performance │
│            Consider dyslexia (section 8.2)                │
└─────────────────────────────────────────────────────────┘
                            │
                            ▼
┌─────────────────────────────────────────────────────────┐
│      ASK ABOUT BEHAVIOUR AT HOME AND IN SCHOOL            │
│              If restless, fidgety, impulsive              │
│  Consider attention deficit hyperactivity disorder (section 8.3) │
└─────────────────────────────────────────────────────────┘
                            │
                            ▼
┌─────────────────────────────────────────────────────────┐
│             ASK ABOUT FAMILY ENVIRONMENT                  │
│ Especially styles of discipline, violence in the home, conflict and arguments │
│                  If problems evident,                     │
│           Consider: child abuse (section 8.4)             │
│          Consider: conduct disorder (section 8.5)         │
│            Consider: depression (section 8.7)             │
└─────────────────────────────────────────────────────────┘
```

Bibliography

Burns, A. A., Lovich, R., Maxwell, J. & Shapiro, K. (1997) *Where Women Have No Doctor*. Berkeley, CA: Macmillan Education.

Graham, P. & Hughes, C. (1997) *So Young, So Sad, So Listen*. London: Gaskell/West London Health Promotion Agency.

Heise, L., Ellsberg, M. & Gottemoeller, M. (1999) *Ending Violence Against Women*. Population Reports, Series L, No. 11. Baltimore: Johns Hopkins School of Public Health.

Hope, R. A., Longmore, J. M., Moses, P. A. H. & Warrens, A. N. (1989) *Oxford Handbook of Clinical Medicine*. Oxford: Oxford University Press.

Hyman, S. E. & Tesar, G. E. (1994) *Manual of Psychiatric Emergencies*. Boston: Little, Brown.

Isaac, M., Chandrashekar, C. R. & Murthy, R. S. (1994) *Mental Health Care by Primary Care Doctors*. Bangalore: NIMHANS.

Murthy, P., Chandra, P., Bharath, S., Sudha, S. & Murthy, S. (1998) *Manual of Mental Health Care for Women in Custody*. Bangalore: NIMHANS.

Murthy, R. S., Chandrashekar, C. R., Nagarajaiah, I. M. K., Parthasarthy, R. & Raghuram, A. (1988) *Manual of Mental Health Care for Multipurpose Health Workers*. Bangalore: ICMR Centre for Advanced Research on Community Mental Health, NIMHANS.

National Institute for the Mentally Handicapped (1988) *Mental Retardation: A Manual for Guidance Counsellors*. Secunderabad: NIMH.

Shader, R. (1994) *Manual of Psychiatric Therapeutics* (2nd edn). Boston: Little, Brown.

Taylor, D. & Kerwin, R. (1995) *The Bethlem & Maudsley NHS Trust Prescribing Guidelines* (2nd edn). London: Maudsley Hospital.

US Department of Education. *Growing Up Drug Free: A Parent's Guide to Prevention*. Washington, DC: US Department of Education.

Werner, D. (1994a) *Where There is No Doctor: A Health Care Handbook* (Indian edn). New Delhi: Voluntary Health Associations of India.

Werner, D. (1994b) *Disabled Village Children* (Indian edn). New Delhi: Voluntary Health Associations of India.

World Health Organization (1992) *AUDIT: The Alcohol Use Disorders Identification Test: Guidelines for Use in Primary Health Care*. Geneva: WHO.

World Health Organization (1996) *Diagnostic and Management Guidelines for Mental Disorders in Primary Care*. Seattle: Hogrefe & Huber.

World Health Organization (1998) *Mental Disorders in Primary Care. A WHO Education Package*. Geneva: WHO.

World Health Organization (2000) *Guide to Mental Health in Primary Care (UK Adaptation)*. London: Royal Society of Medicine Press.

Zeidenstein, S. & Moore, K. (1996) *Learning About Sexuality*. New York: Population Council & The International Women's Health Coalition. (For domestic violence.)

Handouts and leaflets

The Carrier Foundation *About ...* booklet series. New Jersey: Carrier Foundation.

The Mind *Understanding* series. London: Mind Publications (1997).

The Mind *How to ... Find Out More* mental health promotion series. London: Mind Publications/Gaskell (1997).

Child and Adolescent Psychiatry Information Factsheets. London: Royal College of Psychiatrists.

World Health Organization and Alzheimer's Disease International. *Alzheimer's Disease: Help for Caregivers*.

Toronto Child Abuse Centre. *Information Packages on Child Abuse and Domestic Violence*.

Glossary of terms for mental illnesses and their symptoms

The English word	Its meaning	The word in your language that means the same
Acute psychosis	A severe mental disorder which starts suddenly and usually lasts less than a month	
Addiction	See *Dependence*	
Alzheimer's disease	The commonest type of *dementia*	
Anxiety	A state of feeling tense, worried or fearful	
Attention deficit hyperactivity disorder	See *Hyperactivity*	
Autism	A condition in which a child does not speak much and is socially cold	
Bed-wetting	A condition in which a child is wetting the bed well past the age when it is not expected (about 5 years)	
Bereavement	The experience of losing a loved one through death	
Bipolar disorder	See *Manic–depressive disorder*	
Common mental disorders	*Depression* and *anxiety*	
Compulsion	A behaviour that is repeated again and again for no reason (for example, repeated hand-washing)	
Conduct disorder	A condition in which a child (usually a teenager) behaves badly, is undisciplined	
Confusion	A condition when a person does not know where he is, what time it is or who he is	
Conversion disorder	A condition in which a person develops physical symptoms caused entirely by mental stress	
Convulsion	A condition when a person is not fully aware of her surroundings and may show jerky or unusual movements	
Delirium	A state in which a person is confused (see *Confusion*)	
Delusion	A belief that is irrational and untrue but is held with firm conviction	
Dementia	A condition in which the person shows progressively worsening memory and behaviour problems	
Dependence	A state when a person must take a drug regularly in order to avoid a *withdrawal syndrome*	

Depression	A state of sadness, despair or loss of interest in daily life
Disorientation	A state in which a person does not know what day it is or where he is
Drug abuse	The use of a drug in a manner that may cause social, legal, economic or health damage to the person
Dyslexia	A condition in which a child of normal intelligence has specific problems with school tasks such as reading, spelling or writing
Enuresis	A condition in which a child wets her clothes at an age when this is not expected (about 3 years)
Epilepsy	A condition in which *seizures* occur repeatedly
Fit	See *Convulsion*
Grief	See *Bereavement*
Hallucination	An experience in which a person hears, sees, smells or feels things that no one else can
Hyperactivity	A childhood behaviour problem where the child cannot sit in one place for long and is always on the move
Hysteria	See *Conversion disorder*
Impotence	A condition in which a man is unable to get an erection of his penis
Insomnia	Difficulty in sleeping
Irritability	Feeling short-tempered
Manic–depressive disorder	A severe mental disorder where a person experiences episodes of high and low mood
Mental illness	An illness where there is a disturbance of behaviour, feelings or emotions
Mental retardation	A state where a child develops more slowly than normal
Obsession	A thought that comes repeatedly into a person's mind even though she does not want it
Obsessive–compulsive disorder	A condition in which *obsessions* and *compulsions* occur
Panic	A state of severe *anxiety* during which the person feels as if he is going to die or collapse
Phobia	A state in which a person develops an irrational fear of a situation such as crowds or markets
Postnatal depression	A condition in which *depression* occurs in the months after childbirth
Post-traumatic stress disorder	A condition of mental distress occurring in a person who has had a life-threatening experience
Premature ejaculation	A condition in which a man has an ejaculation (semen being discharged from the penis) too soon during sexual intercourse
Psychosis	A severe mental disorder associated with *delusions* and *hallucinations*

Psychosomatic	A term used to describe complaints or a condition in which there are physical health complaints caused by a psychological illness
Schizophrenia	A type of psychosis which often lasts many years
Seizure	See *Convulsion*
Specific learning disability	See *Dsylexia*
Suicide	A person ending her own life
Trauma	A life-threatening or frightening event
Withdrawal syndrome	A state of discomfort in a person who is *dependent* on drugs or alcohol after the drug or alcohol is stopped

The word in your language	**Its meaning**	**The mental illness or symptoms the word resembles most closely**

Please send us your comments

This manual is based on the clinical, personal and research experiences of the author in Zimbabwe and India. These experiences have been supplemented by reviewing other books and papers and by consulting an international panel of reviewers. However, there is no better judge of the book than the reader. Most importantly, the value of this book depends entirely on how practical its style and contents are for each reader. I would be grateful if you write to me with your comments on any aspect of the book. These will be invaluable in revising its contents with the hope that the book will serve the needs of the general health worker where there is no psychiatrist.

Comments can be sent to: Dr Vikram Patel, c/o Gaskell, Royal College of Psychiatrists, 17 Belgrave Square, London SW1X 8PG, UK.

Index

Page numbers for the main references in the book are shown in **bold** type.